The Ecological Context

By the same author:
THE FUTURE OF THE FUTURE, 1969

THE
ECOLOGICAL
CONTEXT

John McHale

George Braziller ● NEW YORK

Preface and Acknowledgments

THIS BOOK is a revised and expanded version of *The Ecological Context: Energy and Materials,* by John McHale, which was Document #6 (1967) in the series of reports issued by World Resources Inventory at Southern Illinois University. The author particularly wishes to acknowledge the work done on this initial report by Carl G. Nelson, who was responsible for research and graphic supervision.

Valued assistance has been rendered in the preparation of the present edition by the staff and students of the Center for Integrative Studies, State University of New York at Binghamton—in particular, by James MacAulay, Joseph Hryvniak, and by Rosalind Forse for her secretarial supervision. Additional graphic services were also carried out by Stanley Kaufman, of Learning Resources Center at the same university.

The work itself develops and underlines the earlier focus on energy and material resources, within a broad framework of considerations regarding the consequences and implications of man's activities on a global scale. Rather than attempting, in any way, to be definitive in the area of ecology, it endeavors to provide a general orientation to the overall ecological context within which these activities are conducted.

JOHN McHALE

Binghamton, New York
February, 1970

Contents

The
Ecological Context

ORGANIC LIFE has been evolving on the planet for billions of years—the human species for but a tiny fragment of that time. It is only in the most recent, and brief, period of his tenure that man has developed in sufficient numbers, and acquired enough power, to become one of the most potentially dangerous organisms that the planet has ever hosted.

Now capable of destroying his own species many times over through consciously contrived means of war, it suddenly becomes apparent that his largely unconscious, and uncontrolled, exploitation of the earth's resources may similarly render the planet unlivable.

It is significant that, at this critical juncture in human affairs, man now turns to "ecology" as a guide towards rethinking his overall relationship to his environment—rather than to the more traditional political and economic viewpoints which have guided and measured his large-scale actions before.

Coined by the distinguished scientist Haeckel in 1873, the term "ecology" is derived from the Greek words *oikonos* (house) and *logos* (knowledge). Though originating in botany to describe the interaction of plants with other organisms, and with their environs, this approach now engages with the study of large-scale regional ecological systems and global interactions and relationships.

The role of man, both as symbiotic component and disruptive agency, has been particularly focused upon in recent years. Human ecology may theoretically embrace the overall study of man's relationship to his planetary earth environment. From the roots of "house-knowledge," we can assume a definition of applied human ecology as "planetary housekeeping."

Such an ecological reorientation may, paradoxically, be as disruptive of man's traditional attitudes and values as his physical actions have been in the environment!

Though seemingly innocuous in its theoretical origins, ecology generates a radical view of human society, which may prove to be more "positively" revolutionary, in its widest implications, than any of the socio-political ideologies which have previously challenged our traditional economic and institutional arrangements.

But such a conceptual and value shift—from the local study of plants, wildlife, and their surroundings to one which suggests responsibility for the viable maintenance of the planet as life-space—is in accord with the kinds of changes in human consciousness and conceptuality that are already underway. Man is now unraveling the life-code at the molecular level. He has left the earth and sojourned on the moon, and moves inwardly to the ocean depths and outwardly to the physical monitoring of other worlds and galaxies.

A fresh awareness of the origins, potentialities, and possible limits of human life and intelligence is engendered in this psycho-physical expansion. Even in our relation to time, we now begin to probe and plan forward into the future as we, in almost equal measure, successively locate the origins of life itself ever more remotely in the past.

The home planet has, by the second half of the twentieth century, become the *minimal* conceptual unit of occupancy for the whole human family—whose planetary interdependence is now seen to be closely interwoven with maintenance of the fragile balance of natural forces which sustain life. Man has converged on man and his home planet as the prime focus of his attention.

The sense of impending crisis and the pressures of accelerating rates of change are part of this process of convergence. Our world has suddenly grown quite small—and the successively impacting waves of reported change, catastrophe, suffering, injustice, and deterioration appear to become claustrophobic.

We are undergoing a vast evolutionary transition whose pace and magnitude of change patterns is unprecedented in human history. This transition may only be achieved by circumventing the various survival crises that accompany it and, are, by their own nature, aspects of that transition—world population has grown to near maximum and the environmental deterioration caused by processes accompanying that growth already threatens those natural-resource-renewal cycles that make life possible on earth.

Medicine has developed from concern with the pathology of dysfunction and disease in individual organisms to larger concerns with preventive medicine and health regulation at the national- and world-health level. So, whatever meta-discipline an "applied ecology" might evolve into, it must also move toward a preventive and regulatory concern with the optimal viability of the planetary ecology.

To rephrase such an analogy: Where the medical-health sciences have grown to encompass overall concern with the *internal metabolics* of the human organism, the approach to human affairs through an ecological perspective must now deal with all the *externalized* metabolic systems of humanity—both the naturally occurring cycles with which man interacts, and the psycho-physical and technological systems through which all of his environmental interactions are conducted.

We need also to extend the physical and biological concepts of ecology to include the social behaviors of man—as equally critical factors within the ecosystem. The earth has not only been changed by scientific and technological transformations for particular economic and industrial functions—but these have been spurred by specific value attitudes, by politico-ethical systems, by art, by religion, by the need for social contiguity and communication as expressed in cities, by highway systems, and so forth. Such "cultural" transformations play more directly causative and formative roles than we customarily accord them.

Human modifications of the planetary habitat extend out into the atmosphere—to the degree that the activities of man have altered and continue to alter the composition of the atmosphere. They extend also to the streams, rivers, lakes, and oceans, to the extent that man has altered these also. And they embrace the overall relationships of water, land, and air, as he has already transformed large areas of the earth surface—removing forests, changing vegetation cover through cultivation, redirecting and damming rivers, redistributing the metals and minerals, and so forth—and so changed the complex relations of animal population and their surroundings, and even the larger cycles of evaporation, transpiration, and precipitation.

The global environment within which some three and a half billion humans exist has already been modified considerably by man, and we may presume that such modification will continue. When we speak of the habitable areas of the earth, at this date, we are required also to take into account that men are presently experimenting successfully with the extension of living to beneath the oceans, around the poles, and beyond the earth's atmosphere.

This modification of his environment by man to his own requirements has both positive and negative aspects. Positive in that it reduces, in considerable measure, the apparent long-term insolubility of many of man's historical and present problems. If we may irrigate the deserts, begin to "farm" the oceans, "interconvert" our resources on a growing scale, and extend our environmental control capacities to living anywhere on, within, or above the earth, then currently gloomy prognostications about "standing room only" in terms of population pressure, and "global famine before the year 2000," and so forth, are less likely to come about.

There is the negative aspect, of course. So far, our modification of the earth has proceeded with little regard for the intricacy of the overall ecological balances which maintain life on earth. We have taken little heed, for example, in modifying the environment for our own use, of the disruption of the populations of animals, micro-organisms, plants, and so forth, with which the maintenance of our own ecological cycle is still closely interwoven. There is presently—

[3]

nothing in untouched nature to compare with our extravagant use of energy and our failure to recycle essential materials. The leaves that fall upon the forest floor, the excreta and remains of animal life, and even the carbon dioxide exhaled in breathing pass through transformations and make them repeatedly available to sustain life, but the effluvium of cities and industrial plants, mining operations and mismanaged soil pour into streams and atmosphere. At best these wastes are often lost beyond recovery; at worse they are toxic. In any event they represent a loss of the ultimate potential of environment to sustain life and thus violate the model which has evolved through geological time. Time, space, motion, matter, the earth and the life upon—these are the phenomena whose inseparable relationship needs to be convincingly appreciated.[1]

The scale and critical magnitude of human activities within the earth system are now such that nothing less than a planetary approach toward "ecological health" may be adequate. The overriding crisis point revolves around the survival of the human and other species of life within the biosphere.

The nature of the crisis is such that no *local* measures can now, in themselves, be wholly effective or sufficient unless they are considered within the whole system. No piecemeal acts of emergency-pressured political legislation can, alone, do more than postpone catastrophe— perhaps, hopefully, beyond the next election! The socio-political understanding of the larger ecological implications of local actions and decision-making must now be set within a more radically framed series of questions on how they affect, and are affected by, other dimensions of the crisis. Their consideration goes, inexorably, from local to regional to national to international and trans-national consequences and implications.

Let no one make the mistake of thinking we can save ourselves by "cleaning up the environment." Banning DDT is the equivalent of the physician's treating syphilis by putting a Band-Aid over the first chancre to appear. In either case you can be sure that more serious and widespread trouble will soon appear unless the disease itself is treated. We cannot survive by planning to treat the symptoms such as air pollution, water pollution, soil erosion, and so forth.[2]

In this sense, there are no *local* ecological issues which may be decided within wholly local and apparently autonomous contexts. Ecology is about the entire web of intricate relationships that make life itself possible on earth; hence, it touches upon, draws together and is affected by the whole spectrum of human activities.

Each separate "issue" must be systematically expanded to explore its

[1] "The Perspective of Time," Paul B. Sears, *Bulletin of the Atomic Scientists,* Vol. XVIII, No. 8, October 1961.

[2] "Overpopulated America," Wayne H. Davis, *New Republic,* January 10, 1970, copyright Harrison-Blaine of New Jersey, Inc.

relationships and ramifications with other "issues." The early uses of DDT were varied, widespread, and local, but the "threat to survival" of higher organisms was first noticed through its accumulation in the tissues of penguins in Antarctica. Pesticide and fertilizer misuse first killed millions of fish in the rivers and lakes of the most prosperous and "locally healthy" nations, *before* its effects and long-range implications on other species and man were seriously considered.

Smog is initially irritating, then deadly! Its prevention and symptomatic implications cannot be confined solely to the legislation of more efficient exhaust systems and the control of local industrial effluents. These measures can be locally effective and palliative—but the core questions, about our overall use of oil, coal, and other fossil fuels in burgeoning energy-consuming economies, remain to be answered.

Again, our examination of the "local question" of energy uses needs to be extended outwardly to link up with the destruction of air and aquatic life and pollution of beaches by ruptured oil tankers, to the growing size of such tankers, and the proliferation of less visible but equally threatening pipelines. In this specific case, it should extend to the overall role of the world oil industry—in terms of support of its operations, of its ownership and control of large areas of the earth surface, to its impending operations on the Alaskan slope and pan-Arctic islands. We need to offset our immediate concerns with hydrocarbon and sulphur-dioxide pollution of local environs with more knowledge of the swift, but relatively invisible, acquisition of oil leases on the continental ocean shelves around the world—or these will be the locus of tomorrow's problems.

This is not to overemphasize any one industry but merely to use an example. In the oil and petro-chemical complex of industries, benefits and flexibility of approach afforded by their more diverse activities may, on the balance, be far more positive than negative in their ecological planning than many other industrial sectors.

Many of our questions need also to be retrospectively oriented. Current reports on the alarming erosion and breakdown of the Great Barrier Reef, and other large coral formations in the Pacific, now couple the delayed effects of W.W.II bombardments as partially responsible for this—through physical damage and subsequent deterioration leading to an ecological imbalance favoring the abnormal growth of a starfish that feeds upon the live coral. If the bombardments *were* a causal agent leading to the loss of all such large reef formations in that area, *and* the bombardments were necessary at the time, how do we gauge the future ecological costs of such operations? They may always be logically defended "at the time."

One of our key ecological imperatives is, of course, that war itself, like smallpox, plague, or the locust on the world scale, will increasingly have to be brought within the spectrum of those large-scale human activities whose immediate and long-range ecological implications require stringent regulatory control. This, obviously, can no longer be achieved through political rhetoric and paper treaties, nor through the proliferation of nuclear, chemical, and biological warfare deterrents whose only total and effective threat is the end of life itself in the biosphere.

It will require the design and enforcement of counter-institutional measures which cut the sinews of modern warfare—access to resources, linkage to communications systems, withdrawal of essential services, and so forth. No nation or region in the world can now "go it alone" in terms of warring upon its neighbors, much less in terms of maintaining its own well-being. All, even the most powerful and prosperous, are dependent upon the global web of interrelated systems which now sustain all.

While defoliation and crop destruction may be militarily defensible— within the short-range dictates of local national posture—their extended implicative relationships in a world under survival threat by food/population pressures are not only ecologically indefensible but, even in their own contextual terms, profoundly irrational.

Deserts are singularly difficult to occupy, and costly to reclaim. The price-and-time tag on coral reefs, lakes, rivers, streams, and the damage to human and animal genes may be forever out of our reach!

Similarly, the various major problems evidenced in the present disparities between developed and lesser developed regions of the world—food, shelter, health, life expectancy, and education—may be more clearly defined in terms of ecological imbalance. From this viewpoint we may be able to define and act upon them in more radical and operational terms. The urgency of solution to these problems needs to be removed from its present level of humanitarian appeals to the more fortunate of us. We need to meet these emergencies in the human global environment in terms of the common self-preservation of all.

Within the closely knit interdependence of our now global community, the continued disparities between have and have-not nations may be viewed as a grave threat to the overall maintenance of the human community. The explosive rises in population, the pressures on food lands and other resources, the scale of wastage, disorganization, and pestilence now accompanying our "local" wars are also linked in due measure to the revolution in human expectations. They are, in turn, a further aspect of the evolutionary transition that we are going through.

If not more realistically dealt with, they will continue to press—in "revolutionary" rather than evolutionary terms—ever more critically upon the resources and social energies of the prosperous nations. As world problems, they also go beyond the capacity of any piecemeal and locally organized attempts to mitigate or solve them in anything but the shortest range.

As we examine not only the local aspects of such problems within the lesser developed areas but also their global effects on the more fortunate, it is clear that they also form part of a larger context of ecological mismanagement.

[6]

Wasteful resource-usage, soil exhaustion and spoliation, air, water, and earth pollution, and so forth, are world phenomena. They have all been contingent factors on human occupancy of the earth during historical time. Until recently, however, their effects were more localized and their scale relatively small. Now they may affect a whole region or continent in a few years—or in a few days, as in the case of radioactive fallout.

Most of the so-called problems of the lesser developed regions are also present in greater or lesser degree in the developed regions. All are, in varying measure, contingent upon the "piecemeal" nature of our present modes of knowledge integration, the gaps between such knowledge, its diffusion and effective application—and the lack of a consistent body of agreement on the physical stewardship of the planet.

In almost every "issue" area that we might touch upon, few, in the larger sense, may be left to exigencies and predilections of wholly local economic convenience or the requirements of national securities or political "convenience." We have now reached the point in human affairs at which the ecological requirements for sustaining the survival of the world community take precedence over, and are superogative to, the more transient value systems and vested interests of any local society.

AN OVERVIEW

The expansion of science, technology, and industry, however their depredations may be viewed, has measurably increased the survival and well-being of greater numbers of people than was ever imaginable in preindustrial times. From this aspect we might account the overall balance as favorable.

We then might consider some of our most pressing priorities, for example:

i. The extension of such "survival" adequacy and range of life possibilities to the much lesser advantaged two-thirds of the world.

ii. The controlled restoration of the quality of the physical environment.

iii. The stabilization of population growth.

iv. The more balanced development of a truly planetary society.

v. And so forth.

This will require an even more rapid and extensive growth in scientific and technological undertakings on a world scale—in parallel combination with those requisite socio-economic and political changes which are as urgently required. There is no way around such proposals to cure technological ills with more technology—though this may be deplored by more pessimistic observers in the more affluent nations. It is not merely more science and more technology but the redirection and institutional reorganization of the goal structure of our present scientific and technological societies. In many important aspects, we are still dealing

[7]

only with the backlash of the first phases of technically oriented societies emerging from their nineteenth century origins—and have not yet approached the beginnings of what might be termed a scientific society, that is, one whose motivations, goals, activities are actually congruent with, and permeated with, anything approaching a truly scientific outlook!

We cannot, at any rate, return to some idealized pretechnological era, "in which the earth, air, and waters were pure and all was benign and serene"—even if this nostalgic picture were historically correct or ecologically viable. We may need a drastic orientation of the scientific enterprise in its relationship to human values and social action. We do certainly need to revise our motivations for, and redesign our uses of, our vast technological potentialities.

The tasks facing world society will require all the human intelligence and developed technical ingenuity which we possess.

Within this task there also lies the necessity for an immense analysis and stocktaking of the "negative" potentials in the present lack of conscious integration and planning of our major industrial and socio-economic activities.

Such activities now comprise not only local industrialization in the sense of mass production factory facilities but all the globally interrelated systems complexes of transportation, communication, production, and distribution facilities. There is no longer a division possible between factory and farm or, in this sense, town and country. All are closely interlocked in a close symbiotic relation—a man-made ecology which we now see, almost for the first time, as an integrally functioning "organic" sector within the overall ecosystem.

Agriculture, until recently viewed as an independent sector of human activity from industry, is now more clearly viewed as a frontier area of scientific and technological attention. It is one, particularly, in which traditional modes are no longer adequate to the complexity and size of immediate requirements.

Though the growth of population has been accompanied by more intensive cultivation and higher food yields per acre, the amount of presently useable soil per capita is declining, and is, in many areas, already impoverished through ill use. As the historical pattern of deforestation, which produced many of the great desert areas, continues, there is added to this the increasing amount of arable land claimed for building dams, roads, industrial installations, mining, and so forth—all of the necessary uses of an increasing technological system. (In the United States alone, urbanization and transportation have been calculated to draw more than a million acres of soil, each year, from cultivation.)

Though we may question these uses from our more comfortable vantage point in the rich nations, it is unlikely that the poorer regions of the world will abjure such developments in the interests of conservation or through fear of technological growth.

The decreasing amount of land per capita, though often cited as an obvious limiting factor of human expansion, is a relative measure—crucial only during our presently critical transition period.

The actual amount of land surface available, and still unused, may be gauged from the fact, for example, that the entire population of the United States occupies much less than 10 per cent of the land area. Also, and importantly, man's increasing ecological mobility suggests that fixed land habitation may only be one of a number of alternative forward patterns.

In relation to food yield—many more people may be feed *off* the land than on it, in terms of fixed agricultural occupancy. Toward the end óf the nineteenth century, for example, one farmer, in the developed countries, provided food and fiber for five other people. By 1930, 60 years later, he could produce enough food and fiber for 10 people. In 1960 this has risen to the provision by one person, in industrialized agriculture, for 26 people. By 1970 this output has risen so that about 45 people may be maintained by *one* person engaged in agriculture.

The depletion of animal populations has also been considerable—a recent estimate suggests that 107 kinds of mammals and 100 species of birds, as well as a vastly greater number of plant species and lesser animals, have been rendered extinct in the past 1900 years. Of these losses, 70 per cent have occurred in the past century and have been mainly due to human agencies—less through hunting than destruction of habitat.

Other uses of the earth, incident on our developed technological capacities, have also increased enormously in the past hundred years. As against approximately 50 tons of raw materials per person consumed in 1880, we now use over 300 tons per person annually. When this is translated into amounts of iron, coal, oil, wood, and other products "harvested" from the earth, processed, and redistributed elsewhere, the operation becomes of considerable ecological magnitude.

For example, of all the coal mined by 1960, only 20 per cent was before 1900, and the remaining 80 per cent since that time. The energies used in the extraction, processing, transportation, and use cycles of all the industrial materials are obtained mainly from burning the fossil fuels— each ton of which used releases large amounts of carbon dioxide and other gases into the atmosphere.

From 1860 to 1960, this has been calculated to have increased the atmospheric carbon dioxide concentration by 14 per cent; during the eight years from 1954 to 1962, the average rate of increase was 5 per cent. During the past century of industrialization, more than 400,000 million tons of carbon dioxide have been introduced into the atmosphere. The concentration in the air we breathe has been increased approximately 10

SOURCES OF AIR POLLUTION U.S.

[In millions of tons annually (1966)]

A Motor Vehicles   B Industry   C Powerplants   Total 142
D Space Heating   E Refuse Disposal

Carbon monoxide 72				Sulfur oxides 26		Nitrogen oxides	Hydro-carbons 19	Partic-ulate matter
B	C	D	E	D	E	E	C,D,E	E
						D		D
			C		C	B	C
					B		
A				B		A	B
			B		A		
			A	A		A	

per cent, and if all known reserves of coal and oil were burned, the concentration would be ten times greater.

Sulphur oxides, a more immediately harmful aerial pollutant in highly industrialized countries, is expected to show a 75 per cent increase over present critical levels by 1980. A single fossil fuel, power-generating plant may emit several hundred tons of sulphur dioxide per day and, under certain weather conditions, locally overburden the air of a whole city. When this effect is increased by larger multiple fuel uses in dense urban concentrations, the results may be lethally apparent—four thousand persons died, directly or indirectly from one week of such intense pollution in London in 1952,[3] and one thousand in 1956. It is estimated that each year the United States has 142 million tons of smoke and noxious fumes pumped into its atmosphere—more than 1400 pounds per person. In addition to aerial pollution, it has been calculated that certain elements, for example argon, neon, krypton, and so forth, essential to life maintenance are now being "mined" out of the atmosphere by industrial operations at a faster rate than they are being produced by natural processes.

[3] In 1956, the Clean Air Act, directed toward industrial and domestic polluters, was passed by Parliament. Its enforcement, and the cost to industry of approximately one billion dollars, has resulted in an 80 per cent cut in aerial pollution in London alone—which is now estimated to get 50 per cent more sunlight in the winter than before the Act was passed.

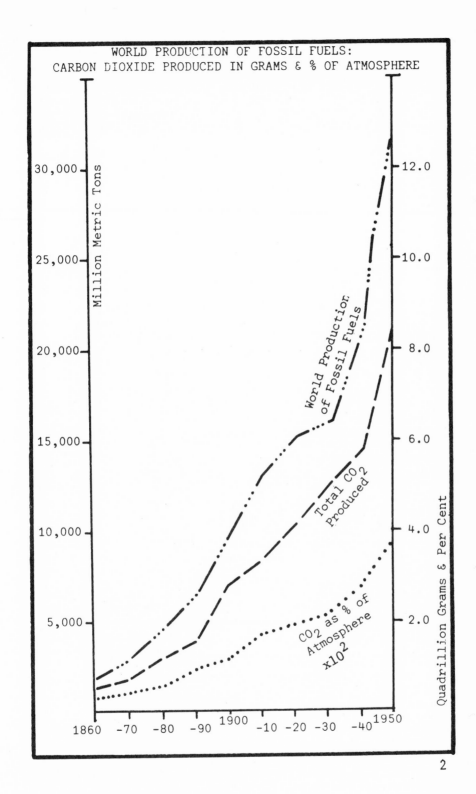

WORLD PRODUCTION OF FOSSIL FUELS:
CARBON DIOXIDE PRODUCED IN GRAMS & % OF ATMOSPHERE

Million Metric Tons

30,000
25,000
20,000
15,000
10,000
5,000

World Production
of Fossil Fuels

Total CO$_2$
Produced

CO$_2$ as % of
Atmosphere
x10^2

12.0
10.0
8.0
6.0
4.0
2.0

Quadrillion Grams & Per Cent

1860 −70 −80 −90 1900 −10 −20 −30 −40 1950

2

[11]

When we speak of increasing the per capita availability of industrial energies and extracting higher performance per pound from our metallic resources, these are key critical factors in the redesign of our use systems. But, even if present generating and production power technologies were converted 50 per cent to nonfossil fuels, it has been estimated that pollutant by-products from the remainder would still double present levels every twenty years.

The dependence of one sixth of the world's food supply on "artificial" nitrogen from the chemical industry is another factor in the overall ecosystem function. There is a tendency to separate agriculture from industry in everyday thinking, but the image of the farmer as conserver and industry as the spoiler of nature is no longer true—if it ever was.

To make each million tons of such nitrogenous fertilizer annually, we use, in direct and related industries, a million tons of steel and five million tons of coal. Some 50 million tons of such support nitrogen are estimated to be required annually by A.D. 2000. The amounts of other agricultural chemicals that will require equally massive support technologies to further maintain and increase crop yields are only now becoming apparent.

The irony, in terms of our present ecological mismanagement, is that in making the chemical fertilizers and other nutrients to render the land more productive, we indirectly destroy the crops through the by-products of similar industrial processes. Each calorie of food produced in highly mechanized agriculture requires roughly another calorie of fuel to power tractors, harvesters, processing, and transportation. Such fuels are usually the fossil fuels used in internal combustion engines and contribute further sources of aerial pollutants to industrial smoke.

> Vegetation damage has been caused in at least half the states in the nation (U.S.) by photo-chemical smog, ozone, sulphur dioxide, fluorides, or ethylene. . . . Livestock damage is usually subtle and chronic. . . . The extent of loss of future forest yield that can be attributed to polluted air is not fully known.[4]

Water, a key resource in daily life, agriculture, and industry is also in critical balance in many world regions. Approximately 95 per cent of fresh waters are presently used at a greater rate than their precipitation replacement in ground surface waters. Though much of this water use is of a multipurpose "cycling" nature, and therefore differs from the single use/discard pattern of other resources, the bulk increases in each use now begins to strain the storage, replenishment, and natural recycling capacities of many acres.

Population growth and urban concentration have been considerable factors of increase—in the United States, consumption has risen from 40

---

[4] *Waste Management and Control*, National Academy of Sciences (U.S.), N. R. C., Pub. No. 1400, 1966, p. 127.

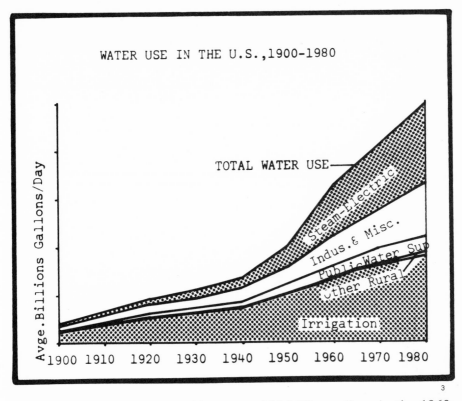

WATER USE IN THE U.S.,1900-1980

TOTAL WATER USE

Steam-Electric

Indus.& Misc.

Public Water Sup

Other Rural

Irrigation

Avge. Billions Gallons/Day

1900 1910 1920 1930 1940 1950 1960 1970 1980

3

billion gallons per day in 1900 to over 300 billion gallons in the 1960s. The average Western per capita use is 150 gallons each day. Industry increasingly requires vast quantities of process water, approximately:

7-25 gallons to produce 1 gallon of gasoline
25,000 gallons to produce 1 ton of steel
50,000 gallons to produce 1 ton of paper
250,000 gallons to produce 1 ton of acetate
600,000 gallons to produce 1 ton of synthetic rubber.

Agriculture still accounts directly for 50 per cent of all usage, requiring 400-500 pounds of water for each pound of dry plant produce. The water-to-specific-crop ratio varies considerably, but, in general, it is important to note that the lesser-developed, agriculturally based regions consume as much water per capita as the technologically advanced.

Health cannot be taken for granted when about 75 per cent of the world's inhabitants are without an adequate and safe supply of water, when 85 per cent depend on the most primitive methods for the disposal of excreta and refuse.

When air, water, and earth uses are compounded with mounting waste and sewage disposal, the emphasis on the required redesign of all such human systems becomes acute. The natural systems of air/water/soil

[13]

AVERAGE COMPOSITION OF MUNICIPAL REFUSE (% by weight)					
Waste Food	garbage				fats
Non-Com-bustibles	metals	glass & ceramics	ashes		
Rubbish	leaves,grass,brush,wood		materials	street refuse	rags house dirt etc
	paper				

[4]

purification are now so overburdened, through increase and misuse in many areas of the world, that concern is now expressed about their overall malfunction for greater areas.

Waste disposal, even in the most advanced countries, is still archaic. Those methods used in our larger urban concentrations are little improved from the traditional systems evolved for much smaller and less waste-productive communities of the preindustrial period. The average city of a half-million people now disposes of 50 million gallons of sewage daily and produces solid wastes of about eight pounds per person each day.

> Pollutants are the residues of things we make use of once and throw away. . . . As the earth becomes more crowded there is no longer an "away" . . . our whole economy is based on taking natural resources, converting them into things that are consumer products, selling them to consumers, and then forgetting about them. But there are no consumers—only users. The user employs the products, sometimes changes it in form, but he does not consume, he just discards it. . . . One person's trash basket is another person's living space. [5]

The use of water courses, of rivers, streams, and lakes, has also been grossly affected, not only in the "discard/residue" process of sewage disposal from cities and the increasing discharges of industrial wastes but from intensified agricultural practices.

[5] Ibid.

[14]

In the U.S. during the past 30 years, more than 20 billion tons of mineral wastes have been generated, and these now compose great slag heaps and mounds of mill tailings.

In summary, the total solid waste load generated from municipal, commercial, and industrial sources in the United States amounts to more than 360 million tons annually.

Altogether, over 3.5 billion tons of solid wastes are generated in the United States every year. [6]

Large amounts of soil additives in the form of fertilizers and chemical nutrients are washed off the lands through rainfall, irrigation, and drainage into the natural water courses where they disturb the aquatic life balances. The undue growth of algae and plant growths decreases the oxygen supply for fish and other organisms, thus attenuating the self-renewal of the water system.

Again, such problems are not localized. In the case of pesticide "runoff" from the land and other toxic discharges from domestic and factory sources, and so forth, these may be relatively isolated and "unobjectionable" where they enter upper reaches of streams and rivers. Their concentrated build-up effects may only be felt thousands of miles away—where rivers enter lakes, or reach the ocean, for example, as in the massive fish kills, of around 12 million, in the Mississippi and Gulf of Mexico in recent years.

Inadvertent poisoning of organic life through the unplanned and uncoordinated introduction of various toxins into the environ is not restricted to plants and animals. The effects on man are, in many cases, greater—but receive less direct attention. Some 500 new chemical compounds, each year, go into widespread usage in the highly industrialized countries with little planned attention to their long-term deleterious effects.

In 1968, municipal and industrial activities caused 88 per cent of fish deaths from pollution in the United States. The total number of fish killed from water pollution was an estimated 15,236,000; up 31 per cent from 1967. Approximately one-half the fish killed by municipal and industrial sources in 1968 died from wastes discharged by cities. [7]

Without going into the more publicized aspects of radioactive fallout, a simpler case may be adduced of "lead fallout"—from tetraethyl lead in auto fuel additives and other uses of lead compounds in domestic areas, and so forth. After almost fifty years of rapidly increasing use, such lead contamination is now being monitored at levels approaching toxicity in

[6] Report of Public Health Service Bureau of Solid Waste Management, U.S. Department of Health, Education, and Welfare, 1969.

[7] "Notes," Center for the Biology of Nature Systems, December 1969.

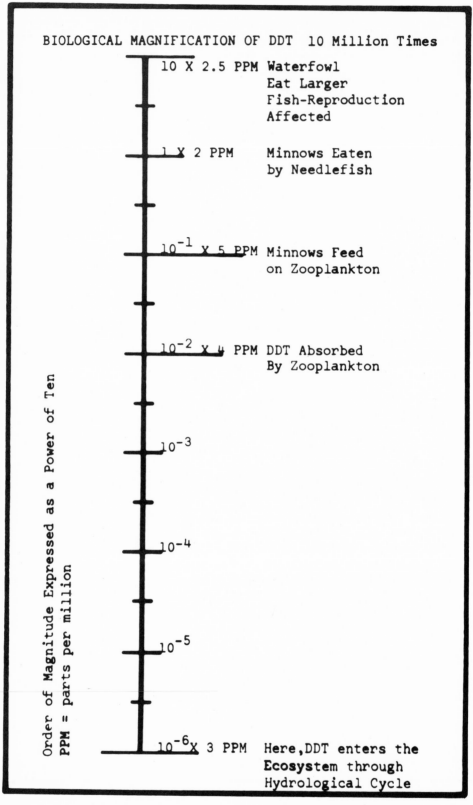

BIOLOGICAL MAGNIFICATION OF DDT 10 Million Times

10 X 2.5 PPM Waterfowl
Eat Larger
Fish-Reproduction
Affected

1 X 2 PPM   Minnows Eaten
by Needlefish

10^{-1} X 5 PPM Minnows Feed
on Zooplankton

10^{-2} X 4 PPM DDT Absorbed
By Zooplankton

10^{-3}

10^{-4}

10^{-5}

10^{-6} X 3 PPM   Here,DDT enters the
Ecosystem through
Hydrological Cycle

Order of Magnitude Expressed as a Power of Ten
PPM = parts per million

5

waters, crops, and the human system. Most recently, evidence of its role in stunting intelligence growth in infancy, and possible linkage to other systemic brain damage in adults, has come to light.

Returning to the more positive aspects of man's ecological activities, it is necessary to redress, in part, the semantic bias on "pollutants, garbage, and poisons." This usually tends to suggest vast quantities of alien substances being injected into an otherwise perfectly functioning system.

Man is perceived as the enemy, science and technology as the evil instruments which rape unsullied and fair nature. This attitude seems to be prevalent in many of the conservation and ecological slogans purveyed, for example, in the U.S. Its latent ties to a kind of "Mr. Clean" syndrome—as a latter-day version of the Puritan ethic—are too obvious to require elaboration here. We do not react to the degree to which technology has made nature accessible and enjoyable to man today—unlike the majority of men in the preindustrial period, when nature was viewed as a capricious and often cruel aspect of human struggle for survival. Poets appreciate nature in the raw more than the peasant, who has to wrest his laborious and precarious lifelong livelihood in closest contact with it.

Rather then—pollutants are as we perceive and designate them. Poisons are natural substances "out of place," or in excess of tolerable levels. The dust and gases of forest fires, volcanic ashes, pollens, marsh effluents, and so forth, are all "natural" pollutants of our natural environments.

> We tend to forget the extent to which nature destroys—and pollutes—segments of itself, sporadically and violently—with man often a major victim in these upheavals. Among the greatest of these were: the earthquake in Shensi Province of China in 1556, killing an estimated 800,000 people . . . the volcanic eruption of 1470 B.C. that destroyed the Minoan civilization . . . the great flood of the Hwang-ho River in 1887 that swept 900,000 people to their death; the famine in India in 1770 that claimed the lives of a third of this country's population—tens of millions of people; and the 1877-78 famine in China that killed 9,500,000. And centuries before man seriously tampered with nature through modern medicine, between 1347 and 1351, the Black Death (bubonic plague) wiped out 75,000,000 people in Europe. History records numerous other types of plagues and natural disasters that have periodically destroyed various forms of life and changed the face of the earth . . . long before man and his new technologie interfered with the balance of nature.[8]

Our concern here is to appraise more fully the role of man-made systems which are also natural systems in the overall functioning of the ecological context.

[8] "The Environment—and what to do about it," Dr. Glenn T. Seaborg, paper given at meeting of the National Academy of Sciences—National Research Council, Argonne National Laboratory, May 5, 1969 (published in *Nuclear News,* July 1969).

Many of the problematic aspects which we stress now are only problems that we have created recently through the "laissez faire" operation of most of our socio-economic and industrial undertakings. They are also due to the lack of anything approaching an integrated policy of environmental design and more thoroughly "anticipatory" planning which would account for the social consequences and ecological implications of our large-scale undertakings.

Our lack of adequate knowledge and equal lack of foresight and control are the main factors that overburden the natural regulatory systems and lead to their malfunction and breakdown. The naturally occurring forces operative in the environ *can* be more selectively and systematically used to absorb pollutants, reduce sewage/garbage, and reprocess discards and residue on a much vaster scale.

Some large-scale sectors, such as the global atmosphere, have enormous absorptive and regenerative capacities; others, such as a local soil area, forest, lake, or watershed, are more precariously balanced and may *not* be renewable or recoverable in anything but very long-range terms.

Some of the mandatory requirements for the merely adequate maintenance of the planetary ecosystem are already clear. We need to redesign our major social, industrial, and agricultural undertakings toward their more efficient and systematic functioning—as ecologically operating systems, rather than "piecemeal" aggregates of unrelated processes.

This would apply not only to environmental controls—such as houses, cities, and other facilities—but to all of those environmental control facilities which now comprise within themselves a vast "socio-agri-industrial ecology." We shall also need to refashion this system within the next few decades so that it may be able to serve many more people—at better material and psycho-social standards than ever before.

Even to note briefly a few of the most urgent of these ecological redesign directions will serve to indicate the massive revision and refashioning of our systems that this will entail:

a. "recycling" the metals and materials in the system—so that there is a swifter turnover with the least lag in scrapping and processing cycles. It is the "lag" aspect that is crucial in certain areas of environmental deterioration, that is, where junked materials are not reprocessed more immediately within the industrial sector. This is also an extremely costly and wasteful mode of using scarce resources. The process of use and re-use needs to be "designed in" to products at the beginning—or in cases where man-made recycling is not required, they should be so designed as to be reabsorbed "naturally" within the ecological processes.

It is also important to note that in high-grade technological processes, each use cycle tends, through overall development, to achieve more, not less, performance per invested unit of materials—hence less wasteful.

b. employing increasingly our "income" energies of solar, water, wind, tidal and nuclear power, rather than the hazardous and depletive fossil fuels—oil, coal, natural gas, and so forth. The latter represent major "capital" investments which, once used, are not replaceable. They are too precious to "burn up" in our currently prodigal fashion, when they may be more efficiently—and more fractionally— employed in indirect conversion to plastics, foodstuffs, and so forth.

c. refashioning our food cycle so that we may more swiftly augment the present starvation diets of more than half the developing world.

We need, however, to go also beyond emergency satisfaction of immediate needs toward the more extensive ecological redesign of our whole agri-industrial system, employing the most efficient "natural" means of food conversion through the plant/animal chains and the possibilities inherent in microbiological, biosynthetic, and other processes.

d. setting up global "ecological overview and alerting" centers which will act as "early warning" systems in relation to our large-scale scientific and technological undertakings—analyzing and evaluating their immediate and largest-range effects on the overall ecological matrix and their positive and negative implications for the quality of the human environ.

e. inaugurating networks of "integrative planning and study" which will function so as to focus, and constantly readdress major problems, priorities, goals, and directions in terms of their larger transnational aspects.

In essence, we have to redesign the presently chaotic elements of our developed and "externalized" human metabolic system into a series of "closed" ecological loops phased in with, and taking gainful symbiotic advantage of, the overall environmental systems.

The wastes of one type of production cycle become the raw materials of another; thus energy converted and dissipated for one purpose may serve many more. The noxious "garbage" of several processes may be valuable "nutrients" materials in another sector.

Each component sub-system now requires critical evaluation and redesign in terms of socio-physical environ costs, higher performance, and more economical function. The quantitative gains implied in this redesign are also even more directly qualitative in terms of reducing pollution hazards, in less "destruction" of the natural environ—and in the increased social and physical advantages available to man.

This may often entail "non-use" as well as redesign and reuse. It may involve accelerated activity and growth in certain areas, for example, of our industrial system—and in others, more deliberate restriction and conservation of resource use.

The scale of our present technological capacities are such that we cannot act without more accurate gauges of their immediate and largest-range effects. Where it may be pleaded, for example, by special interest groups that we have enough coal, oil, and gas reserves for 500 years, any expanded use at the present rate and level of technology is obviously precluded by their adverse side effects on the ecosystem. In such cases, a resource, an invention or process which is so evaluated as to be dangerous, in its widespread and uncontrolled use, to the maintenance of the life systems, should be left in "storage"—until a more evolved society may use it less prodigally and less dangerously!

Such an orientation leads again to our global and long-range—rather than local and immediate—commitments. As repeatedly stated, no large-scale human problem may now be solved outside of this planetary context. Air, water, and soil pollution are not local—the air is not restrained within municipal or national boundaries, nor are the waters.

Where massive imbalances occur—whether bio-physical in terms of earthquakes and other natural catastrophes or socio-physical in terms of hunger, disease, and the catastrophe of war—we need to recall that the resources of the planet can no more belong, by geographical chance, to any individual, corporation, country, or national group than the air we breathe. National ownership of a key watershed, mineral deposit, or scientific discovery is as farcical, and dangerous, a proposition as our supposed national sovereignty of an "air space."

Our evolutionary transition toward a planetary society now faces an analogous situation to that of emerging national or empire societies in the preceding two centuries. Then, the local ideological issues revolved around national control of public health, child welfare, education, pure food and water legislation, and so forth.

The same arguments now prevail, at the world level, regarding the rights and privileges of individual nations, regional groups, and large corporate organizations—as if they were isolated, self-contained, and wholly autonomous physical and social entities. Though such a fiction may be a comforting "prop" for local individual and social identity in a rapidly changing world, it is dangerously removed from reality.

The scale of our global systems of production/distribution, communication/transportation, and so forth, has now gone beyond the capacities of any single national or even regional group wholly to sustain and operate. They require, and are dependent upon, the resource range of the entire planet for the metals and materials of which they are built—and in which no nation is now self-sufficient. Each system is intricately and complexly interlocked with all others—production with transport, with communications, and so forth. The whole planetary "life-support system" is increasingly dependent on the global interchange, not only of physical resources and finished products but of the "knowledge pool"—of research, development, technical and managerial expertise, and the highly trained personnel who sustain and expand this.

We are now poised in the transition between one kind of world and another—literally on the hinge of a great transformation in the whole human condition. The next fifty years may be the most crucial in all of man's history. We have few guides to follow and almost no historical precedents. "Many of the old moralities have suddenly become immoralities of the most devastating character." [9] All of our previously local actions are now writ large on a planetary scale. The knowledge with which we might make the correct decisions is barely adequate—yet the consequences of our gross social, political, and ecological errors may reverberate for many generations to come.

THE VALUES QUESTIONS

One of the usual answers to generalizations about the environmental crisis, the population explosion, war, and so forth, is that available solutions are blocked by the value orientations of individuals. The question is usually phrased in terms of, "How can our personal ethical values control technology, redirect scientific development, arrest environmental deterioration?"

This may be best answered—by turning it around. We may ask, "How do our prevailing ethical values control technology and so forth, and how may we change them? How do we allow our traditional institutionalized set values to override those more positive and personal value commitments which may be in opposition to them?"

The "values" question is generally somewhat misplaced. It is always personal values which must be changed—while the value directions of our core social, political, and economic institutions must be regarded as sacrosanct.

The recent large-scale development and direction of science, technology, economic, and industry systems, in the Western world particularly, have indeed been initiated and sustained by a specific set of institutionalized social and economic values.

Our central questions should, therefore, be applied toward the reexamination of those attitudes and values which have, on the one hand, encouraged and controlled the development of technologies in certain locally preferred modes and directions, and, on the other hand, have failed to take into account the implications and consequences of such directions for the larger human society.

In the main, our current decisions regarding scientific, technological, and industrial development are still considered within a social and political framework that is inherited from the preindustrial period.

The socio-ethical attitudes of preindustrial and early industrial societies in the West were largely based on marginal and competitive survival.

9 Dr. Lloyd Berkner, *Population Bulletin*, Vol. XXII, No. 4, November 1966.

Resources were limited, inequably distributed, and access to them lay mainly through the exercise of physical power or other coercive means.

Individuals, institutions, and communities were considered as relatively autonomous and self-sufficient. Their survival was predicated on the freedom and ingenuity with which they modified and exploited the social and physical environment to their self-determined ends.

Ethical values in such societies tended to confirm the prevailing survival mode and to be constrained within its limited possibilities for choice and action.

Questions regarding the quality of human life, and of the environment, were relegated to individual concern, measured within the short-range criteria of institutional and commercial needs or subsumed under the prior requirements of local national security.

In the mid-twentieth century, the large-scale employment of scientific and technological means has changed almost all of the ethical "ground rules" upon which human society has operated. The use of such means has not only created a new kind of reality but permits the coexistence, and choice, of many different "realities."

Socio-ethical decisions regarding the human condition need no longer be phrased in terms of what we *can* do—but in terms of what we *choose* to do, both individually and collectively.

The most abrupt and significant changes in our period have been those of increased interaction of events, of their scale and magnitude—now reaching out to encompass the entire planet as the only workable context within which to consider the problems of ethical control of technology.

In a few generations the world has undergone the swift transition from a plurality of remote and relatively autonomous "national" societies to one complexly interdependent community. Within this context, many of our older guiding "moralities" may have become not only obsolete but injurious to the continued existence of human society.

It is only in the most recent and brief historical period that we have developed sufficient power to be actually, and even more potentially, dangerous to the overall ecological balance of the earth and to the maintenance of all human life upon it.

Our older ethical modes are no longer adequate toward the controlled exercise of that power—and we no longer have the ecological margins of error which could accommodate the local preferences and expediencies in earlier periods. For example:

1. The explosive increase in human population since the onset of the industrial revolutions has been termed "one of the greatest biological upheavals known in geological, as well as human history."

   Those local moral and religious attitudes that favored large families in the past may now be viewed as dangerously obsolete in the present and future. Questions then regarding the use and dissemination of population-control techniques may go beyond the

[22]

Estimated Annual Housing Needs in Africa, Asia, and
Latin America, 1960 and 1975
(In millions of dwelling units)

	AFRICA		ASIA		LATIN AMERICA	
	1960	1975	1960	1975	1960	1975
Due to population increase:	0.84	1.50	5.30	9.40	1.10	1.70
To eliminate the deficit or shortage in 30 years:	.73	.73	4.80	4.80	.60	.60
To replace the stock:*	1.03	1.03	7.10	7.10	.90	.90
Total new housing needed:	2.60	3.26	17.20	21.30	2.60	3.20

* Average life of a dwelling unit is assumed to be 30 years in urban and 20 years in rural areas. The 1975 figures do not take into account increments of stock between 1960 and 1975.

province of wholly personal and individual ethical concern to their considerations within the larger social morality of the world community.

2. The magnitude of our present industrial undertakings now forms a man-made ecological subsystem whose operation rivals in scale many of the natural processes in the biosphere. No longer constrained to the earth surface, these techno-industrial activities go increasingly into and beyond the atmosphere, beneath the oceans, and transform vast amounts of the material resources of the planet to human purposes.

The processing energies for these undertakings have already polluted the earth's atmosphere on a large enough scale to interfere with natural atmospheric processes.

We have, in recent years, had a rapidly growing chronicle of the degree to which such technological intrusions now prove dangerous to man himself as well as the other populations in the biosphere. The inadvertent poisoning of organic life, through the unplanned and uncoordinated introduction of various toxins into the environment, ranges from pesticide overkill to heightened radioactivity to the "accidental" and deliberate use of chemical and biological warfare agents.

Many such aspects of the deterioration of the earth, air, surface waters, and oceans have already gone beyond being locally contained and may be considered as world problems.

Yet—the social and ethical decisions regarding these relatively massive operations affecting the whole earth system are still made almost wholly on the basis of local, short-range expediency. Attempts to legislate and control such decisions are, therefore, viewed as "immoral" constraints on the rights of corporate industrial

hours in the laboratory and yet not feel committed to the consequences of such change as it enters our daily life. The state of pureness of intentions and non-involvement in consequences will no longer be tenable in a society fully pervaded with science.[11]

One solution for this dilemma of science may well be the assumption of leadership in framing a new ecological ethic that would outline the ground rules that are now required for adequate control of our massive technological capabilities.

It is a task that may be aided considerably by a scientific community that is now globally ubiquitous. Science as an institution, ideally, knows no borders—nor is it constrained within any preferred local idiom. Its laws and methods are, in varying degrees, universally applicable. As a "value-affirming" and goal-setting agency, its status is now equal to and, in many areas, greater than the older social institutions (for example, church, government, family, education) upon which this function traditionally devolved.

The notion that scientific and technological hazards may require as elaborate an early warning system as guided missiles has already been propagated by members of the scientific community in many countries. In the case of air and water pollution, of pesticides, thalidomide, and other drug controls, public attention has been focused upon the ethical issues by individual scientists and their associations—as well as by many journalists and private citizens.

The enlargement of such early warning systems and long-range ethical control of technological development will obviously require the greatest possible concentration of effort by all professional and voluntary associations, by citizens' groups, and by individuals.

To whom may such efforts be addressed and how may they be best forwarded?

The implementation of such ecological-ethical concerns through conventional political mechanisms now available is less than adequate. Political control is restricted to the brief mandate of office terms and is, in many countries, capriciously dependent on local vested interests and ideological expediencies. Increasingly it can only apply "after-the-fact" piecemeal remedies to long overdue local problems.

Within the world community, at a time when organized human knowledge allows man to accomplish the most audacious of yesterday's "impossibles," the so-called "realities" of today's geopolitic are dangerously outmoded. The goal may be then to devise new agencies and forms of organization which might enable us to detour around our largely artificial political and ideological dilemmas.

---

[11] "On the Emergence of a Second Generation Science Policy in America," Jurgen Schmandt, *Science and Policy: A Changing Union*, O.E.C.D. paper, April 1967.

NEGATIVE	vs.	POSITIVE
4 attack submarines at $45,000,000 each	would pay for	1 year of agricultural aid for $178,699,760
One $105,000,000 atomic submarine minus missiles	would pay for	$132,095,000 in famine relief aid including freight costs
One $122,600,000 atomic submarine including missiles	would pay for	$150,000,000 in technical aid
One $275,000,000 aircraft carrier	would pay for	$251,000,000 for 12,000 high school dwellings
One $104,616,800 naval weapons plant	would pay for	35 school buildings at $4,000,000 each
One $104,616,800 naval weapons plant	would pay for	26 160-bed hospitals at $4,000,000 each
One $250,000,000 intercontinental ballistic missile base	would pay for	One 1,743,000 KWH capacity hydro-electric dam
14 standard jet bombers at a cost of $8,000,000 each	would pay for	A school lunch program of $110,000,000 and serving 14 million children
One new prototype bomber fully equipped	would pay for	250,000 teacher salaries this year or 30 science faculties each with 1,000 students or 75 fully-equipped 100-bed hospitals . . . or 50,000 tractors . . . or 15,000 harvesters

Military Personnel - Average Cost Per Man*

	COST
U.S.A.	$4,345
Belgium	1,814
Greece	430
Thailand	400
China (Taiwan)	218
Korea	145

* *Pay, subsistence, housing, and clothing*

The question is addressed, therefore, to the new polity of that world society which already exists—at various stages of growth and awareness—in the many types of formal and informal global networks of individuals and organizations.

We may summarize these comments by stating again that the issue is not whether personal ethical concerns *can* control technology and so forth, but that many of our current social, political, and ethical attitudes which *do* control and largely misdirect our developed industrial, economic, and technological capabilities are dangerously obsolete!

Man in the Biosphere

LIFE ON earth has been possible only during its long billions of years of evolutionary development through the relatively stable interrelationships of the variables of climate, the composition of the atmosphere, the oceans, and the life-sustaining qualities of the land surface, the natural reservoirs, and cycles.

The tenuous envelope of air, water, and soil surrounding the earth within which life can survive has been termed, variously, the bio- or eco-sphere, or the bio-film.

It extends vertically into the air only to about 6¼ miles, downward to the known depths of the ocean around 36,000 feet, and into the first few thousand feet of the earth surface itself where living organisms have been found.

Within this thinly spread bio-film or air, earth, and water space around the planet, then, all living organisms exist in various systems of delicately balanced symbiotic relations. The close tolerances of many of these balances have only become known to us, generally through their disruption, in recent times.

This "life space" of the biosphere is a unitary complex of organic relationships contained with three main layers—*the atmosphere* (or air envelope), *the hydrosphere* (water/oceans, lakes, rivers, and so forth), and *the lithosphere* (the earth/soil surface itself). Within this layered system the balance of life conditions for the various organic forms is characterized by their highly specific "ecological niche" conditions of temperature, pressure, humidity, electrical potential, interface exchanges of liquid-solid, solid-gas, gas-liquid, and so forth.

The overall system is, in turn, conditioned by energy radiation from the sun, providing "power" for all the life exchanges within the biosphere. To this major source of life-sustaining radiation may be added the kinetic and potential energy of the gravitational system of the earth mass itself—and the geothermal energies radiating to the surface from its interior core.

Other major "systems" constants governing optimal sizes, physical configuration, life cycle, and metabolic rate of living forms would be:

   a. Gravity—the physical and structural effects relating to this; pressures of gases, material strengths and stabilities. The ways in which such relationships are stable in various "phase states"—liquid, gaseous,

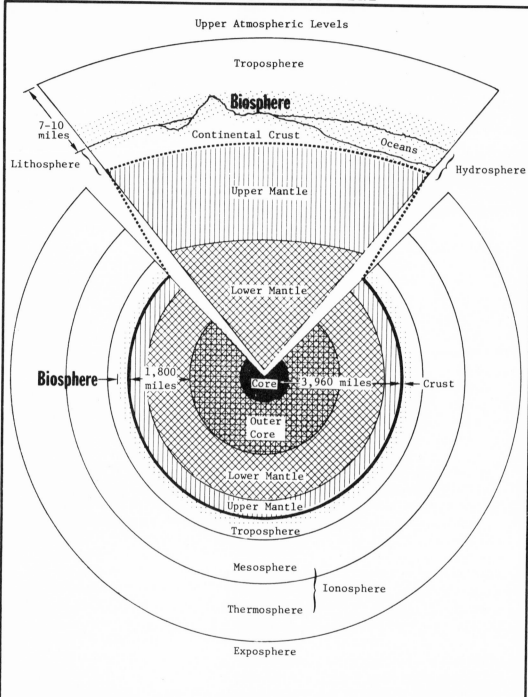

The biosphere is that thin film of air, earth and water around the globe within which most living organisms are found. Within this 'life space' are all the energy patterns and processes of interaction which sustain our major activities. Though extending vertically about seven miles into the air and for thousands of feet below the earth and oceans its most densely populated region is just above and below sea level.

solid—between temperature ranges permit a variety of physiological systems and organic forms within the different earth and water environs.

   b. Temperature—the medium frequency of heat and radiation excitation on the earth's surface allows low temperature energy and materials exchange.

The atmospheric filtering of radiation, the gravitational, pressure, and temperature constants above, provide a median environment for organic life.

Importantly here this median range of environmental conditions has, so far, been in a sufficiently steady state to allow for long evolutionary changes to take place in various species—and yet has provided a sufficient range and diversity of living habitats to allow great species variety to take place. If we were to refer (from our own anthropomorphic vantage point) to an optimal ecological context—it would be defined within the latter terms of diversity of life milieu and a requisite variety of the species, types, and possible developmental ranges of life forms. These twin criteria of diversity and variety are, in this way, inseparable in terms of evolving organic life.

Other systems, or "living process," variables related to the above would be:

   a. Those frequencies of exposure to solar radiation governed by rotation of the planetary mass—the day and night cycles, the seasonal climatic variations, and the distribution of water, land, and air, that is, the geographic location factors.

   b. In turn these may be related to the distribution of energy and material resources of various kinds in different sectors of the biosphere, that is, the local availability of food and so forth, the biogeochemical cycles providing energy and materials exchange between environ and living species.

Other variables in the biosphere that influence life could be varied and multiplied by specification and cross-relation of the above, and by further introduction of altitude, continental mass relations, soils, vegetation distribution, marine environ conditions, and so forth. The extent to which living organisms are also viably affected by the vast electromagnetic systems surrounding, and external to, the earth itself is little known at present.

The planetary surface is relatively "meager"—approximately 197 million square miles, of which 57 million square miles is land and 140 million square miles is water.

In human terms, we live on a small island at the bottom of an ocean of air, surrounded by an ocean of water. Within this life zone, most living forms are held close to the surface of the earth, but the organic evolutionary process has been specifically characterized by the enlargement of occupancy of the vertical and horizontal ranges of the biosphere.

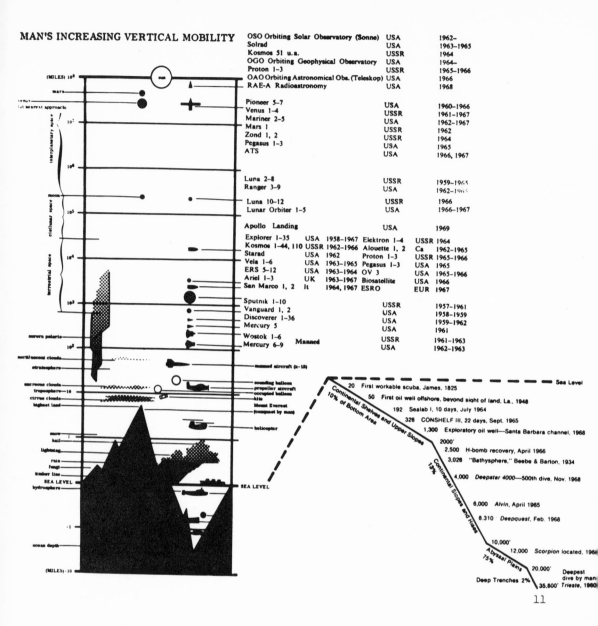

This enlargement of occupancy, life-space, or ecological niche, has been most marked in man—both in the speed of its occurrence, and in the degree to which he has extended this range enormously within a relatively brief historical (rather than evolutionary) time scale. The most singular and recent mark of physical life-space extension in our own period has been to broach the upper limits of the biosphere—by orbiting men, animals, and plants outside the earth's atmosphere, and landing on the moon.

Also, it is important to note that we underline here only physical space extension. Man's conceptual space (that is, his unique ability to transcend space and time bounds through his symbolic thought processes) is, again, of an even more greatly expanded magnitude.

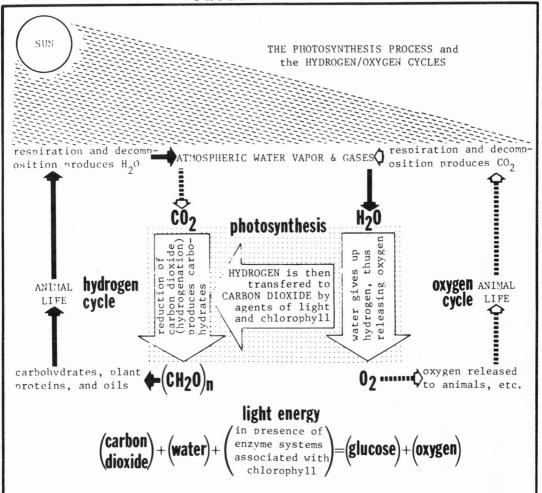

"Chemically the photosynthetic process involves the storage of a part of the sunlight energy as potential or "bound" energy of food...is much more complicated than indicated in the above word formula....The photosynthetic process of food manufacture is...the synthesis of amino acids, proteins, and other vital materials ...this occurs simultaneously with the synthesis of carbohydrates (glucose), some of the basic steps involved being the same. The reverse of photosynthesis, or respiration, results in the oxidation of foods with the release of energy....A part of the synthesized food is used, by the producers themselves. The excess as well as the producer protoplasm is then utilized by the consumers and decomposers, or part of it is stored or transported into other systems." --E. P. Odum.

"...thirty-five percent yield in energy conversion by plants is very respectable -- considering that we do not know of any reaction produced by visible light outside the plant cell which would convert as much as 10 percent of absorbed light into chemical energy. If some economical means could be found to capture and convert even 10 percent of light energy, the discovery conceivably could produce a greater revolution in our power economy than can be expected at present from the much-publicized discovery of atomic energy." --E. I. Rabinowitch.

12

SUN — Solar Energy

$CO_2 + H_2O + N_2 +$ PHOTOSYNTHESIS

PHOTOSYNTHESIS produces 150,000 million tons of Organic Matter (Vegetation) per year on world land surfaces.

89% vegetation presently unused by man

Higher food extraction processes may provide increased food supply.

11%

CULTIVATED CROPS & GRAZING LANDS provide 16,000 million tons of potential food material

4,000 mil tons of Usable Food Materials taken from the land

25%

75% waste cuttings etc.

Approximately 13,500 million tons WASTED per year.

97% animal metabolic processes

Grains etc. fed to livestock with 3% net efficiency

60 mil. tons Animal Products

360 million tons food per year HUMAN CONSUMPTION

75% (300 million tons) plant food

Mechanized Food Processing about 2,000 million tons per year.

80% waste from processing

20%

400 million tons of food in STORAGE & TRANSIT

25% LOST IN STORAGE through rodents, insects, & other vermin.

Percentage of Solar Light Striking a Leaf

reflected 20%
transmitted 10%
transferred 20% to heat

2% used in photosynthesis

used in transpiration 48% & evaporation

100%

Distribution of Photosynthetic Material in Plants

20% respiration

Plants use only about 2% of available light energy in photosynthesis. Man in turn uses only 25% of materials manufactured from this process.

25% usable crops

43% leaves & stalks

12% roots

75% Waste cuttings, etc.

The amount of solar energy received on one acre of land during a 90 day growing season is equivalent to the energy derived from 243 tons of Anthracite Coal.

Energy obtained from 25 bushels of corn is equivalent to 0.33 tons of Anthracite Coal

Converted

(The amount of energy obtained from 25 bushels of corn when converted to alcohol by fermentation is equivalent to 0.20 tons of Anthracite Coal.)

(The amount of energy obtained from 25 bushels of corn when converted to meat by feeding steers is equivalent to 0.033 tons of Anthracite Coal.)

"...The natural chemical storage of solar energy by photosynthesis in agriculture is inefficient. Ordinarily, only about one-fifth of one percent of the annual supply of solar radiation falling on agricultural land is utilized in plant growth. But in devices, with the direct use of the solar radiation, higher efficiencies are possible -- perhaps 40 percent for the distillation of water, 25 percent for solar refrigeration, and 10 percent for conversion into electricity with silicon photovoltaic cells. We can use the sun effectively for cooking, for heating water and heating houses, for cooling and refrigeration, for distilling water, and for producing mechanical and electrical power with heat engines, thermoelectric converters, and photovoltaic cells.

"...Solar energy cannot now compete economically with cheap fuel and electricity as we have it in industrialized countries. But there are 2 billion people in the world who do not now have any electricity; and most of these people live in the sun belt near the equator. In many of these areas there are few deposits of fossil fuel and no opportunities for hydroelectric power. Solar radiation is often the most important, potentially available, natural ressource." -- F. Daniels.

13

Despite the close dimensions of the life zone within the biosphere, and the relatively narrow physio-chemical tolerances endurable by living organisms, there are a countless variety of habitats within which forms of life pursue their cycles of individual growth and decay.

Man, of middle "size" in range, and one of the least specialized of complex living forms, has almost evolved beyond the stage where he is not constrained within any specific habitat or "ecological niche" parameters. These may be distinctly characterized for most other organisms—by differences in medium, of earth, air, and water; in physio-chemical factors of salinity, acidity, and so forth; temperature, pressure, and light availability.

At the gross end of the scale, we may distinguish such ecological habitats as climatic zones, ranging through the tropical, subtropical, temperate, subarctic and arctic, and so forth. At the micro-end, however, we have bacterial spores at the limits of the bio-atmosphere, organisms under several atmospheric pressures in the ocean depths, and those whose "niche" is on, or within, the tissues of another life form.

The fundamental relation between all organisms and their environ (as including other organisms) is the maintenance of life through various types of energy exchanges. The basic life materials are the chemical elements; for example, the human organism is 99 per cent composed of hydrogen, oxygen, carbon, nitrogen, calcium, and phosphorus with various other trace elements in fractional amounts; its mass is 60 per cent water. Such materials are, of course, energy—at varying levels of relatively temporal organization. We could, therefore, refer to all materials as energy whose "mass" and structural characteristics have given stable configurations in the particular material state.

Energy and materials are in constant and complexly regenerative flows between, and within, organisms and the environ. One such major flow in the biosphere is, for example, the process of photosynthesis, through which plant life utilizes solar energy through its enzyme systems to convert, or "build," carbon dioxide and water into the more complex carbohydrates. These, in turn, provide food energy for other organisms which, in the reverse of the photosynthesis process, "break down" such complex materials—on the one hand, into growth/maintenance elements, for example the internal metabolism of digestion, conversion, storage, and so forth, and, on the other, into further external exchanges, for example in respiration and in the mobility necessary to obtain more food energies, and so forth.

In the simple food chain, used as an example—say from plant to herbivorous animal to man—

a. The plant converts the sun's energy within its own tissue-building process—giving back into the atmosphere various gaseous exchanges.

b. The herbivore eats the plant, receiving carbohydrates, minerals, water, and so forth from its ingestion—but using up energy to move

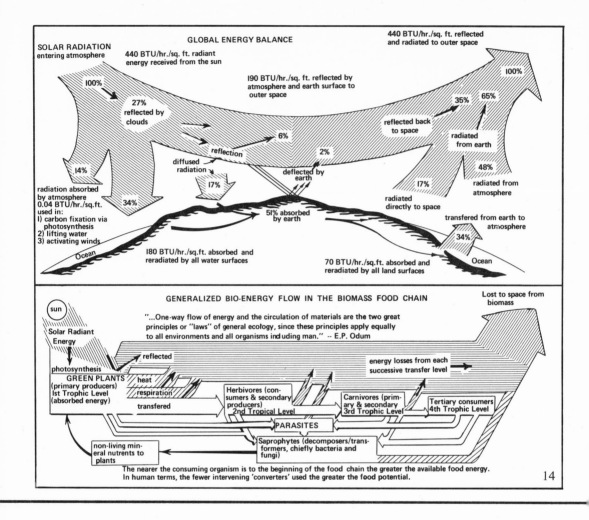

from plant to plant, to chew, digest, and otherwise fuel its overall metabolic process. Part of the range of substances ingested also returns to the environment through excretion, sweat, respiration, and so forth.

c. Man eats the herbivorous animal, but expends more energy in, for example, locating, killing, and processing the meat for his metabolic purposes.

No energy conversion is 100 per cent efficient, so even in such a simple food chain, much is lost, or dissipated back into the environment at each link in the chain. Eventually, of course, plant, animals, and men die and their "stored" tissue energies are dispersed, again, in the earth cycles.

Theoretically the end point occurs when all the energy has been dissipated and the organism's decay converts the initially "built up" elements back into their original state.

However, even at this simple level of consideration, the growth/decay cycles are such that the process is in part regenerative. Decay is in itself a further microbial reduction which produces nutrents for other plants,

EARTH ENERGIES

"Of the solar energy received by our globe, practically all of it is re-radiated to outer space within a few hours. Only a minute percentage of solar energy goes to vegetation, lifts water from the oceans or stirs up the winds. Solar radiations that arrive in the form we normally think of as light, have the highest intensity; but the wide range of heat or infrared radiations reaching the earth comprise the largest quantity.

"Photosynthesis holds the biological key to life. Through the catalytic action of chlorophyll, solar energy sparks the chemical combination of carbon from the air with hydrogen from ground water, to form the carbohydrates of plant fibers. This provides the fuel for all forms of animal life—food. Without food all animal life would perish. But carbohydrates also combine to yield a cellulose fuel that can release heat energy by the process of combustion." —"Solar Radiation Power."

"The transfer of food energy from the source in plants through a series of organisms with repeated eating and being eaten is referred to as the *food chain*. At each transfer a large proportion of the potential energy is lost as heat. The number of steps or 'links' in a sequence is limited, usually to four or five. The shorter the food chain (or the nearer the organism to the beginning of the chain) the greater the available energy which can be converted into *biomass* (=living weight, including stored food) and/or dissipated by respiration. Food chains are of three types: the *predator* chain, which, starting from a plant base, goes from smaller to larger animals; the *parasite* chain, which goes from larger to small organisms; and the *saprophytic* chain, which goes from dead matter into microorganisms. Food chains are not isolated sequences, but are interconnected with one another. The interlocking pattern is often spoken of as the *food web*. In complex natural communities, organisms whose food is obtained from plants by the same number of steps are said to belong to the same *trophic* level. Thus, green plants occupy the first trophic level, plant-eaters, the second level, carnivores which eat the herbivores the third level, etc. . . . A given species population may occupy one, or more than one, trophic level according to the energy actually assimilated. The *energy flow* through a trophic level equals the total assimilation at the level which, in turn, equals the production of biomass plus respiration." —E. P. Odum.

other animals, other men—thus "closing" the cycle and phasing it into a further series of regenerative energy conversion processes.

When we consider the more complex role of man—plus his man-made external energy/material conversion metabolism—this alters the overall process significantly in human ecological terms.

Man, of course, like all living systems, functions basically as an energy-converting organism. Energy is absorbed in one form or another, for example, food, and transformed for internal and external purposes. Part goes toward maintaining the internal processes of the organism, and part is available for external use, for example, to find more food. In terms of external mechanical work energies, man is, however, a relatively inefficient energy converter. Operating at less than 20 per cent efficiency, he can only deliver about one horsepower hour of work per day.[12]

---

[12] *Energy and Society*, Fred Cottrell, McGraw-Hill Book Co., Inc., New York, 1955. Man can convert about 3500 calories per day. About 20 per cent of this is available for mechanical work—roughly one half to one horsepower hour per day per man.

His own mechanical energy conversion capacity has been, possibly, the least important factor in his progress. Man's unique evolutionary pattern has been predicated rather on his ability to convert energies externally.

Through his intellectual capacity, he has designed and employed tools which enable him to do this on a much greater scale than may be accomplished solely by his own unaided metabolism. This gain in energy output through the use of technical advantages has increased enormously in the past hundred years, as the conceptual tools provided by the scientific revolution were phased into new technological tools giving higher degrees of energy conversion than were possible for man before. Though many millions of men still function in the lesser developed countries as "mechanical" energy converters—as their own prime source of survival energy—man increasingly functions mainly as controller and designer of high-energy-conversion systems.

The overall energy flux into and out of the biosphere and its larger containing earth system, by radiation received from the sun and that radiated outwardly from the earth, is roughly in balance. This allows us to consider the biosphere, theoretically, as a locally "closed" system—within which no energy may be lost or gained overall. The energy flow within the biosphere, as a closed local system, should ultimately be reduced through its various exchange losses to an evenly dissipated end state—of entropy or minimal energy flux. The state of minimal order, of the final running down of the system, may be characterized, partially, by the process of organic decay. In this stage, the arrest of material growth and the slowing down of external and internal energy flows is finally resolved in the disintegration of the complex organic structure into its elementary constituents.

Entropy is also used, in terms of information, as a measure of uncertainty, or disorder, of knowledge. To the extent that it increases order and predictability in the system—and reverses the tendency toward "running down"—information is, however, anti-entropic. As the agency or principle of complex ordering in the environ, its role has not yet been fully or clearly defined in relation to energy and material organization. It is significant, for example, that while the amount of available energy and material elements in the ecosystem remains relatively constant, the amount of order increases.

The bio-evolutionary direction appears to be set toward increased complexity of order—information increases and accumulates.

A further interesting characteristic of this process is that:

> The information extracted from the environment by one organism does not in equal measure reduce the amount of information available to any other organism, nor does what is learned by one diminish the amount that can be learned by another. A genetic population in expanding its numbers increases, if anything, its per capita information supply, even if per capita supplies of

materials and energy be reduced. . . . Evolution viewed as a "learning process" entails the incorporation of more information into population systems: "In the long view there has been an increase in the complexity of genetic instructions" (Medawar, 1961).'. . . Social organisms in sharing information increase the amount by increasing the distribution rather than inversely.[13]

Man's function in the ecosystem may then be viewed as:

a. Entropic—in using energies to reduce complex material resources to simpler structures, that is, where he acts as an "unconscious" biological agent as in food processing, reducing and extinguishing other organic populations, disordering toward malfunction of "natural" systems, in air, water, earth, pollution, and so forth.

b. Anti-entropic—where he uses energies more consciously to modify and transform his environ toward higher levels of complexity. Through the application of organized information/knowledge in his "artificial" systems, he increasingly reprocesses, reorders, and redistributes energy and materials in more, rather than less, complex forms.

The balance between his entropic (disordering) propensities and his anti-entropic (ordering) propensities is, in this sense, a central point of our present discussions. We can only surmise, in terms of our brief historical record, that this balance is already tipped, through evolutionary development, toward the anti-entropic as more favorable to the survival of the species.

The concept may also be extended beyond life on earth toward the imminent engagement of man with extra-terrestrial systems. Some of these, such as the moon, are of a different and apparently less complex order and lower energy level. What may be the "evolutionary" effect of introducing anti-entropic bias into such entropically oriented systems? The question enlarges philosophically to the consideration of all life forms, including the non-human, as an anti-entropic process or principle.

Our more immediately pressing consideration is, however, human life and society within the present confines of the biosphere.

Apart from the comparatively local disturbances of natural cycles occasioned through hunting, herding, and primitive agricultural practices, man, until quite recently, did not have the developed capacities to interfere seriously with the major life-sustaining processes of the planet. He could live and find food only under conditions restricted by his technological development. The earth surface available to him, with breathable air, water, and arable land, was less than one-eighth of the earth area; the remainder—of the seas, mountain peaks, glacial and desert areas—was mainly inaccessible to human habitation or large-scale use. Though the evidence of ancient disruption of natural balance is still with

[13] "Social Organization and the Ecosystem," O. T. Duncan, Chapter 2, *Handbook of Modern Sociology*, R. L. Farris (ed.), Rand McNally & Co. (U.S.), 1964, p. 44.

us in the form of man-made deserts, for example, de-forested lands and so forth, these were essentially local in their scope and consequences. It is only in the most recent and brief historical period that man has become dangerous to the overall ecosystem—hence, to the maintenance of the human community within that system.

His acquisition of specifically technological means of gaining control over local aspects of the environ through fire, implements, weapons, and so forth, is accompanied by the swift increase and geographical spread of human populations. This latter and explosive increase occurs most significantly in relation to the introduction of inanimate energies in machine production; to mechanized agriculture and the use of chemical fertilizers, improved sanitation, general health measures, and higher life expectancy.

As each earlier invention expanded the amount of energy and material advantage available to man, so it has adjusted the ecological balance to favor his increase—with corresponding adjustments in all other living populations within the system. The latest growth change in human population since the onset of the industrial revolutions is, within all previous contexts, an extremely "abnormal" one. (In the longer range, of course, this apparently unstable and explosive increase of population may be some unrecognized pattern change in the "natural" evolutionary development of an unique species.)

The first fifty years of this new phase, of adaptation and "species extension" through intensive industrialization, seemed to confirm the notion that man could indeed conquer nature—could free himself from the biological laws governing other species' development. As the series of such technological revolutions has multiplied in frequency and power amplification, this has been somewhat tempered by the equivalent increase of knowledge about the overall effects on the planetary habitat.

Though it has been obvious for some time that we cannot simply extrapolate human development in terms of "natural laws," and the Malthusian and other limits may not strictly apply, there are still many central questions remaining. Since man, as a species, sidestepped the normal biological sequence of evolutionary adaptation through his capacity to externalize his intellectual and physical means, in symbolic and technological systems, he is, in this sense, more directly in control of his own future evolvement. The extent of that control, over the environ and over his own "uncontrolled" activities within the environ, rests on his capacity to apply himself consciously to an adaptive process which has been largely unconscious.

THE PHYSICAL ENVIRONMENT

a. The Atmosphere   That area of the earth's atmospheric shield which is most concerned with the human biosphere is the tropospheric layer—

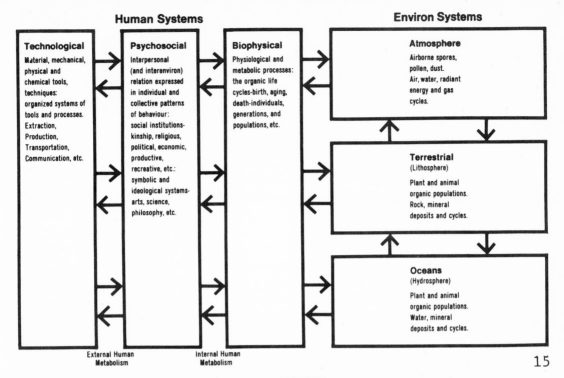

Technological	**Psychosocial**	**Biophysical**	**Atmosphere**
Material, mechanical, physical and chemical tools, techniques: organized systems of tools and processes. Extraction, Production, Transportation, Communication, etc.	Interpersonal (and interenviron) relation expressed in individual and collective patterns of behaviour: social institutions- kinship, religious, political, economic, productive, recreative, etc.: symbolic and ideological systems- arts, science, philosophy, etc.	Physiological and metabolic processes: the organic life cycles-birth, aging, death-individuals, generations, and populations, etc.	Airborne spores, pollen, dust. Air, water, radiant energy and gas cycles.

Terrestrial
(Lithosphere)

Plant and animal organic populations. Rock, mineral deposits and cycles.

Oceans
(Hydrosphere)

Plant and animal organic populations. Water, mineral deposits and cycles.

External Human Metabolism   Internal Human Metabolism   15

THE GLOBAL ECOSYSTEM

We need to extend the physical and biological concepts of ecology to include the social behaviors of man—as critical factors in the maintenance of his dynamic ecological balance. Nature is not only modified by human action as manifested in science and technology—through physical transformations of the earth to economic purpose—but also by those factors, less amenable to direct perception and measure, which are political-ethical systems, education, needs for social contiguity and communication, art, religion, etc. Such "socio-cultural" factors have played and will increasingly continue to play a considerable role in man's forward evolutionary trending and its effects on the overall ecology of the earth.

composing about 70 per cent of the air mass around the planet and confined in a narrow film of about six miles in thickness. This layer is a great "cycling" reservoir which transforms and redistributes the various energies and materials that are swept up into its systematic flows. Within it move all the great wind systems that sweep around and ventilate the terrestrial biosphere system, carrying all the water, gas, and material interchanges around the surface of the earth and playing a major role in the climatic cycle system. It has been calculated that a complete interexchange of all the circulating air masses around the planet in this layer takes about two years—and the passage of an "air parcel," or local air/gaseous system, about one month.

The composition of the atmosphere close to the earth's surface is mainly nitrogen, oxygen, and argon in approximately 75, 23, and 1 per cent by volume. Other constituents amounting to less than a tenth of 1 per cent are hydrogen, neon, helium, krypton, xenon, radon, tritium, and so forth. We are generally not aware of the extent to which the atmospheric environ is freely "mined" of its elements in our various agricultural and industrial technologies. They are, of course, "replaced" by other parts of the organic and inorganic cycle. But we have, as yet, no accurate monitoring of the vastly enlarged scale at which this or that key consituent may be in the process of extraction in excess of renewal by the ecosystem.

Within this layer the condensation of water vapor also takes place, which provides, within its cycling interchanges with the terrestrial waters, all the available waters in the biosphere. The "inward" distributive pattern of this cycle is in the form of rain, snow, hail, dew, and so forth. This evaporation, precipitation, exchange cycle links the atmospheric, marine, and terrestrial areas of the biosphere in massive exchanges and redistributions not only of water and other gas vapors but of all the other elements of material particles caught up in different parts of the major environ cycles. The latter process would include quantities of bacterial spores, soil from wind erosion, dust of all kinds, and all the other materials which the natural and man-made earth processes pour into the air.

Where we referred to the pollution of the atmosphere and water as a global, not local, problem, we may note here that dust particle masses and other materials noted above may be carried almost 3000 miles by a wind of only 10 miles per hour before they are deposited on the earth's surface. Dust and sand storms are a common enough phenomenon—during the United States' dust-bowl storms of 1934, it was calculated that about 700 million tons of topsoil materials were eventually blown out to sea.

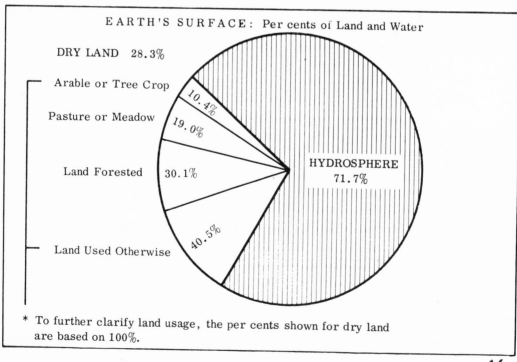

EARTH'S SURFACE: Per cents of Land and Water

DRY LAND   28.3%

Arable or Tree Crop   10.4%

Pasture or Meadow   19.0%

Land Forested   30.1%

HYDROSPHERE
71.7%

Land Used Otherwise   40.5%

* To further clarify land usage, the per cents shown for dry land are based on 100%.

	Percent arable land under permanent crop	Percent meadow and permanent pasture	Percent wasteland	Percent forestland
WORLD	11	19	40	30
AFRICA	9	21	45	25
U.S.S.R.	10	17	34	39
N. AMERICA	10	13	42	35
L. AMERICA	5	20	27	48
SOUTH ASIA	22	13	40	25
EAST ASIA	10	15	63	12
OCEANIA	4	54	33	9
EUROPE	31	18	23	28

17

The decreasing amount of land per capita is a relative measure. The actual amount of land surface available, and still unused, may be gauged from the fact, for example, that the entire population of the United States occupies much less than 10 per cent of the land area. Man's increasing mobility suggests that fixed land habitation may only be one of a number of alternative patterns. In relation to food yield—many more people may be fed *off* the land than on it, in terms of agricultural occupation.

	ACRES	
EARTH SURFACE PER CAPITA	*Total Surface Per Cap:* 40.46	*Total Dry Land Per Cap:* 8.88
		Virgin Forest: 3.15
	Total Hydrosphere Per Cap: 31.58	Grassland: 2.67
	Ocean: 28.68	Desert: 2.07
	Lakes and Rivers: 1.71	Cropland: .85
	Ice-covered Land: 1.19	Accessible Forest: .14

[43]

In addition to the specific function ongoing within the tropospheric layer, there is however the key functional processes of all the combined layers of atmosphere around the planet. These protective shields filter the incoming solar energies bombarding the earth from the sun. In so doing they admit the major part of short-wave radiation, but trap the outgoing long-wave radiation moving upward from the earth's surface. This aspect of their function works like a "greenhouse" screen—slowing up the dissipation of energies from the biosphere and helping to stabilize temperature ranges within the biosphere at the earth's surface.

Critical attention has been given, in recent years, to the way in which the increase of atmospheric carbon dioxide, due to the use of fossil fuels, may further accentuate this heat-trapping "greenhouse" effect. Suggestions have been made that this direct but originally unwitting interference with one of the largest of the ecosystem's maintenance patterns could, eventually, raise average temperatures to a sufficient degree to cause gross climatic changes—even reduce the polar and other ice cap areas.

Past and present human practices have largely misused, or ignored, the enormous potential inherent in the massive and constantly renewed energy circulation patterns in the atmospheric cycles. Wind power at the earth-surface level has been used for centuries, but this represents only a tiniest fraction of the energy potentials available. These are usually only perceived by us at their most awesome and destructive expression in electrical storms, tornadoes, typhoons, and so forth.

Some of the human research and organizational energies presently devoted to further extraction and misuse of the fossil fuels could—if reapplied within this area of "tapping" more directly into the atmospheric circulation exchanges—possibly reap an even greater annual amount of renewable "pollution-free" energies for direct human use.

b. The Earth   Treated here as *land* environ, this occupies only about a quarter of the earth surface and is the primary ecological habitat of man—from which he extracts most of his food and other energies and upon which, until recently, he conducted most of his environ transactions.

Most of the material resources contained within the land surface have been built up over long periods of geological time. The great metal and mineral deposits upon which human society is dependent for its extended technological systems have taken millions of years to accumulate in the earth surface. As a side glance at our present use rate of these non-renewable resources, the following rough figures are instructive. [14]

Of course, in the case of the metals, though these are not renewable in the strictest sense, they are cycled through successive use/scrap processes. The fossil fuel extractions are of a more seriously depletive nature.

The dry land usable by man, which also sustains large animal

[14] *World Balance Sheet,* R. Doane, Harper, New York, 1957, p. 27.

	GEOLOGICAL TIME REQUIRED TO PRODUCE 1 TON (MILLIONS OF YEARS)	MAN'S REMOVAL RATE (MILLIONS OF TONS PER YEAR)
Petroleum	250	600
Coal	1000	2000
Iron	2000	200
Lead	4000	4

populations, is less than a quarter of the available land space—the rest is desert, jungle, ice cap or mountain peaks, and so forth.

The usable agricultural area provides food through direct use of edible crops or through other animal food converters. In terms of traditional food yield uses, this is confined to a thin depth of topsoil where most of the plant nutrients are present in a relatively critical distribution balance. This is a renewable resource base dependent on the various geochemical and climatic cycles; in recent historical time, however, the rapid growth of population, its aggregation in great densities, and the pressure upon the food soils have led to misuse and relatively permanent loss of great areas of this vital soil base.

One of our most critical present limitations remains biological and terrestrial, in this sense, as human society is still almost wholly dependent on the plant/animal food yield from a relatively "fixed" area of arable land.

Recent calculations [15] suggest that the present maintenance of three billion humans in the biosphere requires a plant yield sufficient to accommodate 14.5 billion other consumers. These others, the animal populations, are an essential element in maintaining the humans by acting as intermediate processors for many products indigestible by man. Pigs, for example, consume as much as do 1600 million people, when measured on a global scale; the world horse population has a protein intake corresponding to that of 650 million humans, that is, approximately the population of China.

c. The Oceans   The marine environ covers more than 70 per cent of the planetary surface. In terms of planetary space, food, and other material resources, this is like having several more environs at human disposal. The comparatively shallow areas of the continental shelves alone are equivalent to about half the area of the earth's lowlands where most of humanity lives.

Our knowledge of the oceans is rudimentary. As man's locally, most hostile environ for centuries, only the surface has been travelled upon and

[15] "The Human Biosphere and Its Biological and Chemical Limitations," G. Borgstrom, *Global Impacts of Applied Microbiology*, Mortimer P. Starr (ed.), John Wiley and Sons, Inc., New York, 1964.

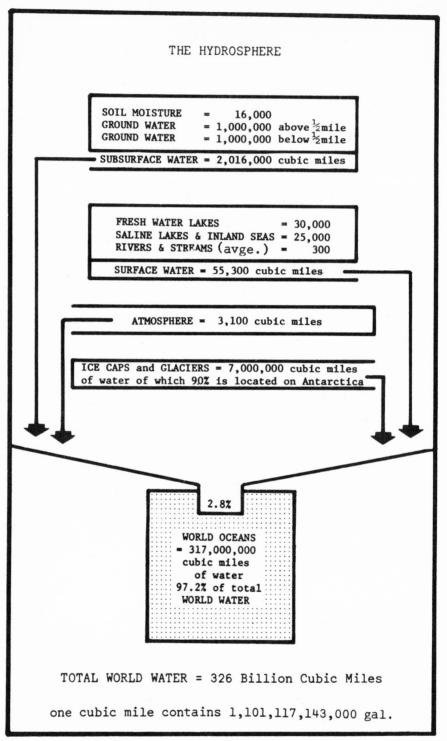

THE HYDROSPHERE

SOIL MOISTURE   =   16,000
GROUND WATER   = 1,000,000 above $\frac{1}{2}$mile
GROUND WATER   = 1,000,000 below $\frac{1}{2}$mile

SUBSURFACE WATER = 2,016,000 cubic miles

FRESH WATER LAKES   = 30,000
SALINE LAKES & INLAND SEAS = 25,000
RIVERS & STREAMS (avge.) =   300

SURFACE WATER = 55,300 cubic miles

ATMOSPHERE = 3,100 cubic miles

ICE CAPS and GLACIERS = 7,000,000 cubic miles
of water of which 90% is located on Antarctica

2.8%

WORLD OCEANS
= 317,000,000
cubic miles
of water
97.2% of total
WORLD WATER

TOTAL WORLD WATER = 326 Billion Cubic Miles

one cubic mile contains 1,101,117,143,000 gal.

18

[46]

the depths not at all investigated until quite recently. Barely 1 per cent of all sea organisms have been studied and the cyclic migrations of its larger creatures have been little charted.

Also pertinent is the fact that about four fifths of the planet's animal life and the bulk of its vegetation are underwater—yet, comparatively little of these are used as food. In this regard, the ecological recycling of such resources in the oceans is much more frequent than on land. Fish and other organic populations have higher growth rates; ocean crops have less variable "weather" problems for possible cultivation and harvesting than the land.

The other material resource potentials of the oceans have hardly been tapped. Vast deposits of pure metal ores have recently been located on the ocean bed, and the waters themselves are a rich source of extractable materials.

> The ocean is the ultimate depository of everything eroded from the continents. Over 40,000 million tons of materials are washed into the oceans every year by rivers. The winds also transport millions of tons of materials per year.[16]

The use of ocean waters for direct irrigation of the land has also been considerably pioneered in recent years. As specifically applicable to the sandy "desert" soils, such research is of extreme importance in the critical area of world food production.

> Arid and semi-arid regions cover a third of the land's surface . . . many of these sandy regions could be made productive with salt water irrigation . . . any advance in making sandy soils productive adds to the resources available for the production of food. And any such addition can be a factor in the effort to keep the production of food abreast of the growth of population.[17]

Desalination, the production of fresh water from sea water, also forms part of the growing use of the oceans. The most promising developments are those combining nuclear power/fresh water generation plants in the same productive units. Such units in present use around the world have a desalting capacity of about 50 million gallons per day—an increase of 100 per cent over the past two years.

In view of these great potentials, it is hoped that planned use of the oceans may come about in time to reduce the spoilage which has already occurred in many areas, particularly of the key coastal shelves. Indiscriminate sewage and industrial wastes have already ruined future developments of considerable areas for some time to come.

This process is further increased by the discharge of fuel oils from sea tankers which contaminate beaches for years and wreak heavy toll of sea

[16] "Mineral Wealth from the Ocean Deep," J. L. Mero, *Discovery*, July 1964.

[17] "Salt Water Agriculture," H. Boyko, *Scientific American*, February 1967.

41 mil. tons (World Catch) of Live Weight Marine Products in 1961		Edible Weight consumed		4,200,000 Asia & Far East
	sold fresh	35%		2,400,000 Western Europe
	frozen	10%	10%	2,000,000 Mainland China
	canned	10%		2,000,000 Russia
	cured	17%		1,200,000 Africa
	meal & oil, etc.	28%		1,000,000 U.S.A. & Canada
				600,000 Latin America
				150,000 Near East
				40,000 Australia and New Zeland
				14,000,000 Metric Tons

28%

5-50%

Discarded at sea, in port or by consumer

"International trade absorbs about a third of the world catch in terms of value. The fact that actual quantities of fish exported more than doubled over the period 1957–64 while their export value rose considerably less, is largely the result of a rapid growth in world trade of low value fish meal, used principally for animal feed and fertilisers. Peru has been the main contributor to this sector of trade.-- Barclays Bank Review.

SOLAR ENERGY

SUN

Attached Plants, kelp, algae, etc... along shore. (littoral)

Primary Producers floating plants in lighted zone only (phytoplankton, dino-flagellates, etc.) yields 100 billion tons per year.

Consumers & Secondary Producers (zooplankton, small crustacea, etc. which live in lighted zone) yield 100 billion tons per year.

C_2O, H_2O and plant nutrients etc.

Primary Carnivores preditory surface fish etc. which feed upon plankton (whales & other nektonic animals) yield 10 billion tons per year.

Secondary Carnivores (bony fish etc.) yield 1 billion tons per year.

Discarded Wastes sinking and detritus food etc.

mid-depth plankton

Mid-Depth Primary and Secondary carnivores, parasites and scavengers.

Bacterial Activity and Decomposition of sinking food.

abyssal zooplankton

Abyssal Fish and Benthic Animals which feed on detritus or are parasitic.

Bacterial Activity and Decomposition of sinking and detritus food.

REGENERATED PLANT NUTRIENTS returned to lighted zone by vertical upwelling

The major fishing waters of the world "...are usually on continental shelves or near to them. Either the water must be shallow enough that the local food chain can be based on food and light at the bottom, or there must be a 'plowing up' or nourishment from the bottom by means of up-wellings."

"...Marine plants, such as kelp, are relatively unimportant parts of the biomass. Microscopic floating plants, the phytoplankton, depends upon the nourishing elements in the water and on sunlight. They are rarely found much below 300 or 400 feet of depth. They form the food of zooplankton, small floating animals. The zooplankton are too small to be used by any but the smallest fish, which in turn are the food of larger fish. Thus there is formed a food chain, in which the largest links are those caught by man. There are of course complex interconnections within the chain: whales actually can feed on zooplankton, as can herring and sardines. But as a general rule, the larger the fish and the more valuable it is to man, the higher it is in the chain.

Just as man makes relatively 'inefficient' use of grass when he eats it through the agency of meat or poultry, so the fish food chain is more and more 'wasteful' of the basic nutrients available to the phytoplankton. With some knowledge of the loss at each stage, and with some idea of the number of links in an average chain, experts have attempted to estimate what the potential harvest of the biomass might be."

"...It is not certain to what extent plankton feed on the nutrients released by the decomposition of dead fish. If their dependence were high, then a more complete utilization of the basic nutrients might soon exhaust the nutrients on which the food chain now depends. The estimates assume that relatively full utilization of the seas would not significantly alter the store of basic nutrients upon which the chain depends."-- A. D. Scott.

birds and other ocean organisms. Old sea mine fields still render large areas of the coastal waters unsafe, and are now accompanied by the new hazard of radioactive waste disposal in offshore areas. Over-fishing and hunting has led not only to greatly reduced catches in many previously well-populated fishing zones but also the near extinction of certain ocean species like the great sperm whale and the fur seal.

Much play has certainly been made of the ocean's inner space as our next great exploratory frontier. The magnitude of the volume and expanse of the seas and oceans, the richness and variety of life in the surface waters and in the depths, certainly encourage this idea. The main critical difficulty, again, may be to regulate and plan their exploration now— *before* unrestricted exploitation, industrial and military misusage render them unfit even for their own organic populations.

The nations already wrangle about how much of the oceans "belong" within their national territories; the weaponeers are already planning for military installations on the ocean floor. A mapping of the oil and other industrial exploitation leases already operative on the shallow continental ocean shelves around the world is an instructive forewarning that the so-called "inner space" frontier is no longer an open option for all humanity—but that much of its potential use has already been foreclosed in terms of various short-range commercial and other interests.

The "ecologically" designed use of the oceans, if vigorously pursued in an integrated way and on a truly transnational scale, could provide man with an enormous expansion of his environs, which would also solve many of his most pressing terrestrial problems of food, scarce and depletible land resources, and increasing water requirements of agriculture and industry. The recreational potential and challenge of exploring the oceans could indeed, then, truly become a new and almost illimitable frontier.

THE MAJOR ENVIRON CYCLES

Mediating, as it were, between the physical environment systems and human systems, it may be useful here to interpose some notes and diagrams on the cycles of biogeochemical exchange. We have mentioned these in referring to the complex interchanges of air, water, and other constituents of the physical environ systems.

The specific importance of the major cycles—of photosynthesis, carbon, nitrogen, phosphorus, and so forth—are that they can provide the working modes for reorganizing and redesigning the critically necessary recycling and reuse systems which are currently lacking in the majority of our man-made industrial systems.

They are also a guide toward seeing more clearly the basic material element exchanges which go on in the natural system around us, and can be used to identify the precise points where the impingement of human socio-economic or technological intrusions enter into, and interrupt, the natural cycles.

[49]

20

WORLD HYDROLOGIC CYCLE

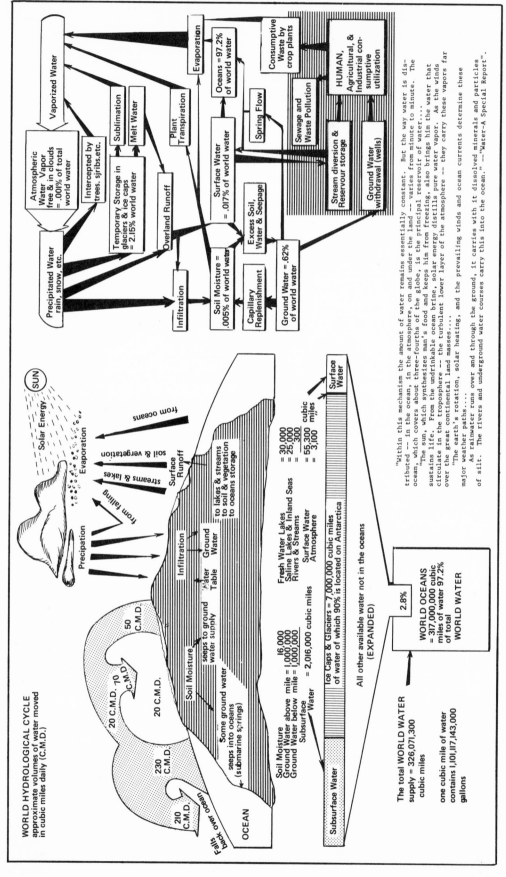

WORLD HYDROLOGICAL CYCLE
approximate volumes of water moved
in cubic miles daily (C.M.D.)

Soil Moisture
Ground Water above mile = 1,000,000
Ground Water below mile = 1,000,000
Subsurface Water = 2,016,000 cubic miles

Fresh Water Lakes   = 30,000
Saline Lakes & Inland Seas   = 25,000
Rivers & Streams   = 300
Surface Water   = 55,300
Atmosphere   = 3,100   cubic miles

Ice Caps & Glaciers = 7,000,000 cubic miles
of water of which 90% is located on Antarctica

All other available water not in the oceans
(EXPANDED)

2.8%

WORLD OCEANS
= 317,000,000 cubic
miles of water 97.2%
of total
WORLD WATER

The total WORLD WATER
supply = 326,071,300
cubic miles

one cubic mile of water
contains 1,101,117,143,000
gallons

"Within this mechanism the amount of water remains essentially constant. But the way water is distributed -- in the ocean, in the atmosphere, on and under the land -- varies from minute to minute. The
ocean, which covers about three-fourths of the globe, is the principal reservoir of water....
    "The sun, which synthesizes man's food and keeps him from freezing, also brings him the water that
sustains life. From the undrinkable ocean brine, solar energy distills pure water vapor. As the winds
circulate in the troposphere -- the turbulent lower layer of the atmosphere -- they carry these vapors far
over the great continental land masses....
    "The earth's rotation, solar heating, and the prevailing winds and ocean currents determine these
major weather paths....
    As rainwater runs over and through the ground, it carries with it dissolved minerals and particles
of silt. The rivers and underground water courses carry this into the ocean." --"Water-A Special Report".

As may be noted, most of the cyclical patterns chosen for comment here are concerned with the main critical "element" exchanges, modifications, and reuses in the environment.

Of the inventory of chemical elements in the universe, between 30 and 40 are known to be essential to life forms. Some are required in large quantities—carbon, hydrogen, oxygen, and nitrogen—others in minute or trace quantities. All are in more or less constant circulation within the biosphere and, though local "shortages" may occur, as in the loss of critical soil components, all elements are potentially inexhaustible as recirculating in the eco-cycles or "in reserve" in the great reservoirs of the ocean, air, and earth crust.

It has been suggested, in this regard, that man is unique in his use of the elements. He not only employs in his internal metabolism the range of approximately 40 elements essential to biophysical maintenance but, in his external metabolism of extractive, productive, and redistributive processes of agricultural and industrial activities, he employs all the other naturally occurring elements in the universal inventory, as well as their isotopes.

Man is, however, only one of the species of organic life in the biosphere, and, like all life forms, exists only in interrelation with all others. The precise degree of interdependence may seem remote and tenuous between a briefly viable colony of micro-organisms in a large area of virgin jungle on one side of the globe, and a community of human beings on the other—but it is, nonetheless, real.

Plants, animals, men, and their environs are bound together in a complex web of relations. Animals depend on plants and other animals for food; man depends on both. The plants draw nutrient elements from the soil and these are, in part, returned from various stages in the food chain. The soil-plant-animal-soil cycle is only one aspect of the larger cycling of essential elements in the system. The soils themselves become exhausted of various elements through repeated plant/animal populations, and it has long been man's practice to fortify the natural cycling of essential soil elements with "natural" or "chemical" fertilizer elements.

One of the greatest revolutions in human society, the agricultural revolution, comes through increased understanding of the fundamental growth patterns of plants and their relation to the natural cycles of energy and materials in the ecosystem. The second and more recent wave of industrial revolutions was also predicated on increased understanding and gainful advantage of the energy cycling principles.

The major cycles in the biosphere are, therefore, of key importance to all aspects of our ecological considerations. Almost all of our major societal undertakings are affected by or, more importantly, affect the natural cycling of energies and materials in the system. In some cases the cycling patterns are so large and their "reserves" and compensating mechanisms of sufficient latitude to correct any maladjustment through

[51]

21

WORLD CARBON CYCLE
in tons per year (T.P.Y.)

STAR-DUST

730,000 T.P.Y. of STAR-DUST enters earth's atmosphere and adds some carbon

Returned to atmosphere from earth, ocean, biosphere & man's processes.

Atmospheric Free Carbon

Solar Energy Oxygen

Elaborated into living plant materials through photosynthetic process.

Returned through other processes.

Plant acids decompose limestone particles in soil.

Returned to atmosphere through plant & animal respiration & decay.

Chalk & limestone deposits formed with carbon by marine organisms.

Microbial Activity & further Decay

cultivation aerates soil & increases the release of carbon.

Ocean Food Chains
Approximately 90% of world photosynthesis is carried out in sea by algae.

Terrestrial Food Chains
Plants take in carbon animals exhale carbon.

Excreta & Cellular Carbon in Humus

Fossil Fuel Beds created through time under influence of heat and pressure

industrial combustion for processing, heating & transportation.

industrial processing that decompose limestone, etc.

wood, grasses, animal oils & dung burned as fuel.

household heating, etc.

FREE ATMOSPHERIC CARBON
2,300 x 10⁹ tons and increasing

160 x 10⁹ T.P.Y.

169 x 10⁹ T.P.Y.

100 x 10⁹ T.P.Y.

Ocean Photosynthesis

60 x 10⁹ T.P.Y

TERRESTRIAL PHOTOSYNTHESIS 60 x 10⁹ T.P.Y.

PLANT and ANIMAL RESPIRATION released from

from Tilled Soil 2 x 10⁹ T.P.Y.

from Homes & Industrial Combustion 6 x 10⁹ T.P.Y.

from Hot Springs & Volcanoes 1 x 10⁹ T.P.Y.

from Oceans 100 x 10⁹ T.P.Y.

Geothermal Activity

Rock Weathering .1 x 10⁹ T.P.Y.

Decay

New Fossil Beds .1 x 10⁹ T.P.Y.

Fossil Fuels 40,000 x 10⁹ T.

World Ocean Carbon in Solution = 130,000 x 10⁹ tons

Ocean

...The geological record indicates that the huge capacity of the biosphere to store and turn over carbon dioxide has also had its effect upon climatic change. We know that plants borrow 60 billion tons of carbon dioxide yearly for photosynthesis. Under present conditions the organic world repays nearly all of this debt each year via respiration and decay. The formation of new fossil fuel deposits withholds at most only 100 million tons of carbon dioxide, or less than .2 percent of the annual amount used for photosynthesis.... ...The earth's hot springs and volcanoes pour about 100 million tons of carbon dioxide back into the atmosphere per year. The earth in turn recaptures approximately the same amount each year by the weathering of the rocks.... ...Quite accurate records of the amount of fossil fuel consumed in the world each year show that in the past 100 years man has added about 360 billion tons of carbon dioxide to the atmosphere. As a result the atmospheric concentration has increased by about 13 percent.... ...If fuel consumption continues to increase at the present rate, we will have sent more than a trillion tons of carbon dioxide into the air by the year 2000. This should raise the earth's average temperature 3.6 degrees....
--G. N. Plass.

ERRATA: Input of atmospheric carbon dioxide is 168.1 T.P.Y.; 0.1 x 10⁹ T.P.Y. emerge from volcanoes etc.;

ATMOSPHERIC CO₂ (parts per million)

CARBON DIOXIDE CONCENTRATION

360
340
320
300
280

1860 80 1900 20 40 60 1980

"Each year the plants of the earth combine about 150 billion tons of carbon with 25 billion tons of hydrogen, and set free 400 billion tons of oxygen. Few are aware, that perhaps as much as 90 percent of this giant chemical industry is carried on under the surface of the ocean by microscopic algae. Only 10 percent of it is conducted on land by our familiar green plants. ...A tiny fraction of the organic material synthesized by plants is later utilized as food by animals. A much larger amount is used in the respiration and other life activities of the plants themselves. The greatest part, however, is decomposed into water, carbon dioxide and mineral salts by the decay of leaves and dead plants on land and in the sea.
--E. I. Rabinowitch.

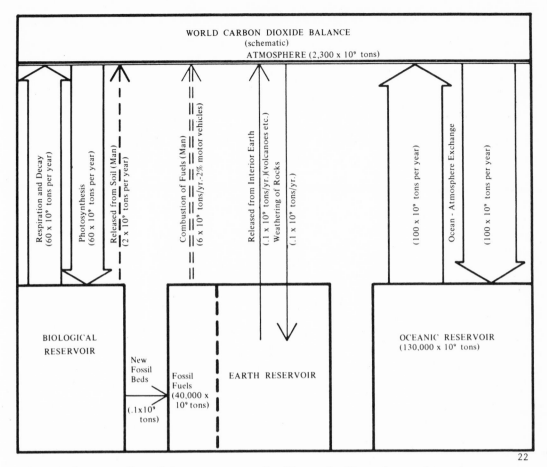

WORLD CARBON DIOXIDE BALANCE
(schematic)
ATMOSPHERE (2,300 x 10⁹ tons)

Respiration and Decay
(60 x 10⁹ tons per year)

Photosynthesis
(60 x 10⁹ tons per year)

Released from Soil (Man)
(2 x 10⁹ tons per year)

Combustion of Fuels (Man)
(6 x 10⁹ tons/yr.-2% motor vehicles)

Released from Interior Earth
(.1 x 10⁹ tons/yr.)(volcanoes etc.)

Weathering of Rocks
(.1 x 10⁹ tons/yr.)

Ocean - Atmosphere Exchange
(100 x 10⁹ tons per year)

(100 x 10⁹ tons per year)

BIOLOGICAL
RESERVOIR

New
Fossil
Beds

(.1x10⁹
tons)

Fossil
Fuels
(40,000 x
10⁹ tons)

EARTH RESERVOIR

OCEANIC RESERVOIR
(130,000 x 10⁹ tons)

22

human intervention. Others are naturally "imperfect" cycles, and require careful attention to avoid serious disequilibrium and, locally occurring, disparities in the essential elements with which they are concerned.

Apart from the hydrological, carbon, and photosynthesis cycles already discussed or illustrated, it may be pertinent to give two other key examples.

The Nitrogen Cycle   Though one of the most abundant elements in the atmosphere, nitrogen requires chemical change to enter the soil and be utilized by plants in the food cycle. A further series of changes returns nitrogen to the atmosphere and completes the circular process. We may view the pattern from any point in the cycle.

   a. It is emitted into the air from nitrogenous compounds in organic materials that are broken down by a chain of specialized bacterial actions. Some of this reduced nitrogenous material is taken up by plants, as nitrate for example, some used in other forms by other organisms.
   b. The above reduction of nitrogen-bearing materials is complemented by the return cycle of nitrogen from the atmosphere and other

[53]

sources by the action of nitrogen-fixing bacteria, fungi, and plant forms in the soil, pond waters, and so forth. This aspect of the cycle is a relatively closed, self-regulating pattern.

c. Further nitrogen exchanges occur, for example, in the atmosphere as ammonia and nitrates are formed by electrical discharges, in the earth from excretion/decay cycles, and in the marine environ.

We may note that the complex regenerative pattern of even this single element requires interaction from each level and every component of the ecosystem, including both living and nonliving forms of matter.

The major importance of nitrogen for the food cycle of plants—hence, animals and man—cannot be exaggerated. The increase in agricultural plant yields through the application of "artificial" nitrogenous compounds to augment and increase the cycle locally is now marked. Adequate protein supplies for the present world population are thus no longer predicated entirely on the natural cycle—but require millions of tons of nitrogen fertilizer produced by the chemical industry. This is a particularly clear-cut example of the ways in which the extended industrial metabolism of man is interlocked with the natural cycles to maintain his increased requirements.

> Approximately one sixth of the world population is presently dependent on artificial nitrogen for its survival. It can safely be assumed that the world's soils via residues and soil micro-organisms can hardly be expected to take care of more than half the additional 3000 million people expected before the end of the century. This would imply that in the year 2000, the world would need artificial support along the nitrogen front of no less than 50.5 million tons. . . . The annual production of 1 million tons of nitrogen requires at least 1 million tons of steel and no less than 5 million tons of coal, calculated as energy equivalents. This is a most crucial factor for the energy-poor parts of the world.[18]

It may be noted that in terms of the usual solutions advocated in relation to the "food problem," such industrial components are not so closely gauged. Further, with the added amount of other agri-industrial support chemicals, the amount required would be closer to 500 tons by the year 2000. Stating the problem in these terms, one can calculate more accurately the logistical parameters of the problem—the increase in fertilizer production, in energy/plant expenditures, transportation, distribution, and the ancillary requirements of raw fertilizer materials, extraction processing, transport, and so forth.

Whereas in the nitrogen cycle the element is returned to, and circulated within, the soil in large amounts by natural means, other elements have less locally regenerative cycles. They may be "lost" through leaching or erosion to the oceans or redistributed in unfavorable balances through

[18] Op cit., Borgstrom.

THE NITROGEN BIOGEOCHEMICAL CYCLE

NITROGEN GAS in the air

ELECTIFICATION (lightning) and Photochemical Fixation

Industrial Nitrogen Fixation

MARINE BIRDS

Fresh Water and Marine Life

Shallow Marine Sediment

Deep Sediment

Igneous rocks

NITRATES

NITRITES

gain from Volcanic action

AMMONIA

NITRITE Bacteria

AMINO-ACIDS and Organic Residues

aminifying BACTERIA

BACTERIA & fungi of decay

EXCRETION AREA, Etc.

PROTOPLASM — animals plants

Protein Synthesis

Denitrifying Bacteria

NITROGEN GAS

PROTOPLASM

AMINO-ACIDS

AMMONIA

NITRITES

NITRATES

energy barrier

heat

Basic steps of nitrogen circulation in ascending, descending order, with the higher energy consuming forms on top and energy releasing forms below.

—— steps requiring energy from other sources
--- steps providing energy to the decomposer organisms

"It has been calculated that a ton of wheat extracts on the average from the soil about 47 lbs. of nitrogen, 18 lbs. of phosphoric acid and 12 lbs. of potash; and unless these losses are replaced the fertility of the soil is decreased." --W. R. Jones

"The self-regulating, feedback mechanisms, shown in a very simplified way by the arrows, make the nitrogen cycle a relatively perfect one, when large areas or the biosphere as a whole is considered. Thus, increased movement of materials along one path is quickly compensated for by adjustments along other paths. Some nitrogen from heavily populated regions of land, fresh water, and shallow seas in lost to the deep ocean sediments and thus gets out of circulation, at least for a while.... This loss is compensated for by nitrogen entering the air from volcanic gases...."

"According to Hutchinson (1944a), the amount of nitrogen fixed from the air (non-cyclic nitrogen) is estimated to lie between 140 and 700 mg. per square meter, or between 1 and 6 pounds per acre per year for the biological; only a small portion (not more than 35 mg. per square meter per year in temperate regions) is non-biological (electrification or photochemical fixation). Biological fixation in fertile areas may be much greater than the biosphere average, up to 200 pounds per acre, according to Fogg (1955)." -- E.P. Odum.

THE PHOSPHORUS BIOGEOCHEMICAL CYCLE

Marine Birds

GUANO DEPOSITS

FRESH WATER & MARINE LIFE

Ocean Water contains $6 \times 10^{-5}\%$ phosphorus

SHALLOW MARINE SEDIMENT

Deep Sediment

streams

dissolved phosphates

exposed through geologic activity

SEDIMENTARY ROCKS (Often highly phosphatic and enriched by replacement and concentration.)

phosphate rock

leaching

weathering & erosion

PHOSPHATING BACTERIA

fossil bone deposits

METAMORPHIC ROCK

IGNEOUS ROCKS

APATITE (a complex form of calcium phosphate.)

Agricultural Fertilizers

Protoplasm Synthesis — animals plants

excretion

PHOSPHORUS makes up about 0.1% of the earth's crust.

"A portion of the earth's phosphorus is continually passing out of the mineral reserve into living substance, and similarly, phosphorus is continually passing out of living matter to re-enter the mineral reserve. This movement of the element has been pictured as taking place within two cycles, a land cycle and a marine cycle, or one general cycle with its complicated circulations of the element since the two cycles are definitely interrelated. Actually, the losses of the one cycle become the gains of the other. The cycle of matter is not completely reversible, that is to say, all matter is not restored completely to its original state, but it has a large measure of forward movement which permits a redistribution of chemical elements and states of matter."

"The cyclic phenomena of the life processes and the transport of phosphatic material by streams to the ocean waters give a broad picture of how biologically available phosphorus has been distributed over the face of the earth. The phosphorus content of sea water has been derived chiefly from soil erosion and the processes which dissolve fish bones, shells, and the vast amount of debris from dead tissues."

"Goldschmidt estimates that on an average, ocean water contains $6 \times 10^{-5}\%$ phosphorus. Authorities recognize that phosphorus is the most important limiting factor or for the growth of plankton, and therefore, that it controls almost entirely the production of life in ocean waters. The quantity of phosphorus is always very small owing to its continual utilization by sea life and it is said to vary between zero and 0.07 ppm." --Vincent Sanchelli.

example, where large herds of livestock are "harvested" from the same pasture area over many years and shipped elsewhere for consumption. Without human intervention, trace elements they have taken up would be returned to the local soil via the growth/decay cycle—these are now "lost" at their various other use/consumption destinations elsewhere on the earth surface.

Man speeds up the extraction and widens the circulation pattern of a great many materials so that in certain critical cases the local cycles are disturbed—the process becomes acyclic. As we have so far emphasized, we are fast acquiring capacities to disturb other major cycles in similar fashion. The prime function of designed and ecologically oriented man-made systems would be that they make acyclic processes more cyclic.

Though we deal elsewhere and more specifically with the problems of human population growth and food, one author, G. Borgstrom, whom we have already quoted, makes the plea that research is "now needed on the scale of a space project . . . to broaden the potential of the biosphere." Suggesting that we learn to operate with nature, not against it, he lists an "action program" whose emphasis on the systematic study and utilization of the organic cycles is of key relevance to large-scale environmental planning in the comprehensive and ecologically oriented sense.

A. *Foods*
  a. Review the status of fermented foods to improve and broaden the use of present methods in order to find simple and cheap procedures.
  b. Institute a systematic search for methionine-rich fungi or, possibly, bacteria.
  c. Expand engineering studies for the transformation of sewage plants into food-producing centers (via algae, yeast, fungi, bacteria, fish, and so forth).
  d. Determine the nutritive contribution by intestinal flora.
B. *Soils*
  a. Broaden the attack on improved microbial nitrogen-fixation in tropical and temperate climates with the specific aim of reducing artificial application of fertilizers or, still better, making this superfluous. This is the greatest contribution microbiology could make to the developing world.
  b. Establish more precisely the role of microbes in the mineralization process and the release of bound mineral nutrient resources (phosphorus, calcium, and so forth).
C. *Seas*
  a. Detailed mapping of nitrogen and sulfur cycles of the oceans.
  b. Study of the role of nannoplankton.
  c. The microbial mobilization of the nonliving organic matter of the oceans.
  d. The role of autotrophic microbes in the oceans.
D. *Lakes*
  a. The sulfur and nitrogen cycles (determine the role of microbes).
  b. The immunization mechanism of fish under the stress of the seasonal build-up of microbes in the surrounding waters.[20]

[20] Op cit., Borgstrom, p. 163.

In terms of our focus on energy and material efficiencies, it may be interesting to note certain of the energy-conversion efficiencies obtaining in the naturally occurring cycles.

Estimates vary considerably, but the generalized figure for plant fixation of solar energy is given as roughly 1 per cent in the overall photosynthetic process on the earth's land surface. This seemingly low average is due, partially, to variation in plant cover—as limited by sunlight, rainfall, and the availability of nutrient elements in the soil.

Of this total converted solar energy: (a) approximately 30 per cent is used in the plant's own growth and maintenance; (b) 10 per cent is transferred to herbivorous animals; (c) the remainder (60 per cent) is reduced in plant decay by bacterial composition.

The overall efficiency for the oceans is estimated at 0.18 per cent of the solar energy reaching the ocean surface.

The seemingly low energy-conversion efficiencies in such an overall view of the total ecosystem are not strictly comparable with those obtained in man-made energy-converting mechanisms. There are great differences in physical and time scales between the two forms. The naturally occurring forms are self-renewing and self-perpetuating and achieve more "production" growth per unit and time interval than man-made forms—whose efficiency calculation does not include renewal, autonomous growth, repair, and replacement.

THE HUMAN SYSTEMS

Man, and his "systems," organizations, institutional arrangements, and so forth, should be regarded as a wholly integral process. For convenience, for various analytical and practically oriented purposes, we may isolate some feature of man and consider this as a major aspect of the whole. But, as in dealing with different parts of the physical environment complex, we need to remind ourselves constantly that the analysis and classification into "parts" or "subsystems" is merely a labeling convenience.

The use of the term "system" always needs qualifying in this regard. The complex richness of human activities often forces us back onto simplistic models—particularly for measurement and accounting purposes. Though these may function well as limited conceptual supports, and help reduce human complexity into some neat disciplinary format, we usually end up with "mechanical systems": models like economic man, behavioral man, political man, technological man, and so forth. Such concepts abstracted for convenience tend to become "reified"—that is, they tend to assume an autonomous reality in themselves, "a life of their own," for which they are unfitted. This is particularly dangerous when we attempt to solve human problems in such reified terms. We often assume that many critical human problems may be solved wholly within the artificial divisions set up for intellectual convenience.

[59]

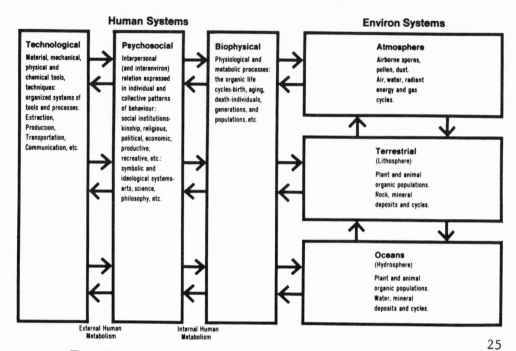

Technological	Psychosocial	Biophysical	Atmosphere
Material, mechanical, physical and chemical tools, techniques: organized systems of tools and processes. Extraction, Production, Transportation, Communication, etc.	Interpersonal (and interenviron) relation expressed in individual and collective patterns of behaviour: social institutions- kinship, religious, political, economic, productive, recreative, etc.: symbolic and ideological systems- arts, science, philosophy, etc.	Physiological and metabolic processes: the organic life cycles-birth, aging, death-individuals, generations, and populations, etc.	Airborne spores, pollen, dust. Air, water, radiant energy and gas cycles.

Terrestrial
(Lithosphere)

Plant and animal organic populations. Rock, mineral deposits and cycles.

Oceans
(Hydrosphere)

Plant and animal organic populations. Water, mineral deposits and cycles.

External Human Metabolism   Internal Human Metabolism

25

Though we may have schematized our overall ecosystem relations by labeling certain areas of the environ system and the "human systems" through which we relate to these, this should be treated as an extremely limited conceptual convenience. Such schematic models, in which divisions or "boxes" are set out in linearly connected fashion, can in no way approximate the dynamic complexity of our simplest relationships in which every aspect of every activity is interconnected.

No social problem of small or large scale, and all human problems are axiomatically social, may be "solved" within the terms or models of any single field or discipline.

A wholly technological solution, however logical and seemingly efficient, may fail by overlooking some elementary socio-cultural require-ment. Solutions conceived solely in economic or even biological terms, for example, in the case of population and food, may fail through lack of adequate technological considerations. The point seems an obviously simple one—but examples could be drawn out, at length, of our present failures to solve human problems through inadequately conceived solutions.

The basic biological functions that we share with other organisms only furnish some of the parameters of our overall ecosystem requirements. Our distinctly human needs are complicated by the high degree of social development of the human species. Social patterns are more determinant of biological events than we generally concede.

The divisions used here—biophysical, psycho-social, technological—are adopted for present convenience. They overlap considerably, and are in no way suggested as an exhaustive classification of the major aspects of human activities in the biosphere.

Biophysical   From the viewpoint of biological and physical apparatus, there are few characteristics which give man any uniqueness as a life form. We could elaborate here on the specific anatomical and physiological features which describe his species position, for example, as a mammalian primate of medium size, with certain kinds of individual variability, brain size, psycho-physical capacities, temperature/pressure tolerance, and so forth. Such detailed information may be more easily referred to in many specialized texts.

Some discursive notes on basic human needs may, however, be pertinent. The biophysical requirements for optimum maintenance of human life fall within a relatively narrow and specific range. The basic energy process, as with other organisms, is that of consuming food energies in combination with the oxidation process in respiration. Air, water, and food within various degrees of temperature and pressure are the key requirements. Individuals' daily needs vary with age, weight, health, activity, and so forth (figures given below are for an average 140-pound male adult):

Air—Life may be sustained without food and water for some time as the organism may draw upon nutrients and liquids stored in the tissues, but air intake cannot be postponed for more than a brief interval. Respiration supplies oxygen to the tissues via the lungs and eliminates carbon dioxide and other oxidation products from the tissues. Oxygen intake need per day is approximately 1.35 pounds under normal conditions, and about 2.2 pounds of carbon dioxide are exhaled—that is, taken up largely by plants and reconverted into oxygen and food in the photosynthesis cycle.

Water—Though somewhat less immediate than air, the organism's need for water is still more stringent than food.

> The body can lose practically all stored animal starch or glycogen, all reserves of fat and about one half of the protein which is stored or built into structures, and not be confronted with great danger. But the loss of 10 per cent of body water is serious and a loss of 20 to 22 per cent means certain death.[21]

The daily water need is approximately 5 pounds per day. Depending on cultural context, much larger quantities are used for various other physiological functions, for example as in washing, general hygiene, and so forth.

Food—The various basic food requirements may be summarized briefly under these headings:
1. Carbohydrates, including starches and sugars, are the main energy fuel sources which compensate for the oxidation and heat energy losses in the general metabolism. Such "fuel" requirements, depend-

[21] *The Ways of Man*, J. Gillin, Appleton-Century-Crofts, Educational Division, Meredith Corp., New York: 1948, p. 290.

IMPORTANT ELEMENTS IN MODERN MAN WHICH REQUIRE INVESTIGATION

ELEMENTS	Daily intake micrograms	Amount retained micrograms	Accumulation with age	Systems or tissue affected
FLUORINE	1,000	?	Bone	Bone
SILICON	3,500	4	Lung (A)	Integument
VANADIUM	2,000	0-0.2	Lung (A)	Lipids
CHROMIUN	60	0-0.3	Lung (A)	Glucose, lipids
MANGANESE	5,000	0	No	Brain, several
IRON	15,000	0	Lung (A)	Blood, storage
COLBALT	75	0	No	Blood
COPPER	2,000	0	No	Storage, liver, brain, blood
ZINC	12,000	0	No	Skin,many
SELENIUM	?	?	No	Muscle
STRONTIUM	2,000	1	Bone	Bone
MOLYBDENUM	1,000	0	No	Purines
IODINE	150	0	NO	Goitre
BARIUM	16,000	?	Bone	Bone ?
LANTHANUM	?	0	No ?	Coagulation

(microgram = 0.001 milligram)

"There are 9 essential inorganic micro-nutrients for mammals; 7 are metals and 2 are non-metals. Four have been or are being considered as causing deficiency diseases, and only 3 as causing diseases of accumulation. There are 10 trace elements with requisite capacities to act as essential micronutrients for mammals, but which have not been investigated as such, either because of ubiquity in foods or because of lack of interest; 7 are metals. There are 4 alkali metals or alkaline earths which may exert biological activities, either beneficial or antagonistic. There are 13 heavier elements to which modern man is exposed; his ancestors had minimal exposures to at least 7 of these. All are more or less toxic; 4 are known to accumulate in tissues with age, and 6 are more highly concentrated in man's present environment than on the earth's crust. Only 2 so far are considered to influence a disease." --H. A. Schroeder.

26

ing on activities, average about 3000 calories per day—to balance daily energy output/loss of approximately the same amount.

As a general note on food-energy conversion, man converts food intake into available "mechanical" work energies at about 20 per cent efficiency. Part of the food energy intake is consumed in respiration, circulation, digestion, and so forth—part is given off as heat—part is used in nervous-system activity—and part is indigestible and voided as waste.

2. Protein is required for the repair maintenance of organic structure and tissue. Though less in volume-demand than carbohydrates, an average of 100 grams per day (or 1.5 grams per kilo of body weight) is estimated as the minimal need.

3. Minerals, vitamins, and a number of "trace elements" are required for adequate human function. Some daily minimal quantities are:

      iron   0.015 grams
      calcium   0.45 grams
      phosphorus 0.86 grams
      salt   2.0   grams

Much attention has been given in recent years to the question of trace elements, the part played by mineral deficiencies in growth retardation, and so forth. Attempts have been made to correlate such "trace" resource availability in different soils and food plants with variation in social and cultural growth rates, to the extent that this factor observably affects other animal populations. Vitamin intakes of different types and quantities are also essential to adequate function and maintenance. There is little need for detailed comment on these here.

Temperature and Pressure—with narrow physiological adjustment to temperature variability, man can only survive within a median high range of cold heat. He is, in this sense, a "subtropical" animal functioning best where twenty-four-hour temperatures average between 63 and 73 degrees F. Function and "survival" would be defined here in terms of health and activity output.

Acclimatization plays a considerable part and though much evidence has been accumulated on higher physical activity as sustained in temperate climatic zones, this may well be due to other social and cultural factors. Pressure is also a limited adjustment area for the human organism and may be noted particularly in physiological difficulties, high altitudes, or in underwater working.

Sleep requirement varies directly with age more markedly, perhaps, than other requirements in relation to body size, and so forth. From 18 to 20 hours per day when newborn, the need declines through 12 to 14 hours in the growing child, 7 to 9 hours for the mature adult, and thence to 5 to 7 hours in later ages.

There is some division of opinion on whether adult requirement for sleep varies with activity function or with cultural "conditioning." Sleep deprivation experiments have recorded only up to around fifty hours maximal time without sleep, and then only if the subject was kept in continuous activity of some sort.

Our emphasis in the biophysical requirements above has been on basic individual physiological requirements. Even in terms of simple physiological requirement, we cannot avoid considerable overlap with the "technological" system. Various biophysical modifications through sophisticated technical means are already routine. Artificial organs and extensions of organs are now operating as well as electronically controlled artificial limbs and "natural" organ transplants.

The artificial limb prosthetic attachment is one of the most interesting examples which, though produced in response to human defect through birth or amputation, is capable of much wider application. The problems of delicacy of control and requisite power of manipulative and holding action have now been largely solved. Turning the body's own energy to use, scientists have amplified bio-electrical muscle currents in limb "stumps" to trigger servo-mechanisms for hand movements—versatile enough to unscrew a light bulb, bend each artificial finger joint, and lift relatively heavy weights.

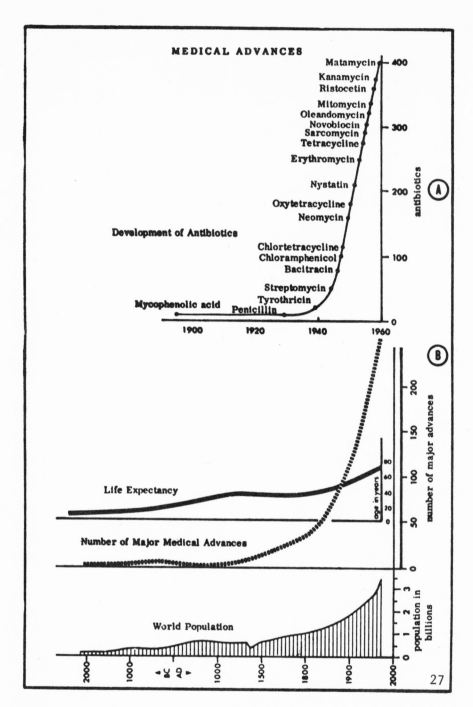

MEDICAL ADVANCES

Development of Antibiotics

Matamycin — 400
Kanamycin
Ristocetin
Mitomycin
Oleandomycin — 300
Novobiocin
Sarcomycin
Tetracycline
Erythromycin
Nystatin — 200
Oxytetracycline
Neomycin
Chlortetracycline — 100
Chloramphenicol
Bacitracin
Streptomycin
Tyrothricin
Mycophenolic acid   Penicillin
— 0

1900   1920   1940   1960

antibiotics   (A)

(B)

Life Expectancy

Number of Major Medical Advances

World Population

number of major advances

population in billions

27

The use of electrical energy drawn directly from the body itself (to power various internal and external organs directly, or to use for remote control of other mechanisms outside of the body) has far-reaching consequences. Apart from self-powering artificial organs, heart pacemakers, and so forth, it could also be used for transmitting signals for

[64]

operating other controls at a distance, or to act internally as receiver/activator of metabolic control signals from remote medical centers.

With new valves for damaged hearts, synthetic tubes, clips, organs, and assists and metabolic amplifiers of various kinds, the biophysical organism may now enter a new era of synthetic regeneration. This field is now more than simply "spare parts" medicine, but has evolved swiftly into bio-engineering.

> Surgery is essentially an engineering discipline . . . the integration of electronic circuits into the human body as functioning and permanent parts . . . is going to become very important within the next ten years.[22]

The most striking extension of all has been the general increase in human life expectancy and improved physiological function throughout the lengthened life span—in the advanced regions of the world. This capacity to prolong life, however, already has attendant problems in population control. We may anticipate further problems when prolongation is expanded toward genetic control of bio-physical characteristics before and after birth; and when we increase our capacity to modify, by

[22] *Electronic Physiologic Aids,* A. Kantrowitz, Director, Cardio-Vascular Surgery, Maimonides Hospital, New York, 1963.

LIFE EXPECTANCIES

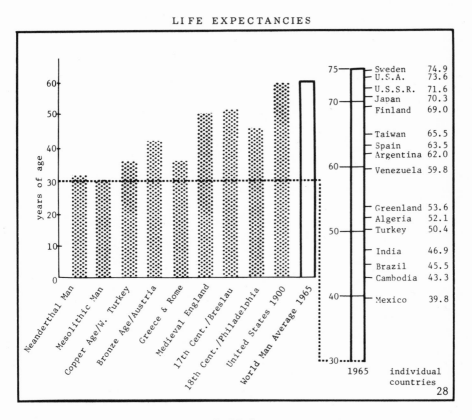

many present and emergent means, the emotional, mental, and physical aspects of the human organism. Coupled with this is the possibility of creating new types of "living" systems based on quite different bio-chemical configurations.

These advancements in bio-physical "control" are specific aspects of the general advance in man's knowledge of himself—as a biological organism. The interaction of biological, medical, and engineering sciences which this entails is also underway in other areas such as water supply, waste disposal, air pollution, food preservation, and public health.

We may sense, again, the growing ecosystem's approach as beginning to operate at both the micro and macro extremities of human environ control—within the human body itself and outwardly to encompass the entire planetary body.

Note: Our emphasis in the above bio-physical requirements has been on basic individual needs. We have only mentioned, in passing, the way in which these basic needs are subject to psycho-social adjustment. Though we "hunger" biologically, we are generally "hungry" at socially designated intervals and for a definite range of culturally defined foods prepared in quite specific ways.

> In the very process of responding to environmental stimuli, each individual human being creates his physical and mental personality from the biological attributes that are shared by all men. Human societies and culture emerged from the progressive integration of these responses.[23]

The needs may be biological, the responses to the needs, and their satisfaction, social and cultural—are learned responses. This brings us over into the area of the psycho-social.

Psycho-social All that we have to say in this text is dependent on this central aspect of man. We have noted that "social patterns determine biological events." In the case of man, this is strikingly evident.

Man is human by virtue of his social existence—that he lives in, by, and for human society. This is not to devalue individual man, but to underline that man's nature, that is, his humanity, is socially produced. Society, in this case, is not confined to local society, but to the awareness of, and sense of belonging to, the larger human society—to the continuity of human cultural experience. Meaning, even for the individual, cannot be separated from its location within this societal context.

Man is made human by his earliest experiences of human contact. He learns to be a human being. When acutely deprived of such early periods of socialization, the organism exists, but is so limited in mental and even physical development that basic survival itself is impaired.

---

[23] "Humanistic Biology," R. Dubos, *American Scholar,* Vol. 34, No. 2, 1965, p. 197.

Though we may stress an "ecological" approach, this remains almost exclusively man-focused—a bias we cannot escape. We perceive the environment only in human-related terms. No matter how "objective" we may strive to be, the formulation of objectivity is itself a peculiarly human symbolic process.[24]

All of our environmental transactions are conducted inescapably through elaborate symbolic screens. Objective "truths" about such transactions are most clearly expressed in a series of highly abstracted symbol systems, whose claim to truth and objectivity is almost in due ratio to the degree of abstraction of their symbology—as in mathematics, the expression of the fundamental physical elements and their periodicities, the electro-magnetic spectrum, and so forth.

These symbolic constructs are the highest "ordering" principles that we know, and though we refer to their "discovery" in nature, they are only apprehensible to us as conceptually "created," and communicated, symbols.

> ... the qualities and characteristics that constitute the visual sensations of which we are conscious ... are not inherent in the so-called external "things" at which we are looking. The origin of our sensations is in the prior experiences and the characteristics and qualities of our sensations are determined by our unique personal (social) history, etc.[25]

The prime vehicle for all our environmental interpretation and the basis for human action is some form of language. Both verbal and nonverbal symbolic languages "order" our perception of the environ and control the interpretation and communication of what we perceive. Language now constructs our reality.

The biological evolution of man is marked by the development of his nervous system and its associated organs for monitoring, controlling, and adjusting the environ to his purpose—from the brain to the eyes, skin, limbs, and so forth. It is suggested that though man stopped physically evolving about 150,000 years ago and is now a social animal evolving only through his extensions, much of his apparently irrational behavior is explicable as "instinctual" responses which were biologically meaningful in early development—but are no longer appropriate to his changed condition. Fears and insecurities, expressed in certain "dominance, territoriality, crowd and flight responses," and so forth, which had survival value in the past, may often appear to act negatively in a more

[24] "A symbol is something the meaning of which is not determined by its intrinsic physical properties, nor whose meaning has been established by the neuro-mechanism of the conditioned reflex, but something whose meaning is freely and arbitrarily determined by those who use it; let the color black indicate mourning. Only man is able to use symbols in this way." "The Symbol, Origin and Basis of Human Behavior," L. A. White, *Philosophy of Science,* Vol. 7, 1940, p. 451.

[25] "Experiments in Perception," Adelbert Ames, Jr., *Progressive Architecture,* December 1947, p. 20.

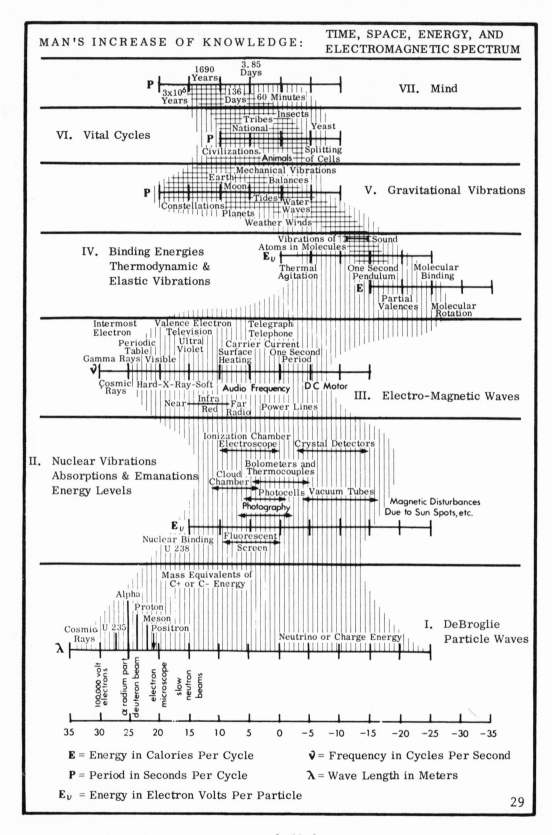

MAN'S INCREASE OF KNOWLEDGE: TIME, SPACE, ENERGY, AND ELECTROMAGNETIC SPECTRUM

VII. Mind

VI. Vital Cycles

V. Gravitational Vibrations

IV. Binding Energies Thermodynamic & Elastic Vibrations

III. Electro-Magnetic Waves

II. Nuclear Vibrations Absorptions & Emanations Energy Levels

I. DeBroglie Particle Waves

E = Energy in Calories Per Cycle   𝒱 = Frequency in Cycles Per Second

P = Period in Seconds Per Cycle   λ = Wave Length in Meters

E_ν = Energy in Electron Volts Per Particle

29

(The chart to the left). "Everything in nature has motion—not just casual motion but motion that is rhythmic and unending, following a precise pattern or cycle. If we set a pendulum in motion it is not difficult to count the number of strokes, or cycles, in a given period of time. Similarly it is quite easy to observe and time such natural cycles of natural phenomena become greatly faster or slower, or as the phenomena being studied become impossible to observe with man's unaided senses, then we must find other means of observing or calculating these cycles.

Much of all basic scientific knowledge can be encompassed within what man has learned of these cycles of motion. The darker shaded area on the chart represents the frequencies observable with man's unaided senses. The lighter shaded area represents the total observable up to the present day through such tools as the microscope, the telescope and all of scientific devices.

Near the periphery are the cycles of the infinitesimal particles within the nucleus of the atom whose motion is so rapid that their vibrations per second are reckoned up to 10 to the 23rd power, which, in more unwieldy figures, would be 1 followed by 23 ciphers. Near the center are the movements of the stars and planets, some of whose movements are so slow that they may take millions of years to complete a single cycle.

Those portions of the various scales covering unshaded areas represent the unknown—the yet-to-be-explored frontiers of basic science." (John J. Grebe: see ref. opp.)

socially secure present. Their measurable physiological reactions are acute and often stressful. Taken as part of the total human system, they are, however, powerful sources of social energy when appropriately channeled. Language and other "symbolic responses" are, for example, now interposed between physical stimuli and "action" response.

We may, more accurately, characterize the key evolutionary stage of man, not as tool-making or -using, but as communication through symbolic languages. Though ". . . language may be termed the first industrial tool, as it involves a plurality of men, and is a prior requirement for the integrated efforts of many men,"[26] tool-using in man is a cumulative and progressive activity unlike that of the tool-using animals.

Language, as a tool, extends our control over the environ as demonstrably as any physical artifact—by naming and ordering, we control as effectively. Organized information is now our major tool resource.

Man's ecological expansion has been particularly characterized by the role in which accumulated knowledge about the environ is preserved and passed on through succeeding generations. This would form part of the major evolutionary step, referred to above, in adaptability of the organism. Such generational transmission of socio-cultural experience, of that which makes man human, was possible only through the evolved "family" unit—within which a relatively fragile organism with an unusually long period of defenselessness and dependency on others could

[26] *Ideas and Integrity*, R. B. Fuller, Prentice-Hall, Englewood Cliffs, New Jersey, 1963.

be effectively nurtured till able to survive as an individual. The period of nurture is also that of socialization, of forming the human personality.

This function of transmitting social and cultural experience and of regulating social interaction also led to the complex growth of other human institutions—to human society as we know it. There is little to suggest that human society evolved "instinctually" in the strict biological sense.

Rather, when we refer to the evolution of society, it may, perhaps, be more accurately meant in the sense of more consciously adaptive development. Animals have forms of society, but these lack the evolutionary capacity that has allowed human society to be more plastic and variable in its responses to particular environ situations. Change has been of key importance in this process and allows of the interaction of individual change agents within the society as influencing and modifying the overall societal orientation.

Social evolution in this sense may be likened to a "cybernetic" process, one that is oriented to its goals by "feedback." Increased, and more highly organized, information about the environ and the society as an integral ongoing process is fed back in due proportion so as to "guide" forward development. As including the role of individual agents—in monitoring the signals, suggesting and predicting the changes of course required, and so forth—we might more properly refer to "psycho-social evolution" as more clearly defining this process.

All human action is, in this sense, social action. Contemporary social theory generally analyzes human behavior as occurring, therefore, in a system of socially interactive relationships, that is, even where the specific interaction is with a physical resource, its form and purpose is socially determined. Further division of the psycho-social environ system would include three subdivisions to account for *individual* action, the *society* as an aggregate or collectivity of such action, and the *culture* as an environ continuum within which individual and societal actions take place. The symbolic processes of communication make all social action possible and furnish the matrix within which all such action takes place.

1. *the personality system* of the individual as motivated toward action by his needs in terms of various goals, commitments, and socialized patterns of behavior. Different needs, situations, purposes elicit different roles or learned patterns of "successful" response behavior.
2. *the social system*, or structured order of social actions, consisting of the basic human institutions—family, kinship, religious, political, economic, and so forth—and their related organizations.

   These consist of sets of defined roles or patterns of behavior with their appropriately "sanctioned" contingencies in different social systems. All human actions are related in one way or another to these institutionalized sets. They should not, however, be viewed as

30

SHRINKING OF OUR PLANET BY MAN'S INCREASED TRAVEL AND COMMUNICATION SPEEDS AROUND THE GLOBE

YEAR	500,000 BC	20,000 BC	300 BC	500 BC	1,500 AD	1,900 AD	1925	1950	1965
Required time to travel around the globe	A few hundred thousand years	A few thousand years	A few hundred years	A few tens of years	A few years	A few months	A few weeks	A few days	A few hours
Means of transportation	Human on foot (over, ice bridges)	On foot and by canoe	Canoe with small sail or paddles or relays of runners	Large sail boats with oars, pack animals, and horse chariots	Big sailing ships (with compass), horse teams, and coaches	Steam boats and railroads (Suez and Panama Canals)	Steamships, transcontinental railways, autos, and airplanes	Steamships, railways, auto jet and rocket aircraft	Atomic steamship, high speed railway, auto, and rocket-jet aircraft
Distance per day (land)	15 miles	15-20 miles	20 miles	15-25 miles	20-25 miles	Rail 300-900 miles	100-900 miles	Rail 500-1,500	Rail 1000-2000
Distance per day (sea or air)		20 by canoe	40 miles by sea	135 miles by sea	175 miles by sea	250 miles by sea	3,000-6000 air	6000-9500 air	105,000 air
Potential state size	None	A small valley in the vicinity of a small lake	Small part of a continent	Large area of a continent with coastal colonies	Great parts of a continent with trans-oceanic colonies	Large parts of a continent with transoceanic colonies	Full continents & Transocean Commonwealths	The Globe	The globe and more

Communica- tions	① The Gutenberg 1440 printing press	② The rapid print Web 1800(newspaper) press	③ The Bell 1876 telephone	④ The Marconi 1895 telegraph	⑤ First commercial 1920 radio broadcast	⑥ National 1926 Television	⑦ Transcontinental T.V. with the introduction 1962 of Early Bird Satellite

Word of mouth, drums, smoke, relay runners, and hand printed manuscripts prior to 1441 A.D.

THE RELATIVE SIZE OF THE WORLD AS TRAVEL TIME DECREASES

15,000 AD - 1840 AD

1850-1930

The best average speed of horse drawn coaches on land and sailing ships at sea was approximately 10 m.p.h.

Steam locomotives averaged 65 m.p.h. while steamships averaged 36 m.p.h.

1950's Propeller aircraft averaged 300-700 m.p.h.

1960's Jet passenger aircraft averaged 500-700 m.p.h.

Man on foot : mph

Curved 5 mph

This toned area represents population growth

Rome was the only metropolis of over 1,000,000 people from this date forward until 1800 AD.

Rome's population declined by 20,000

Bubonic plague wiped out ½ of Europe's population

For the first time in history it began to be safe for men to live in large cities because of advances in medicine and sanitation. Life was made more secure and comfortable by the Industrial Revolution & mechanized farming

5,000 years (300BC-1500AD) in which towns slowly evolved into cities, and then into metropolises.

5,000 years of villages & towns and then

Coach · Horse · Steam locomotive · Automobile · First flight across the Atlantic · Jet · Super sonic · Jet · XB-70

static forms, but as temporal configurations undergoing various rates of change according to their "dynamic" content of idiosyncratic individual actions.

3. *the culture system* contains the "heritage" of customs, habits, belief systems, and so forth—in various ideologies, values, standards. These are all expressed in various symbolic modes—in more and less tangible physical forms as the arts and sciences, in less tangible form in the religions, mythologies, philosophies, and so forth. We might even include technology as a cultural artifact in this manner—with its system of social action as a form expressly concerned with the control of the physical environ through tools. Such tools are, themselves, also "symbolic" artifacts—increasingly dependent upon environ information input refined through symbolic language processes.

The above divisions are, needless to say, another series of convenient abstractions from a fused process of integral human action. A prime characteristic of the psycho-social system(s) is their transmissibility through nonbiological means. They are socially, rather than biologically, inherited.

Culture, used in the more generally inclusive sense to describe the whole system, may be termed the "symbolic ecological context" which encloses and screens all human activity within (and without) the biosphere.

The social behaviors of man are now among the most critical factors in the maintenance of the planetary ecology. We not only modify the environ by human action as manifested in science and technology— through physical transformations of the earth to economic purpose—but, all social institutions play their part in orienting the direction, goal, and purposes that guide such environmental transactions.

Following our line of "evolutionary" development, it may be noted that it is only recently that we have acquired the social awareness that we may from this time forward exercise a more consciously direct control of our forward development. We generally forget the extent to which past historical societies were unaware of this, believing that such control lay more with capricious agencies external to man. The future was predestined, cyclically returned to past forms, or was oriented to life after death. In this sense we have "invented" the future—almost as a consciously orienting strategy for our forward survival.

We have become aware that the forms of our social organizations and whole societies are also man-made and may be redesigned to fit our emergent needs and purposes. Our social "technologies" will now require precedence as control agencies for the developed capacities of physical technology. In terms of environ control, the tribal village, the city state and, latterly, the nation state, were inventive adaptations toward our present ecological dominance.

At our present level of planetary interdependency, the nation-state form, however, may now be as dangerously obsolete as the self-governing autonomous tribal and city principalities that preceded it. The necessary growth of transnational social organizations seems to indicate this.

The vital organizations that maintain the human ecosystem are no longer national in any real sense—world health, communications, transportation, and so forth, are, by agreement, vital to all and decisions relative to their governance may not be abrogated by any local agency. The continued growth of such world organizations may not, however, be left to emergency-pressured need, but must become the object of conscious design, taking gainful cognizance of the evolutionary developments and trends toward such global forms.

We may view this trend in another aspect relative to knowledge/information. In general, human survival has been evolutionarily successful through the bias toward integrative function, for example, the manner in which the differentiated-out and specialized organic functions are integrally directed toward the overall end purposes of the organism.

Man is one of the least specialized biological organisms. Extreme specialization in evolutionary, or ecological, terms of a highly differentiated set of "special" habitat requirements is usually accompanied by lack of adaptability. The organism tends toward extinction or remains low in the species hierarchy.

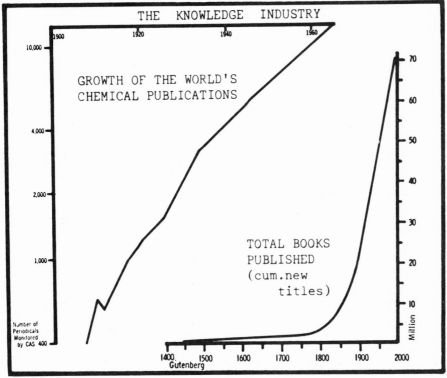

THE KNOWLEDGE INDUSTRY

GROWTH OF THE WORLD'S CHEMICAL PUBLICATIONS

TOTAL BOOKS PUBLISHED (cum.new titles)

31

Our present discussion of "the ecological context" emphasizes in various ways that certain trends toward increased differentiation and specialization may be dangerous through lack of integration of our overall environ activities, that is, as evidenced in air, water pollution, and so forth.

The extremely swift and relatively uncontrolled growth of our array of socio-economic and technological systems—as including forms of social organization—has not been accompanied by a corresponding extension of our integrative "tools" and systems. Fortunately, this negative trend seems to be in the process of reversal where our very large-scale environ undertakings, as in the space programs, have forced a return to consideration of human activities as whole systems. The accompanying increase in global monitoring of the earth system through satellites, and the swift diffusion and interchanges in the world communications network, engender an integral awareness of the essential unity of the planetary community.

The psycho-social extension of man throughout the biosphere has been characterized as adding to this a "noosphere" layer.[27] This idea of organized human thought now covering the globe as a functional part of the overall ecological system is, to an extent, physically demonstrable in our present global communications networks, in the enormously accelerated growth of human knowledge, with its parallel increase in the numbers of messages, meetings, journals, and so forth, ceaselessly circulating around the earth.

The growth of man's knowledge, and his structuring of that knowledge into conceptual tools for the understanding and control of his environment, have tended to follow a cyclical pattern of analysis and synthesis—of differentiation and integration. Both are interactive aspects of the whole process, of man's concern with the understanding of the nature of his world.

In science, for example, the discovery of new knowledge is usually described as proceeding from the elucidation of detailed pieces of information about particular aspects of experience to their organization and verification in terms of new conceptual hypotheses about larger areas of experience.

But, even in science, this method has been somewhat idealized as occurring in such a specifically linear sequence. In many cases, the sequence may be inverted. The discovery of significant detail may attend and be preceded by what is usually referred to as an "intuitive" apprehension of a whole process. Both parts of the cycle obviously feed back upon one another in a way that we do not as yet fully understand.

---

[27] First described by W. I. Vernadsky in *La Biosphere,* 1929; more recently discussed by Teilhard de Chardin in his various works, notably, *The Phenomenon of Man,* The Cloister Library, Harper & Row, 1961.

The trend of scientific development seems presently to favor integration, as evidenced by the fusion of many existing differentiated disciplines into new relationships, that is, bio-chemistry, psycho-biology, bio-physics, and so forth.

It appears as if our accumulation of detailed parts-knowledge, due to vastly increased investment in scientific research—has reached a stage when further elucidation of data must be paced, more and more, by the conscious integration of such data into meaningful wholes. This may be necessary simply in order to restore more communication within science itself as a collaborative enterprise. As many of the routine tasks in research, previously performed by human specialists, are increasingly off-loaded through computer assistance, this may occur naturally.

Relative to education, or "literacy" regarding our present world, it seems essential that we seek to apprehend and communicate our knowledge much more in terms of the larger whole systems. In terms of primary integrative concepts embracing large areas of knowledge:

> Concepts are discoveries as well as—indeed more than—inventions . . . and unifying our thoughts over a vast area of facts . . . enable certain aspects of the enormous complexity of the world to be handled by men's minds.[28]

"The Big Alphabets" is the title used by the distinguished astronomer Harlow Shapley to describe some of the main configurations of knowledge that man has put together. His listing is as follows:

A. Elementary and Fundamental:

The Letters
Ordinal Numbers
Calendars
Terrestrial and Star Maps

B. The Four Major Summaries:

Energy—The Electro-magnetic Spectrum
Matter—The Periodic Table of the Elements
Time—The Geological Timetable of the Earth
Space—The Series of "Material" Organizations

We may note, also, that the notion of an "information explosion," however, is not borne out by this knowledge expansion. Such knowledge is not simply accumulated facts, but the reduction of unrelated, and often apparently irrelevant, facts into new and more compact conceptual wholes. The overall process does not tend toward greater complexity but, rather, toward simpler and more "inclusive" concepts. Recent revolutionary concepts in biology are an example of this—DNA/RNA formulation "impounds" a great number of separate biological facts and relates biology via bio-chemistry to bio-physics—and thence to more elegantly

---

[28] "The Two Aspects of Science," Sir George Thompson, *Science,* Vol. 132, October 1960.

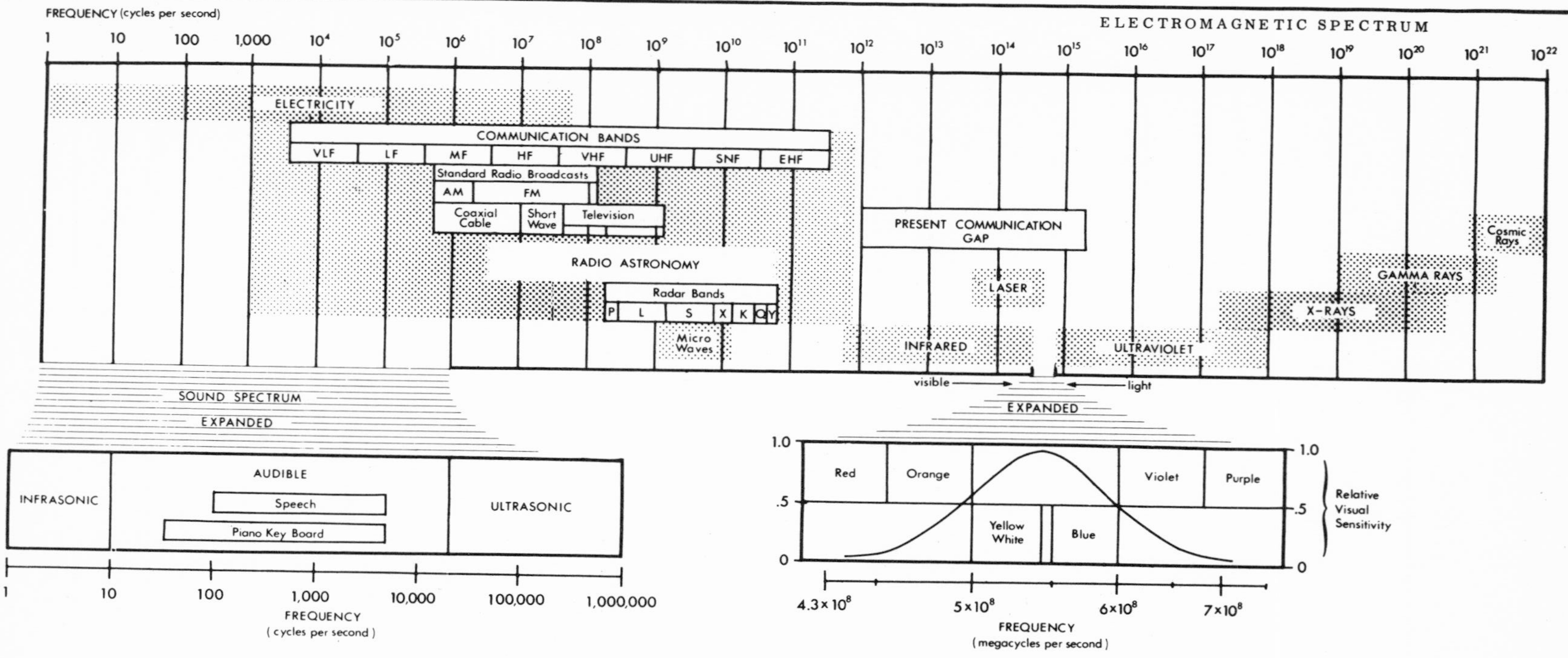

32

ELECTROMAGNETIC SPECTRUM
FREQUENCY (cycles per second)
1 10 100 1,000 10^4 10^5 10^6 10^7 10^8 10^9 10^{10} 10^{11} 10^{12} 10^{13} 10^{14} 10^{15} 10^{16} 10^{17} 10^{18} 10^{19} 10^{20} 10^{21} 10^{22}
ELECTRICITY
COMMUNICATION BANDS
VLF LF MF HF VHF UHF SNF EHF
Standard Radio Broadcasts
AM FM
Coaxial Cable
Short Wave
Television
RADIO ASTRONOMY
Radar Bands
P L S X K Q Y
Micro Waves
PRESENT COMMUNICATION GAP
LASER
INFRARED
ULTRAVIOLET
X-RAYS
GAMMA RAYS
Cosmic Rays
visible light
EXPANDED
SOUND SPECTRUM
EXPANDED
INFRASONIC
AUDIBLE
Speech
Piano Key Board
ULTRASONIC
1 10 100 1,000 10,000 100,000 1,000,000
FREQUENCY
(cycles per second)
Red Orange Yellow White Blue Violet Purple
1.0 .5 0
Relative Visual Sensitivity
4.3×10^8 5×10^8 6×10^8 7×10^8
FREQUENCY
(megacycles per second)

RELATIONSHIP OF MAN TO ELECTROMAGNETIC SPECTRUM

(The chart above). The visual pattern recognition capacity of the eye lens and correlated brain function has been progressively extended and amplified through the simple magnifying lens to the microscope and telescope, through the camera lucida and obscura to the photographic and television camera, and towards sophisticated systems which record, amplify and relate complex visual and aural patterns of great magnitude

This development also encompasses the ways in which man has widened his 'sensorial' monitoring of the electro-magnetic spectrum through instrumentation. He can now 'see' into the infra-red, ultra-violet and Xray frequencies, 'hear' in the radio frequencies, and, may more delicately 'feel' through electronic metering than with his most sensitive skin area.

simpler structural hierarchies. The increasing interrelation and inter-dependence of other "separate" disciplines is further evidence of this direction.

We may hypothesize that as information increases exponentially—explodes—conceptuality implodes, becoming increasingly more simplified.

The effect of this accelerated process on the life space and life style is quite marked. Where tribal man became disoriented when separated from his locality and early city and local state man could barely conceptualize his externally surrounding environment beyond these limits, we are now in a period when many men think easily and casually in terms of the whole planet.

Such emerging world men are not confused by the explosion of information about the earth and its peoples, but are able to deal with this in whole terms, as easily as one previously conceived on one's neighborhood, home town, and surrounding country.

Our basic critical impasse in global terms is, however, our inability to use our swiftly occurring knowledge. The block is to be found most often in the persistence of obsolete social forms and attitudes. To circumvent traditional but now inadequate modes of social action, we need to experiment with new forms of social organization—to learn how to invent socially. We need to refashion the psycho-social environ as vigorously through new social inventions as we have transformed the physical environ in the past century through technical invention.

THE TECHNOLOGICAL SYSTEMS

We have referred to the basic organic enterprise as that of securing energy and materials from the environment to maintain life. A rather simple statement, but one that accounts, in part, for most historical human activities.

At the lowest level of early human survival we find evidence of cultural activity, but its more durable and widespread forms are associated with access to more energies than could be provided solely by unaided human physical effort. As we have noted, language is the tool that enables men to combine together to perform tasks, or convert energy collectively, which would be impossible for an isolated man. The symbolic gesture or sign is, therefore, a first "technological" extension. Second, perhaps, would come fire, as it is difficult to see how the knowledge of fire could be transmitted without language. Fire is a way of gaining access to stored solar energy, of extending the internal oxidation of the body metabolism to provide an external source of heat, predigest food, and so forth—also providing one of our most durable symbols in the process.

The earliest men seem to have subsisted by hunting and food gathering, simply tapping into locally available, naturally cyclic energy supplies. Such techniques would seldom provide the energy surpluses necessary to give

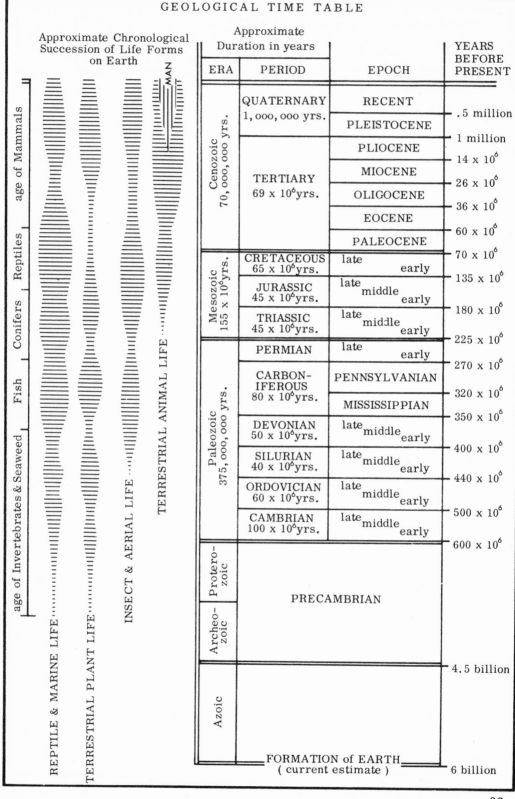

GEOLOGICAL TIME TABLE

Approximate Chronological Succession of Life Forms on Earth				Approximate Duration in years			YEARS BEFORE PRESENT
				ERA	PERIOD	EPOCH	
			MAN	Cenozoic 70,000,000 yrs.	QUATERNARY 1,000,000 yrs.	RECENT	.5 million
						PLEISTOCENE	1 million
age of Mammals					TERTIARY 69 x 10⁶yrs.	PLIOCENE	14 x 10⁶
						MIOCENE	26 x 10⁶
						OLIGOCENE	36 x 10⁶
						EOCENE	60 x 10⁶
Reptiles						PALEOCENE	70 x 10⁶
				Mesozoic 155 x 10⁶ yrs.	CRETACEOUS 65 x 10⁶yrs.	late early	135 x 10⁶
Conifers					JURASSIC 45 x 10⁶yrs.	late middle early	180 x 10⁶
					TRIASSIC 45 x 10⁶yrs.	late middle early	225 x 10⁶
Fish				Paleozoic 375,000,000 yrs.	PERMIAN	late early	270 x 10⁶
					CARBON-IFEROUS 80 x 10⁶yrs.	PENNSYLVANIAN	320 x 10⁶
						MISSISSIPPIAN	350 x 10⁶
					DEVONIAN 50 x 10⁶yrs.	late middle early	400 x 10⁶
					SILURIAN 40 x 10⁶yrs.	late middle early	440 x 10⁶
age of Invertebrates & Seaweed					ORDOVICIAN 60 x 10⁶yrs.	late middle early	500 x 10⁶
					CAMBRIAN 100 x 10⁶yrs.	late middle early	600 x 10⁶
				Protero-zoic	PRECAMBRIAN		
REPTILE & MARINE LIFE	TERRESTRIAL PLANT LIFE	INSECT & AERIAL LIFE	TERRESTRIAL ANIMAL LIFE	Archeo-zoic			
				Azoic			4.5 billion
					FORMATION of EARTH (current estimate)		6 billion

33

sufficient leisure for large-scale cultural pursuits except in particularly favorable habitats.

Higher sustained yields and surpluses first come from the deliberate cultivation of selected plants and the herding and domestication of animals. This allows for more permanent settlement, storage of food energies, and the leisure with which to experiment and forward further survival strategies, for example, in association with such settlements are usually found evidence of recording of seasonal and other periodicities to allow future planning.

In close conjunction with such early technologies of cultivation and domestication comes the development of boats. The extended voyages possible with food stores, animals, and so forth, plus the navigational aids drawn from, and giving rise to, more accurate measurement of environment periodicities—the movements of the stars, phases of the moon, and so forth, added greatly to human knowledge.

Whatever the origins of technology, it is patent that the system of artifacts which this now connotes has developed in a unitary, evolutionary manner. We have referred to this idea as presented by many contemporary thinkers, but the following quotation from La Barre conveys it in succinct form:

> Since man's machines evolve now, not anatomical man, he has long since gone outside his own individual skin in his functional relatedness to the world. The real evolutionary unit now is not man's mere body; it is "all mankind's-brains-together-with-all-the-extrabodily-materials-that-come-under-the-manipulation-of-their-hands." Man's physical ego is expanded to encompass everything within reach of his manipulating hands, within sight of his searching eyes, and within the scope of his restless brain. An airplane is part of a large kinaesthetic and functional self . . . and airplanes are biologically cheap (as evolutionary devices). Without being, through specialization, a biological amputee, he attaches all sorts of prosthetic devices to his limbs. This evolution-by-prosthesis is uniquely human and uniquely freed from the slowness of reproduction· and of evolutionary variation into blind alleys from which there is no retreat.[29]

The augmentation of organic capacity is, however, not confined solely to the evolution of physical tools but includes also those "invisible" tools which have had as powerful an effect in transforming man's condition. Such invisible tools as language, number, symbol, and image systems are also extensions of human internal processes and have, through the larger conceptual systems—religion, philosophy, science, and so forth—extended man's control over environment.

We might even view the growth of social institutions as part of such psycho-physical extension—the development of cities, states, "families" of nations. Certainly the development of the "systems" capability of

[29] *The Human Animal,* W. La Barre, University of Chicago Press, 1954, p. 92.

① SPACE SCALE OF THE UNIVERSE

Volumes in powers of a minimal unit volume (left vertical axis)

Power	Object examples	Linear distances	Diameter in meters
150	possible universe (?) spherical "horizon" of knowledge		10^{27}
140	a group of supergalaxies supergalaxy	one billion light years	10^{24}
130	minor group of galaxies large galaxy small galaxy	one megaparsec one million light years	10^{21}
120	galactic satellite cluster globular cluster of stars distance to Regulus	one kiloparsec one thousand light years	10^{18}
110	distance to nearest star multiple star system inner reservoir of comets	one parsec one light year	10^{15}
100	orbit of Pluto orbit of Jupiter orbit of the earth	one billion kilometers	10^{12}
90	outer corona of the sun the sun (an average star) Jupiter (a large planet)	one million kilometers	10^{9}
80	the earth average moon large asteroid	one thousand kilometers	10^{6}
70	medium asteroid or mountain all mankind (a cubic kilometer) great pyramid	one kilometer	10^{3}
60	whale man (a cubic meter) grapefruit	one meter	1
50	cherry grapeseed (a cubic millimeter) flea or grain of sand	one centimeter one millimeter	10^{-3}
40	ovum or dust particle bacterium virus	one micron	10^{-6}
30	protein molecule sugar molecule atom	one millimicron one angstrom $(10^{-10}$m.$)$	10^{-9}
20	inner atom	one thousand fermis	10^{-12}
10	atomic nucleus elementary particle	one fermi	10^{-15}
0	possible field entry (?)		10^{-18}

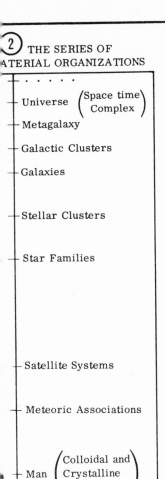

(2) THE SERIES OF
MATERIAL ORGANIZATIONS

· · · · ·

Universe (Space time / Complex)

Metagalaxy

Galactic Clusters

Galaxies

Stellar Clusters

Star Families

Satellite Systems

Meteoric Associations

Man (Colloidal and / Crystalline / Aggregate)

Molecular Systems

Molecules

Atoms

Corpuscles

· · · · · ·

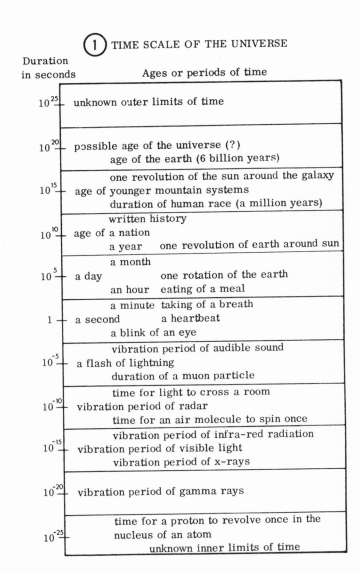

(1) TIME SCALE OF THE UNIVERSE

Duration
in seconds   Ages or periods of time

10^{25} — unknown outer limits of time

10^{20} — possible age of the universe (?)
          age of the earth (6 billion years)

          one revolution of the sun around the galaxy
10^{15} — age of younger mountain systems
          duration of human race (a million years)

          written history
10^{10} — age of a nation
          a year   one revolution of earth around sun

          a month
10^{5} — a day   one rotation of the earth
          an hour   eating of a meal

          a minute taking of a breath
1 — a second   a heartbeat
          a blink of an eye

          vibration period of audible sound
10^{-5} — a flash of lightning
          duration of a muon particle

          time for light to cross a room
10^{-10} — vibration period of radar
          time for an air molecule to spin once

          vibration period of infra-red radiation
10^{-15} — vibration period of visible light
          vibration period of x-rays

10^{-20} — vibration period of gamma rays

          time for a proton to revolve once in the
10^{-25} — nucleus of an atom
          unknown inner limits of time

34

STAGES OF TECHNOLOGY

35

①

FIRST	SECOND	THIRD	FOURTH	FIFTH	SIXTH	SEVENTH
FIRST Technological revolution — The discovery and use of the wheel	SECOND Technological Revolution — The discovery of methods for smelting ores and for making alloys and forged tools and weapons	THIRD — The Industrial Revolution	FOURTH — Chemicals & Chemical Engineering	FIFTH — Electrical Transmission & Telecommunications	SIXTH — Transportation	SEVENTH

Rows (hand tools / materials):
- Tusk, horn, and bone hand tools
- All purpose stone & wood fist axes
- Special purpose stone & wood hand tools
- Metal handtools with energy supplied by man and animals
- Bronze | Iron Age

War / event markers: end of Franco-Prussian war | World War I | World War II | controlled atomic fission

Societies:
- STAGE V, STAGE IV — DEVELOPED SOCIETIES: Industrial Economies
- STAGE III, STAGE II, STAGE I — UNDERDEVELOPED SOCIETIES: Agriculturally Based Marginal Economies

Process bands: AUTOMATION · MECHANIZATION · DIVERSIFICATION · DOMESTICATION · ADAPTATION

②

Time scale (bottom): 10^6 … 5×10^5 … 10^5 … 5×10^4 … 10^4 … 5×10^3 … 2,000 BC … 965 AD … 10 11 12 13 14 15 16 17 18 19 … 1965 — 1,965 Years Before Present

THE LINE OF HIGH ADVANTAGE MOBILE ENVIRON CONTROL DEVELOPMENT WHICH GOES FROM SHIP, TO AIRPLANE, TO ROCKET, TO MANNED SPACE VEHICLE

MODE	Sailing Ships						Clippers		Steam Ships		Airplanes		Saturn V Rocket
TIME PERIOD	2,500 BC	500 BC	1,000 AD	1400	1500	1600	1700	1800	1900	1940	1940	1950	1965
AVERAGE TONNAGE	150	250	30	300	100-500	1000	1,000	2,100	2,500	4,500	Propeller	Jet	3,000 Tons
HORSE POWER	80	120	30-90	150-250	....	500	750	....	1,200	1,400	3,500	12,000	200,000 lbs. thrust
AVERAGE SPEED	8 knots	8 knots	12 knots	10 knots	10 knots	11 knots	12 knots	17-22 knots	16 knots	20 knots	300 m.p.h.	600 m.p.h.	25,000 m.p.h.

③

DOMINANT AGES	MODERN CRAFT 1,000 - 1784	MACHINE AGE 1785 - 1869	POWER AGE 1870 - 1952	ATOMIC AGE 1953 -
POWER	Human and Animal Muscle Wind and Water	Multiple Horse Teams and Steam Engines	Gasoline Engines and Electric Motors	Atomic Energy and Fossil Fuel Burning Equipment Used to Produce Electric Power and Heat - Fuel Cells
TOOLS	Hand Wrought Iron and Wooden	Machine Wrought Iron and Steel	Multiple Machine Tools and Automatic Machines	Cybernated Factories with Computer Closed Feedback Control Loops
WORK SKILLS	All-Around Skilled Craftsmen and Unskilled Manual Workers	Subdivided Manufacturing Processes Replace Skilled Craftsmen With Semiskilled Machine Operators	Human Feeder or Tender Replaced by Skilled Inspector - Mechanic	Highly Trained Engineer - Designers and-Skilled Maintenance Technician Systems Specialist and Programmer
MATERIALS	Wood, Iron and Bronze	Steel and Copper	Alloyed Steels, Light Alloys, and Aluminum	Plastics and Super Alloys (32 New Metals Used, Notably Magnesium and Titanium)
TRANSPORTATION	Walking, Use of Animals by Dirt Road or Via Waterways by Sailboat	Horse and Buggy, Steam Trains Via Steel Rails, and Steam Ships Via Ocean Ways	Automobile Via Paved Highways, Diesel Trains and Ships, and Airplane Via World Airways	Rocket and Jet Vertical Take Off Aircraft, Atomic Ships, Ground Effect Craft, Helicopters and Automobiles
COMMUNICATION	Word of Mouth, Drum, Smoke Signals, Messenger and Newspaper	Mail by Train and Ship, Mechanically Printed Newspaper, Telegraph, and Telephone	A.M. and F.M. Radio, Movies, Television, Magnetic Tape, Trans-ocean Telephone, and Microfilm	Video - Phone, Data Phone, Telstar & Syncom, World Wide Communication Satellites, 'Graphic' Computers

coordinating large-scale and long-term complex enterprises, as in aero-space, in national and international planning, emerges as a powerful new technology. Also, where the hand tool, lathe, grinder, and so forth, extend physical capacities, our communication networks of radio, telephone, television, and linked computer systems are extensions of the human senses and nervous system. Through his instrumented monitoring of the electro-magnetic spectrum, man can now "see" in the infrared, ultraviolet, and X-ray frequencies, "hear" in the radio frequencies, and more delicately "feel" through electronic metering than with his most sensitive skin areas.

The latest phases of socio-technological development now return upon the organism itself as man begins to directly repair, restore, and to replace his internal organs, either through transplantation from others or by artificial devices.

Most of the extraordinary evolution of our complex industrial tools has taken place in the last two hundred years. Though the process of technological development predates history, our present accelerations may be located as taking off toward the end of the eighteenth century with the steam engine.[30]

The brevity of this period probably accounts for the widespread apprehension that technological developments now threaten man, that technologies are out of control, and so forth. Such dire prophecies possibly result from a lack of understanding of the evolutionary and organic nature of technological development that we have emphasized so much in our present discussion. This idea is, in itself, probably somewhat alien to the understanding. Man has always assumed that an "evolving" technology would be of the mythological robotic variety—formed in his own image. It is, rather, more difficult to observe the evolution of the airplane from single person/single engine with multiple wing surfaces, to multi engine/single wing, to propellerless jets of enormous size, speed, and 400-passenger-carrying capacity—almost in one human generation. It is as difficult to equate the evolution of the family of "extended eyes"—from bulky, tripod, wetplate still cameras to microminiaturized television scanners spinning around the globe outside of the earth's atmosphere.

As "powered," renewed, and ultimately directed by human life, technology is as organic as a snail shell, the carapace of a turtle, a spiderweb, or the airborne dandelion seed. In many respects, it is now more ubiquitous as a functional component of the ecosystem than any organic life form other than man himself. The amounts of energy converted by machines, the materials extracted from the earth, processed, recombined, and redistributed in the technological metabolism, and the gross effects of such increased metabolic rates on the ecosystem are now

---

[30] While recognizing the long build-up toward this point, particularly in the medieval period, the first industrial revolution is a convenient bench mark for large-scale industrial and urban expansion.

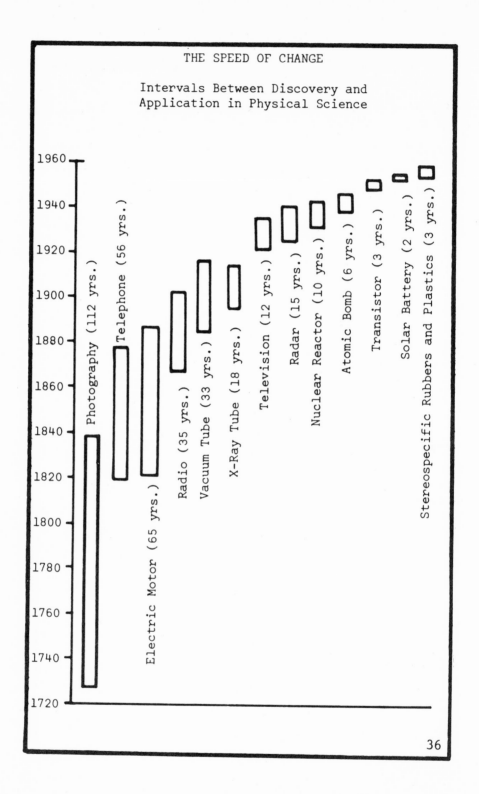

THE SPEED OF CHANGE

Intervals Between Discovery and
Application in Physical Science

Photography (112 yrs.)

Telephone (56 yrs.)

Electric Motor (65 yrs.)

Radio (35 yrs.)

Vacuum Tube (33 yrs.)

X-Ray Tube (18 yrs.)

Television (12 yrs.)

Radar (15 yrs.)

Nuclear Reactor (10 yrs.)

Atomic Bomb (6 yrs.)

Transistor (3 yrs.)

Solar Battery (2 yrs.)

Stereospecific Rubbers and Plastics (3 yrs.)

36

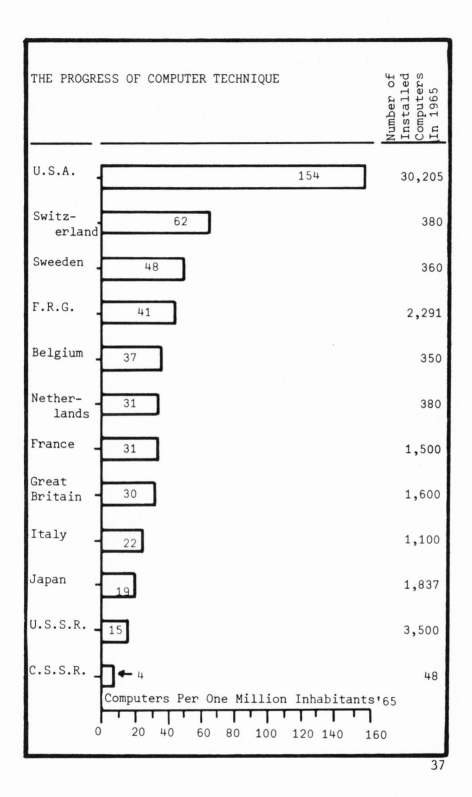

THE PROGRESS OF COMPUTER TECHNIQUE

	Computers Per One Million Inhabitants '65	Number of Installed Computers In 1965
U.S.A.	154	30,205
Switzerland	62	380
Sweeden	48	360
F.R.G.	41	2,291
Belgium	37	350
Netherlands	31	380
France	31	1,500
Great Britain	30	1,600
Italy	22	1,100
Japan	19	1,837
U.S.S.R.	15	3,500
C.S.S.R.	← 4	48

0   20   40   60   80   100   120   140   160

37

[85]

greater than the effects of many global populations of other organic species.

When we come, therefore, to the question of "control" we must seek to find, as we have not yet consciously done on a large enough scale, the fundamental principles and "laws" that govern the evolution of physical technologies. These would include not only science and technology as related processes but the many other organized institutions which are "technological" by nature, for example, cities in their aspect of extended metabolic units, social organizations as extended control units, and so forth.

When we apparently underline *physical* technologies, we should also bear in mind the parallel growth of more intangible technological means, as implied above in urban and social organizations. Almost every ordered aggregate of human actions whose effects modify the physical environ is, in this sense, a "technology." The application of the methodology of the physical sciences to the systematic scheduling of a series of technological operations, for example, in the "systems" approach, is often termed a "soft" technology. In the same regard, historically, so was a rain dance, or the ceremonies attending crop fertility, or a ritual socio-religious drama—all systems for attaining to greater predictive understanding and extended control of the human environ.

To emphasize the organic nature of technology in this fashion is not simply to pose some technological determinism as accounting for all human development and change. Rather, the purpose is to emphasize and reemphasize the integral nature of all human processes—whether labeled technological, economic, cultural, or whatever.

Given the nature of the organism and its enclosing environ, and some notion of the history of its development within that environ, we may observe certain periodicities and orders of growth. So far, our understanding of the larger patterns of the human ecological transformations has been limited by our tendency to compartmentalize our knowledge of the process. The "periodicities and orders" of one discipline are usually left unrelated to those of another. Archaeology, a seemingly remote and quite academic field, has taken the lead in this manner recently. By bringing to bear the data and conceptual means of many disciplines—and their ancillary techniques of bio-chemical and physical analysis, radiation technologies, aerial and satellite photography, and so forth—archaeologists are beginning to "reconstruct" the past as vigorously as we now document the present and probe the future.

The most recent and spectacular area of technological evolution has been the introduction of cybernetics—significantly, and symbolically, derived from the word for "steering" in the navigational sense. Defined as the mechanization of sensory thought and other psycho-physical processes, cybernetics is an extension of the control capacities of the human nervous system into electro-mechanical devices.

LABOR FORCE SHIFT IN TYPICAL ADVANCED ECONOMY

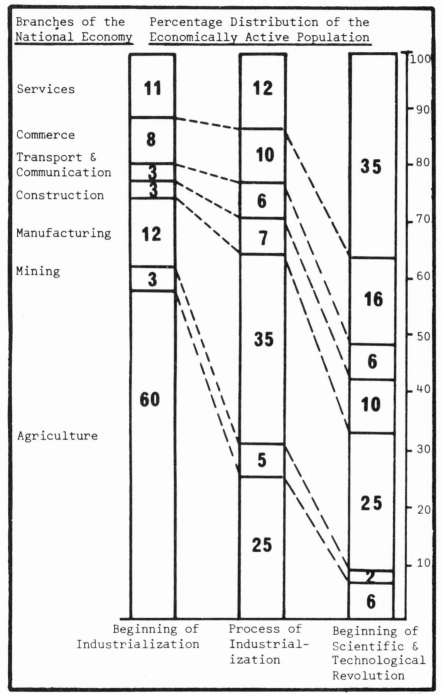

Without elaborating on its technological ramifications here, we may underline its importance in ecological terms. As the mechanical and chemical energy converters of the first series of industrial revolutions freed human muscle from routine tasks, so the computer potentially frees man from comparable routine "intellectual" tasks—of monitoring, supervising, controlling many simultaneous and complex technical processes.

All of our most advanced large-scale industrial enterprises are now service oriented rather than product-manufacturing and marketing institutions. This trend has been further accelerated by the introduction of automated production.

Products may now be manufactured in astronomical quantity runs, with less and less input of human and machine energies. The role of major public or private "business" utilities is therefore not so directly concerned with the creation of "wealth" through material products manufactured— but rather with the organization and regulation of the wealth distribution.

There is then the shift in emphasis from production and product sales marketing to the wider concept of the service industry—whether this is in the service of supplied products (auto) or service in the full rentable (telephone) facility sense.

These developments are paced by changes in occupation and shift in society's orientation to work, production, leisure, and so forth. The manual production work declines obviously as more mechanical energies are poured into production. Supervisory functions vanish as the machine regulates its own work. Inventories no longer need small armies of clerical workers—and so on, up through the hierarchy of functions, to include executive control of marketing and distribution functions. There is a corresponding shift of manpower to the service industry sector, but this again may only be viewed as a temporary phenomenon when automated facilities begin to take over large areas of such servicing.

In reducing the direct link between work and physical maintenance, automation/cybernation also obsoletes many of the basic premises for our major social and economic institutions. These have been largely borne of a past when it was necessary to persuade, coerce, or otherwise "sanction" the bulk of men into spending the greater part of their lives just producing the basic products for human physical survival.

From this time forward, we may potentially produce, in abundance, all such material life-sustaining requirements—without need to "extract" or demand human life-labor in equitable return. Instead of spending most of his years merely maintaining himself, man is potentially freed to address himself to the larger purposes and enormous range of activities implicit in the larger human enterprise.

The cybernetic revolution has occurred largely within the past two decades. It is important to underline this and to recognize its evolutionary significance in the light of our discussion above. We sense this period of change and transition as one of the most critical in human history—and

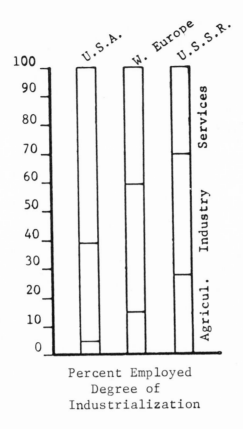

Percent Employed
Degree of
Industrialization

the focus of our discussion has centered around our capacity to control the enormous scale of our present global undertakings in a more positive, efficient, and naturally advantageous manner.

It is of key relevance, therefore, that this new change agency of cybernetics is also specifically developed for massive control and decision-making in handling large-scale systems with many complex and variable factors.

At the point then, where man's affairs reach the scale of potential disruption of the global ecosystem, he invents, with seeming spontaneity, precisely those conceptual and physical technologies that enable him to deal with the magnitude of a complex planetary society.

Population and Food

THE CRITICAL magnitude of population pressure in relation to food supply within the biosphere certainly merits rather more extended and separate consideration here.

We tend to think of the "food/population problem" as one peculiar to our own century. In certain aspects it does indeed reach critical dimensions today—but in other aspects the balance between population growth and the amount of food available to sustain human increase has been a constantly shifting dynamic factor in human development.

Much of what we call the historical development of science and mathematics was bound up with the prediction of the availability of food supplies. The earliest magical rites involve fertility and hunting success, the coming of the rains, the propitiation of deities which safeguard the continuance of food supply. Early astrology, mathematics, and engineering were directly concerned with the prediction of the seasons, the cycles of flooding, times of planting, harvesting, and so forth.

Notwithstanding all of these attempts toward predicting and organizing his forward survival—most of man's historical experience in relation to food-supply adequacy is one of relatively uncontrolled "feast or famine" of "lean years or fat years." Most historical communities lived on a narrow margin between survival and starvation.

The width of that margin—controlled and predictable survival—depended upon the successive adoption of various technologies—not only in the "hard" technology sense but, for example:

a. The change from hunter to herder. That is, the domestication of animals is the development of a form of animal behavioral technology.

b. The change from migrant herder to fixed farmer in the first introduction of agricultural technology. Seed selection, planting, irrigation, soil husbandry, harvesting, and so forth, is a very complex set of technological adaptations.

c. Pacing these progressive developments in control of the external environment was the ancillary series of advances in food storage, preservation, cooking, smoking, pickling, and so forth—the domestic technologies.

But, right up till our own period of the nineteenth-century Industrial

Revolution and the introduction of mechanized agriculture, man lived on a narrow margin of food resources.

Until the beginnings of scientific soil chemistry, the use of fertilizers, the introduction of machine-powered agricultural implements, increased transport speeds, and so forth—the size of human communities was relatively restricted by their close relation to adequate food supply. For example, before the middle of the nineteenth century few cities got beyond a million inhabitants; by the end of the nineteenth century, many European cities had multiplied six-fold in two generations.

This beginning capacity to feed more people off the land than on it is, then, directly attributable to a related series of technological developments.

> The paleolithic hunter required 10 square kilometers per person to feed himself. The neolithic herdsmen required 0.1 square kilometers (or 10 hectares). The mediaeval peasant two thirds of a hectare of ploughland—to produce cereals for subsistence, plus his woodland. The Indian rice grower one fifth of a hectare to produce subsistence. The Japanese one sixteenth of a hectare or only 640 square meters.[31]

Paradoxically, of course, the increased gains in food production have been most recently accompanied by developments in medical science—which made for lower infant mortality, longer life, higher health expectations—all culminating in an explosive increase in overall population.

World population, which had already begun to quicken when the checks and balances in the "feast or famine" cycle were removed, with the increase of settlement and improved agricultural practice, about the year A.D. 1200, began its present upswing in the 200 years between the sixteenth and eighteenth centuries—rising most sharply in the nineteenth century to our present growth rate.

Though we have bracketed food and population growth in a direct relation historically—we may note that, in effect, at a particular point in time this relation is not so directly associated.

For example, just at the time when Malthus predicted that population was increasing geometrically (2,4,8 . . .), and food supply only arithmetically (2,3,4 . . .), and that population would increase beyond the earth's capacity to supply enough food—man was beginning to *triple* his food yield per acre and continuing to expand his numbers. In fact, since the nineteenth century, we have accommodated more and more people at higher standards of living than was ever thought possible in any previous historical period.

---

[31] "Agricultural Productivity in Relation to Population," Colin Clark, *Man and His Future,* Gordon Wolstenholme (ed.), Little, Brown and Company, Boston/Toronto, 1963, p. 30.

This does not lessen our currently critical food and population pressure—but we will only get through that crisis by clearer understanding of the whole process.

In effect, there are three great evolutionary transitions in the human occupancy of the earth which are critical to understanding the food vs. population problem.

1. The Agricultural Revolution—in which man achieved a greater degree of long-range predictive control over his food supply through entering into a more directly symbiotic relation to intensive local land use—this gave rise to the early city civilizations, and so forth.

2. The Industrial Revolution—which freed man from direct dependence on his own and animal muscle energies—and, to a degree, freed him from local dependence on the land itself.

3. The Ecological Revolution—in the past hundred years the various successive and overlapping strands of the industrial-social-electro-chemical and electronic revolutions now constitute the emergence of man and his systems at magnitudes capable of large-scale interference with the overall ecological balance of the earth.

    a. In human population growth alone this represents one of the largest biological revolutions in geological time.

    b. In transformation of the planet to human use, man has now pushed his frontiers—

        (i) below the surface of the land to extract more energy, metals, and other materials in one brief period than all history;

        (ii) expanded vertically into the air—to extract its nitrogen more directly—travels above the earth surface, goes below the surface of the oceans—to exploit its food, minerals, and other potentials;

        (iii) he now deals also in radioactive, electronic, and sonic energies which expand his control into new areas of the electro-magnetic spectrum.

Within this vast and swift ecological transition, the food/population problem is no longer one of the relationship of city to farm land—but of farm to factory to chemical laboratory to orbiting satellite environ. As already underlined repeatedly, all elements of the human enterprise are now closely interlocked in a large-scale "man-made" ecosystem which should be considered as an integrally functioning "organic" sector within the ecological context.

From the social viewpoint, we have advanced swiftly to the point where our socio-agricultural-technological systems of extraction, production, distribution, transportation, and communication have turned the whole world into a single community—a directly perceptible whole system.

Within this context there are, then, no wholly separate problems, that is, there is no *food* problem as such; no *population* problem as such; no *pollution* problem; no *war* problem, and so forth. Each problem area may only be defined adequately in relation to other "problem areas"—as part of man's overall socio-ecological function.

Oceania

AUSTRALIA & N. ZEALAND

MELANESIA
 New Guinea
 Papua

POLYNESIA & MICRONESIA
 Fiji Islands
 Western Samoa

East Asia

MAINLAND REGION
 China (Mainland)
 Hong Kong
 Mongolia

JAPAN

OTHER EAST ASIA
 (Korea (N. & S.)
 China (Taiwan)
 Ryukyu Islands

Soviet Union

North America
 Canada
 United States

Latin America

TROPICAL S. AMERICA
 Brazil
 Colombia
 Peru
 Venezuela
 Ecuador
 Bolivia
 British Guiana

MIDDLE AMERICA
 Mexico
 Guatemala
 El Salvador
 Honduras
 Nicaragua
 Costa Rica
 Panama

TEMPERATE S. AMERICA
 Argentina
 Chile
 Uruguay
 Paraguay

CARIBBEAN
 Cuba
 Haiti
 Dominican Republic
 Puerto Rico
 Jamaica
 Trinidad and Tobago

South Asia

MIDDLE SOUTH ASIA
 India
 Pakistan
 Iran
 Afghanistan
 Ceylon
 Nepal
 Bhutan
 Sikkim
 Maldive Islands

SOUTH EAST ASIA
 Indonesia
 Viet-Nam (N. & S.)
 Philippines
 Thailand
 Burma
 Malaysia
 Singapore
 Cambodia
 Laos

SOUTH WEST ASIA
 Turkey
 Iraq
 Saudi Arabia
 Syria
 Yemen
 Israel
 Jordan
 Lebanon
 Cyprus
 Kuwait

Africa

WESTERN AFRICA
 Nigeria
 Ghana
 Upper Volta
 Mali
 Ivory Coast
 Senegal
 Guinea
 Niger
 Sierra Leone
 Dahomey
 Togo
 Liberia
 Mauritania
 Gambia

EASTERN AFRICA
 Ethiopia
 Tanzania
 Kenya
 Uganda
 Mozambique
 Madagascar
 Southern Rhodesia

 Nyasaland
 Zambia
 Rwanda
 Burundi
 Somalia
 Mauritius

MIDDLE AFRICA
 Congo (Leopoldville)
 Angola
 Cameroon
 Chad
 Central African Rep.
 Congo (Brazzaville)
 Gabon

NORTHERN AFRICA
 Egypt (U.A.R.)
 Sudan
 Morocco
 Algeria
 Tunisia
 Libya

SOUTHERN AFRICA
 South Africa

Europe

WESTERN EUROPE
 Germany (West)
 France
 Netherlands
 Belgium
 Austria
 Switzerland
 Luxembourg

SOUTHERN EUROPE
 Italy
 Spain
 Yugoslavia
 Portugal
 Greece
 Albania
 Malta

EASTERN EUROPE
 Poland
 Romania
 Germany (East)
 Czechoslovakia
 Hungary
 Bulgaria

NORTHERN EUROPE
 United Kingdom
 Sweden
 Denmark
 Finland
 Norway
 Iceland
 Ireland

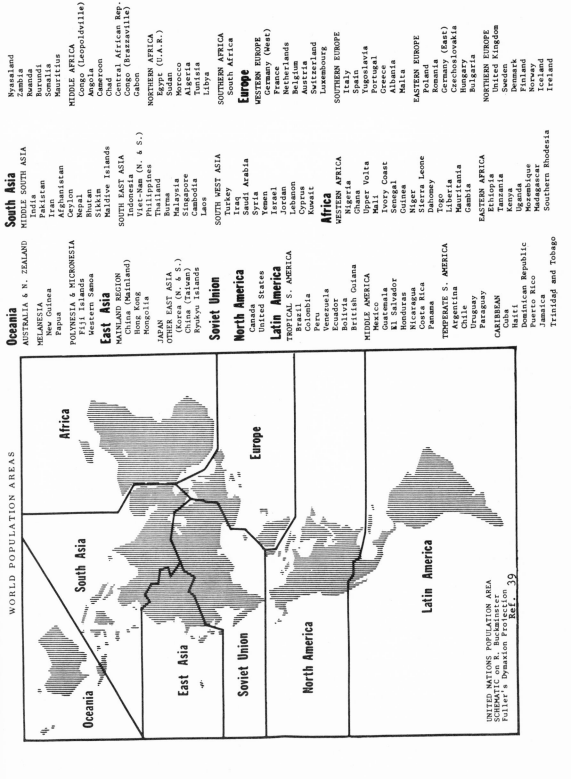

UNITED NATIONS POPULATION AREA
SCHEMATIC on R. Buckminster
Fuller's Dymaxion Projection
Ref. 39

This, in no sense, diminishes the immediate need to tackle these problems separately in the most direct and radical fashion. Rather, it suggests that the urgency of each area be linked to the other to underline their inextricable relationship—otherwise we may be deluded into "cleaning up our own local house system"—while continuing to destroy that of others on the other·side of the world. Or we may be led to decry the need for "more affluence and material growth" when our fellowmen's lives both locally and worldwide remain stunted by malnutrition and lack of the basic material needs for physical health and survival. Each goal direction and priority must be rigorously examined in the light of the range of the human problems with which it is related.

As we note in discussing population and food specifically:

(i) adjusting the *health* problem increased the *population* problem;

(ii) raising living standards in the West—with increased communication of those standards—has assisted "the revolution of rising expectations" around the world;

(iii) increased yield per acre locally in the U.S. caused surplus problems, created farm subsidies, increased government supervision, led to food-production restriction, and so forth.

This emphasis is important in terms of the future. We cannot predict or plan forward in terms of a series of problems—to be solved one at a time in isolated, piecemeal and compartmentalized fashion. The integrated interrelationship of problems and prospects is the key approach to the solution of current problems and thus to their predictive and anticipatory future avoidance.

Let us turn again briefly to the population/food question in more detail.

First—population. What are the established facts and predictions? This is obviously an area in which expectation of future trends is based on extrapolation of past trends. We have mentioned the sharp upward trend of population in the recent past. In 150 years man has added approximately 2 ½ billion increase to a world population—which had been running at approximately ½ billion for about one thousand years.

In rough figures, present world population is just over 3 billion. The current rate of increase is about 1.8 per cent, which means a doubling of world population in about 30 to 40 years. The agreed median estimate is that world population will be doubled by the year 2000, that is, 6 billion.

If this growth rate is sustained, then in 70 years there would be 12 billion people on earth—and by 2070, more than 30 billion!

The cause for alarm about the population explosion is that this doubling within one generation means not only, say, double the food supply—but doubling housing requirements, doubling—and tripling city sizes, highways, industrial extraction production, distribution, transportation of goods; more than doubling energy consumption of the various fuels—and so on.

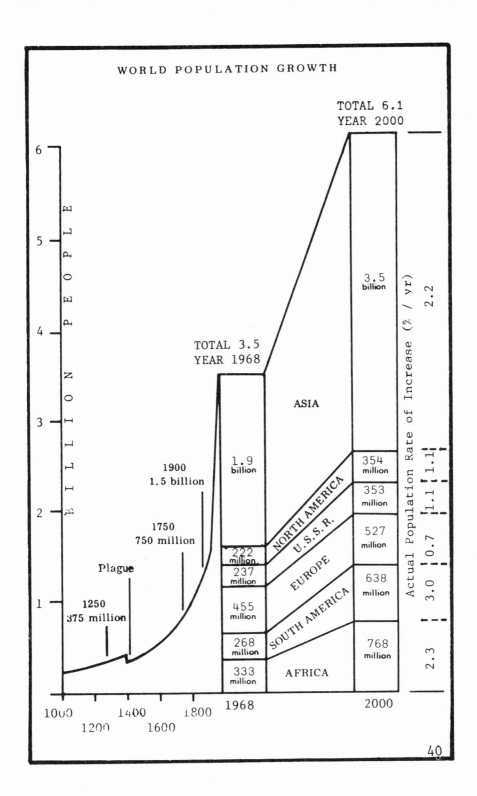

WORLD POPULATION GROWTH

The argument goes that if this exponential increase were to continue unchecked, then we need to ask ourselves: How many people can the earth actually sustain? What are the upper food balances of the total system; what would the permissible densities per area be; what kinds of stress syndromes would this lead to, and so forth?

Extrapolating forward in this way three scientists in 1960 produced a date for "Doomsday: Friday 13 November A.D. 2026" in which, as they suggested, "our great great grandchildren would not starve to death, they would be squeezed to death." [32]

Complicating this kind of projection of continued exponential growth is the fact that exponentials are as we observe them: We may take any rising trend and extrapolate it to obtain this progression toward very large numbers, "infinity," or saturation point, for any given environmental situation.

Taking them thus in isolation denies the fact that such growth rates in the real world are, in effect, changed by many other factors, that is, human population is not, like a colony of fruit flies in a laboratory jar, isolated from the real world system.

Human choice now plays a much greater role in determining human developments than ever before.

Furthermore, all of our growth estimates are based on relatively recent and incomplete records. For example, demographic reports in the past few decades are 90 per cent complete, for only about $1/3$ of the estimated world population. Among 14 per cent of that population birth/death registration is fragmentary. We also have no very accurate records of the larger patterns of population growth and decay over long time spans.

Other factors which may be concealed in usual "straight-line" projections are that: in the West particularly, records of increased population include higher life expectancy—more people are alive at older ages; "death control" through improved health measures lowers infant mortality—but where accompanied by higher living standards also decreases the number of children born per family unit, that is, related to social expectations, changes in family structure, and so forth.

Population-growth patterns also vary considerably in different world regions. At their simplest version these patterns tend to reveal that:

(i) Growth is highest in those countries:
    a. which are technologically deficient
    b. have a high population to useable resource ratio
    c. low physical life expectancy
    d. low social expectations
        for example, China, India, Egypt, and so forth, and to an extent—Africa and Latin America.

---

[32] "Doomsday, etc." H. Von Foerster, P. M. Mora, L. W. Amiot, *Science,* Vol. 132, No. 1436, November 4, 1960, pp. 1291-1295.

As often where life is hardest and most precarious—nature covers her bets!

(ii) Growth is lowest (or more stable) in countries:
    a. technologically advanced
    b. with low population to usable resource ratio
    c. high physical life expectancy
    d. higher social expectations—that is, in mobility, education, life style, and so forth.

This pattern has been generalized in studies of countries such as Sweden, England, and more recently Japan—to suggest a rather crude index—that where the per capita production/consumption of inanimate industrial energies is high (and access to implied high living standards available to a wide range of the population), then "fertility energies" decline. In simpler terms, where people live better and have more life chances, they tend not to have large families.

Detailed studies suggest that the sharpest decline in birthrate, and stable use of birth control, correspond to those social sectors receiving the largest share and access to industrial productivity, and so forth.

Whether feasible or not, then—according to the evidence—the most effective and realistic long-range mode of stabilizing world population and avoiding the implications of "population explosion" would be to raise the living standards and life-chance expectations of the whole world as rapidly as possible!

The question of "feasibility" here is, of course, considerably obscured by the older moralities of national competition, local insecurities, and a lack of understanding of changes in world society itself. Whether such advances could come quickly enough to avert the present unfavorable balance is also questionable in these terms.

When we turn to the food side of the question, the situation here is even more complex. First might be the definition of nutritional adequacy. Though we in the West generally speak in terms of basic adequacy—we consume roughly five times the basic nutritional requirements that we suggest as minimal for the hungry nations.

> Whilst constituting only about one third of the world's population we consume two thirds of the world's agricultural production as well as more than two thirds of the ocean produce.[33]

Of the other two thirds of the world population, the greater majority live on a marginal basis—either close to physical starvation or dependent on the vagaries of local climatic variation for their feast or famine years.

When we refer to the pressures of population—that is, the doubling of world population in the next thirty years—over 80 per cent of that

[33] "Food—The Great Challenge of This Crucial Century," Georg Borgstrom, *The Centennial Review*, Vol. XI, No. 3, Summer 1967.

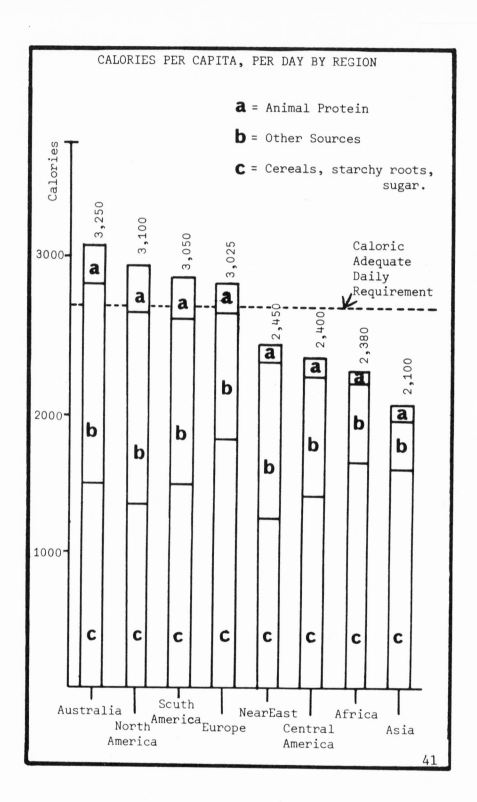

CALORIES PER CAPITA, PER DAY BY REGION

a = Animal Protein

b = Other Sources

c = Cereals, starchy roots, sugar.

Calories

Caloric Adequate Daily Requirement

3,250 3,100 3,050 3,025 2,450 2,400 2,380 2,100

3000

2000

1000

a a a a a a a a
b b b b b b b b
c c c c c c c c

Australia North America South America Europe NearEast Central America Africa Asia

41

[98]

increase will be in those world regions which cannot or are not receiving adequate food now—in Asia, Africa, and Latin America.

Let us try to summarize the actual food position more closely. Grain is a useful yardstick. Cereal grains occupy more than 70 per cent of the world's crop land. Consumed directly they provide more than half of man's total food energy and indirectly, via animal foods, take care of the remainder. This is the preferred adequate balance. In the less advanced world regions the direct consumption of grains provides *over two thirds to three fourths* of the total food supply.

The food anomalies, then, are first in the balance of regional diets; for example, the North American diet includes 25 per cent of livestock products and the European diet includes 17 per cent of livestock products—while the Asian diet includes *only 3 per cent* of livestock products. Also, the average Western city dweller consumes approximately 4¾ pounds of food per day to the Indian/Asian's one to two pounds. Within that the Western balance is still greater in animal products—and the Asian may be up to 85 per cent deficient in protein fats and vitamins.

This is regional comparative adequacy—what about overall world food production in relation to population growth?

Again, the gross figures do not tell the whole story.

The overall rate of increase in the production of food has been around 3 per cent per year—and many compare this favorably with the population increase of an average 1.8 per cent per year.

But, of course, the regional variation of production and consumption is considerable.

We have noted the reliance on a bulk diet of cereal grains in the poorer world regions. Given that world production of grains in overall food production does not rise in any one year there are, then, in addition to the 60 or 70 million extra mouths to feed in these regions, those who slip over the margin into outright starvation.

A further complication is introduced for the hungry two thirds of the world in that not only does malnutrition in early years stunt physical growth, but, as has been shown in recent years, it also retards mental growth. The chronically hungry are thus in a double bind—with insufficient physical energies and a possible decline in mental energy resources to cope with their problem locally!

When we refer to their problem as "local," we should bear in mind that our own more fortunate Western circumstance, at this time, comes not from hard work, greater foresight, and a greater way of life—but from a lucky combination of timing and fortuitous circumstances. Our major recent historical development has taken place in the temperate zone region—which has enabled us to industrialize swiftly on locally available resources—and to draw heavily on the colonized human and physical resources of the lesser developed areas.

This aspect of uneven exchange continues today. At a time when public

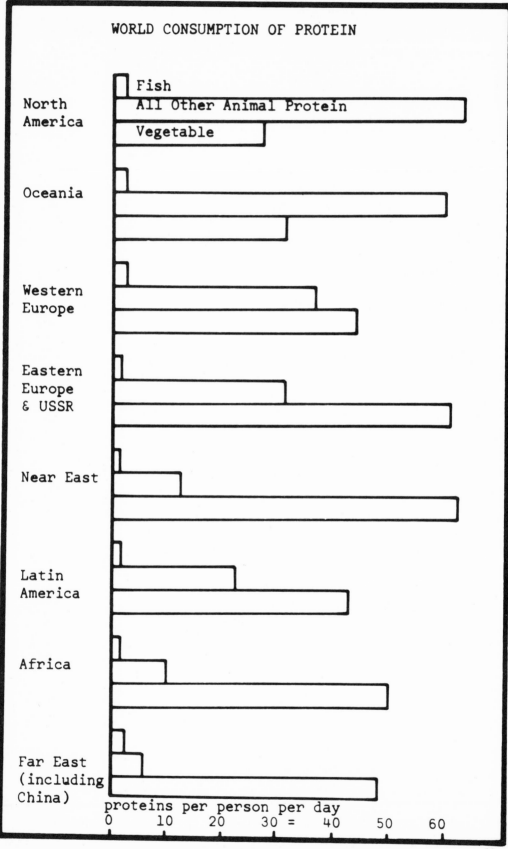

Gross Food Needs and Requirements
1975-2000

YEAR	INCREASE IN TOTAL FOOD SUPPLY NEEDED TO MAINTAIN PRESENT DIET LEVELS	INCREASE IN FOOD SUPPLY NECESSARY TO IMPROVE PRESENT DIET LEVELS	
		TOTAL SUPPLY	ANIMAL FOODS
1975	35%	50%	60%
1985	50%	85%	130%
2000	75%	124%	210%

Required Production Increases
1975-2000

PRODUCT	INCREASES 1975	NECESSARY 2000
Cereals	35%	110%
Pulses & nuts	85%	225%
Animal products	60%	210%

43

attention is focused on the two to three million or so tons of grain protein delivered to the less developed regions—less attention is given to the three to five million tons of other proteins, soybeans, oilseed cake, and fishmeal which are imported *from* the lesser developed regions by the Western world for animal feedstuffs. In Europe, Denmark, for example, imported more than 300 pounds per capita—ten times more than eaten as plant protein—and exceeding in total an amount of protein represented by the milk production of South America. This situation further exaggerates the difference between the haves and have nots.

Many of the developing countries in which great numbers are undernourished are forced to export food to pay for manufactured goods and materials which they cannot produce. Millions of food producers in the tropics are still forced to raise cash crops of cotton, bananas, coffee, tea, cocoa, and so forth, to exchange indirectly for food proteins they might otherwise produce themselves. In turn, many of the industrial goods they purchase are manufactured from material resources they have also exported.

Actually in overall ecological terms, the imbalanced and improvident use of food, metals, and other physical resources, one of the key critical factors is the parasitic relation of the more advanced countries upon the poorer regions.

The rich get richer and the poor get poorer!

Still we may assume that even if all the world's food production were shared out equally—there would still not be enough at the present time to feed everyone adequately—and this situation advances in seriousness day by day—and year by year.

In terms of general prognosis, none of the piecemeal measures, so far, however salutary, has made much of an improvement—or really afford undue optimism. Such measures include:

(i) increased yields per acre through intensive cultivation

(ii) introduction of miracle grains giving much greater yields

(iii) the bringing of more land under cultivation, for example, through use of forest, jungle lands, the deserts through saline irrigation, and so forth

(iv) the export of surpluses by richer countries

Against this also we may note the intensive birth-control campaigns—the intra-uterine devices, the pill, and so forth. These depend even more on radical changes in social attitudes—which are slower to effect than technological developments.

What kinds of alternatives can we see then in the future? What are some of the possible future directions which may be adduced in terms of the ecological context?

World population depends presently for its food on about 3 per cent of the earth's surface of arable crop land and about 6 per cent of the earth's

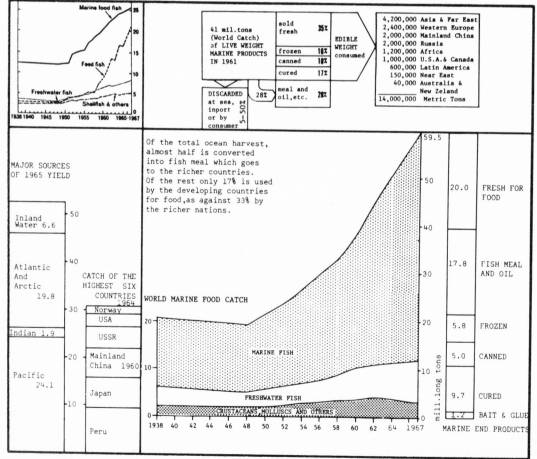

surface of forest land. Within this area, it depends on a thin topsoil layer of approximately nine inches.

Any very large addition of arable land through conversion of deserts, jungle, or rain forest seems unlikely in the immediate thirty-year future—yet it has been calculated that simply to keep up with current population increase we need 30 to 40 million new acres or food-production equivalent each year. Also merely to improve nutrition in both the lesser developed and over-developed world regions, we need to increase "balanced quality" food provision considerably in the next two decades and to increase dramatically our overall food production by the year 2000.

Obviously this cannot all come from new lands. More intensive land use by local means through traditional agriculture will help some—where this compares favorably in some areas with Western mechanized methods. But the breaking in of new lands, for example, in South America, and the parceling out of smaller land lots to smaller scale tenant farming has often been fruitless and discouraging.

Some of the answers will have to be sought "off the land." No country has progressed toward adequate nutritional levels, and avoidance of recurrent famine, for example, in the West, until at least half its population has shifted from direct dependence on marginal agriculture to industry.

Increased crop yields? Again this can go a long way toward "stop-gap" help and longer range adequacy—but even with the new "miracle grains" that have been developed, this is slow and tends to confirm the traditional agricultural use pattern. It also requires an elaborate "back-up" system of pest control, fertilizer, and so forth.

The latter item alone, fertilizer—in overall world terms—is calculated to require about a 30 per cent increase to attain food production adequacy. But there may be an upper limit on its present use! Almost 500 million people now depend on high chemical fertilized land use. To increase fertilizer production in the short run to accommodate 3 billion more people in 30 years may be impractical.

We also use large quantities of other industrial materials and fuels to make it; for example, for each million tons of fertilizer we use approximately 1 million tons of steel and 5 million tons of fuel (mainly fossil fuels). With increased fertilizer, herbicide, and other agricultural chemicals in current practice there is also the mounting danger of ecological imbalance—and many key minerals, such as phosphorus, are being leached from the intensively cultivated soil at a greater rate than they can be replaced.

When we turn to animal produce—the imbalance between the two-thirds vegetarian and one-third animal products food in world diet has been noted. This has interesting ecological side relations in terms of the overall biosphere. As we earlier noted, the maintenance of 3 billion

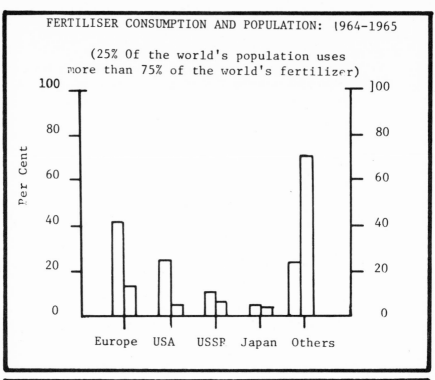

FERTILISER CONSUMPTION AND POPULATION: 1964-1965

(25% Of the world's population uses
more than 75% of the world's fertilizer)

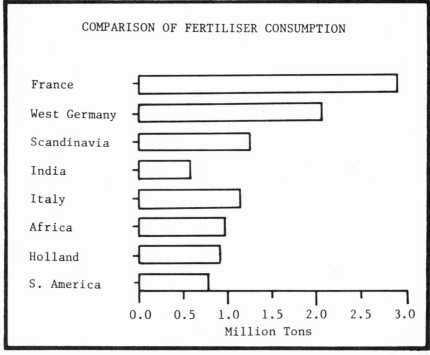

COMPARISON OF FERTILISER CONSUMPTION

45

humans requires a plant yield sufficient to accommodate 14.5 billion other animal consumers, for example, as intermediate processors.

Though environmental pollution is generally laid to industrial functions, we may note that, in the U.S. alone, more than a billion tons of agricultural wastes are produced each year—including logging debris, field crop residue, animal manure and carcasses. Only a relative fraction of this is "recycled" in practice. Discussing the U.S. animal wastes produced each year, Orville Freeman notes that "... the disposal facilities to cope with the staggering amount of animal wastes from highly concentrated feeding operations [feedlots] just don't exist." Another commentator adds, "This is a largely unrecognized problem ... Missouri has about as many pigs and cattle as people—four million. Yet the animals produce sewage equal to that produced by 40 million people! ... It's clear that any efforts to clean up our own wastes will be largely cancelled by an army of well-fed farm animals." [34]

To this we may add the other pollution effects of intensive agricultural practices—fuel use directly in agriculture and in food processing factories; pesticide and fertilizer run off into rivers, lakes, and so forth.

Clearly traditional agricultural practice, even where mechanized, remains largely a one-way "open" system of exclusive and competing market interests.

Again the only realistic solution direction will be to reconceptualize and redesign our whole food-production system—through a more integrated and ecologically oriented approach which regards agriculture-industry-food processing-distribution, and so forth, as a combined service utility.

Other future directions which have been advanced have been to increase ocean fish yields and their by-products through more scientifically controlled catch methods and a more intensive farming of the oceans. Clearly, considerable augmentation of food supply could come in this way—but it may not be sufficient, or fast enough, for the next few critical decades.

The same caveats might be applied to the production of artificial protein, food synthesis, the use of microbial food systems and leaf/waste protein sources. In varying combinations, all these directions offer the promise of solving the world's food problem. To be really effective, however, they will require to be linked together with agri-industry system development, on a scale approaching that of the combined space programs of the U.S. and U.S.S.R.—whereas, at the moment, overall expenditures in this vital research area probably do not amount, in world total, to one day of our current wars.

[34] *Missouri Conservationist,* April 1968.

Energy

OUR OVERALL contextual emphasis has been on the dynamic functioning of the ecological system and the central role of energy conversion as the key to basic life processes. The fundamental relationships governing energy input to the system and some of its main uses have been sketched, for example, in the photosynthetic and other cycles.

In this section, we are primarily concerned with energy as work and production energies—those prime movers used in the industrial system, their fuels, and efficiency of conversion. The vast increase in the amounts of energy required to sustain our present levels of productivity and the necessary augmentation of such levels to accommodate even more people, at better standards of living, lead to questions of the most efficient types of energy conversion, transmission, and process uses. The nature of the fuels used and their possible pollutant by-products are now an important factor. The amounts required in the immediate and long-range future call into question certain preferential uses of specific fuels and the more economic conservation of others.

Let us consider, first, the overall supply of energy to the ecosystem. The prime sources are radiant energy from the sun, the kinetic and potential energy of the earth gravitational system, and that which is radiated from the interior of the earth. Of these, our central focus is on solar energy. Gravitational energy enters into all energy transactions on the earth surface, but this is considered less of a direct source other than through its secondary derivatives of water and tidal power. The interior earth energies, geothermal, have not been used on a large scale so far.

To these three main sources, we might add those energies accruing from the earth spin and atmospheric circulation—wind energies and differences in temperature and pressure related to climatic change—now less widely used than in former periods.

In dealing with solar energy input, we note that this has been ongoing for millions of years and that successive layers of such energies have been "impounded," or stored, in the earth from the organic energy conversions of animals and plants. These are now usually referred to as the fossil fuels—oil, coal, and types of natural gas associated with such deposits. The bio-mass, that is, the entire complex of all life forms on earth, also represents a long and continuous impounding process of solar energies.

In addition to this organic process of energy storage, both past and

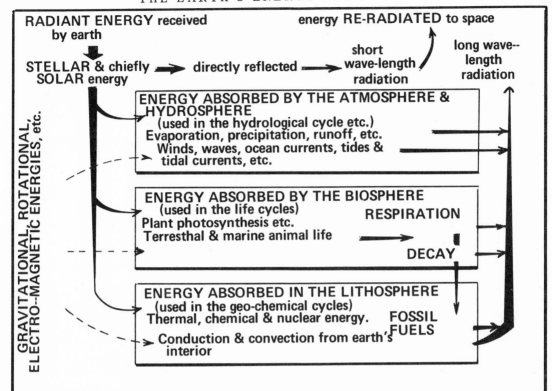

"... The earth may be regarded as a material system whose gain or loss of matter over the period of our interest is negligible. Into and out of this system, however, there occurs a continuous flux of energy in consequence of which the material constituents of the outer part of the earth undergo continuous or intermittent circulation. The material constituents of the earth comprise the familiar chemical elements. These, with the exception of a small number of radioactive elements, may be regarded as being nontransmutable and constant in amount in processes occuring naturally on the earth.

The energy inputs into the earth's surface environment are principally from three sources: 1) the energy derived from the sun by means of solar radiation, 2) the energy derived from the mechanical kinetic and potential energy of the earth-sun-moon system which is manifested principally in the oceanic tides and tidal currents, and 3) the energy derived from the interior of the earth itself in the form of outward heat conduction, and heat convected to the surface by volcanos and hot springs. Secondary sources of energy of much smaller magnitude than those cited are the energy received by radiation from the stars, the plants, and the moon, and the energy released from the interior of the earth in the process of erecting and eroding mountain ranges.

...With the exception of an insignificant amount of energy storage, the energy which leaves the earth by long-wavelength thermal radiation into space must be equal to the comined energy inputs from solar and stellar radiation, from tidal forces, and from the earth's interior." -- M. K. Hubbert.

present, we should also consider that the materials mass of the earth itself represents a vast store of cosmic energies locked in a myriad of chemical combinations from the major geological periods of the earth's physical formation.

We have, thus, a division as above into:

a. stored energies such as the fossil fuels and fissionable elements in the earth crust

b. those energies in constantly renewed income from solar radiation and other sources.

Before proceeding to examine the implications of this overall view of the energy system, we should consider man's role as central to our analysis. His individual unit efficiency as a food energy converter has already been discussed—about one half to one horsepower hour per day. The development of human society has, therefore, been predicated

1. on the use of collective human energies to perform tasks beyond the individual's capacity;

2. on the use of animal energies;

3. on the use of inanimate machine energies.

The process of development has been from low energy conversion to high energy conversion.

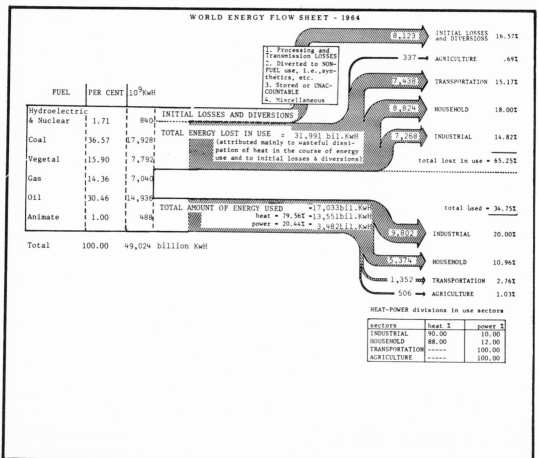

WORLD ENERGY FLOW SHEET - 1964

FUEL	PER CENT	10^9KwH
Hydroelectric & Nuclear	1.71	840
Coal	36.57	17,928
Vegetal	15.90	7,792
Gas	14.36	7,040
Oil	30.46	14,936
Animate	1.00	488
Total	100.00	49,024 billion KwH

1. Processing and Transmission LOSSES
2. Diverted to NON-FUEL use, i.e., synthetics, etc.
3. Stored or UNACCOUNTABLE
4. Miscellaneous

INITIAL LOSSES AND DIVERSIONS

TOTAL ENERGY LOST IN USE = 31,991 bil.KwH (attributed mainly to wasteful dissipation of heat in the course of energy use and to initial losses & diversions)

TOTAL AMOUNT OF ENERGY USED -17,033bil.KwH
heat - 79.56% -13,551bil.KwH
power - 20.44% - 3,482bil.KwH

8,123	INITIAL LOSSES and DIVERSIONS	16.57%
337	AGRICULTURE	.69%
7,438	TRANSPORTATION	15.17%
8,824	HOUSEHOLD	18.00%
7,268	INDUSTRIAL	14.82%
	total lost in use -	65.25%
	total used -	34.75%
9,802	INDUSTRIAL	20.00%
5,374	HOUSEHOLD	10.96%
1,352	TRANSPORTATION	2.76%
506	AGRICULTURE	1.03%

HEAT-POWER divisions in use sectors

sectors	heat %	power %
INDUSTRIAL	90.00	10.00
HOUSEHOLD	88.00	12.00
TRANSPORTATION	-----	100.00
AGRICULTURE	-----	100.00

The use of human muscular energies, even collectively, is not very economical and, like that of animal energies, diminishes the stock of food energies necessary to maintain further energy conversion. Inanimate or mechanical energy converters were the obvious direction which gave greater amounts of work energy and did not diminish food energy stocks; thereby surpluses could be built up and further survival advantage gained.

Possibly the first large-scale energy converters were ships drawing upon wind energies to move large quantities of goods and men. We have commented earlier on the importance of sea technologies historically, and this is a further example:

> The energy costs of operating a ship are only those of building, maintaining and manning it. The surplus energy derived from the sails is potentially enormous as compared with the cost of producing the sail and hoisting it ... men, using the sailing ship came into control of very large amounts of power largely independent of plant life or of the number of persons in the population using it.[35]

As the above author details further in his text, the most efficient sailing ships were able to produce a maximum of 200 to 250 times the human energy required to operate them. Land energy converters such as the water and windmills, which provided the major sources of inanimate energies up till the introduction of the steam engine, did not match such levels of conversion efficiency.[36]

For the greater part of human history, until a scant few hundred years ago, most energies available to man were organic sources from his own muscles and that of his domesticated animals. Our own period is peculiarly marked off from all others as the first in which man has had access to abundant energy supplies from inanimate sources.

Through accumulated knowledge his gain in energy has increased enormously in the past hundred years—as the conceptual tools of science formed new technological means giving higher degrees of energy conversion than ever before. Though many men in the lesser developed regions of the world are still constrained to spend their lives as "mechanical" energy converters dependent for survival on their own muscle power, man's role is increasingly that of a designer of high energy-conversion systems—even now passing the routine control of such systems to other electro-mechanical agents.

The gain from low to high energy converters is not confined to quantity only, but to the speed with which energy is available for a given task and

[35] *Energy and Society,* F. Cottrell, McGraw-Hill, 1955.

[36] *Medieval Technology and Social Change,* L. White, Jr. (This generalization is not to discount the advances in energy conversion technology which occurred in both East and West in early periods), e.g., "In 1086 the Domesday Book lists 5,624 [water] mills for 3,000 English communities." O.U. Press, New York, 1966.

the conditions under which inanimate high energy converters can operate, for example, round the clock with no "organic" rest required.

Zimmerman gives an interesting comparative example of the speed and energy costs differential between wholly animate and human plus inanimate energies.

> If we assume that the building of an Egyptian pyramid required the work of 50,000 slaves for twenty years, while a skyscraper of comparable size can be built by 5000 laborers in six months, the number of workers at a given moment is as 10 to 1; but if the time element is taken into account, the ratio is 400 to 1. This means that it took approximately 400 times as much food to generate the manpower that built the pyramid.[37]

Though the building manpower ratio has already been decreased, the notion of inanimate slave energy as replacing human labor is a fruitful concept which has been particularly explored by R. Buckminster Fuller. His energy slave unit is arrived at by taking the total energy income for the earth as measurably consumed by man in one year, and dividing this by 25 to give a 4 per cent figure of energy gainfully employed at present rates of overall efficiency. This (4 per cent) net energy used, as expressed in kilowatts per year, is divided by one manpower year, that is, by the amount of energy which could be provided by the world population of the year, working 8 hours per day per year. This gives the number of electro-mechanical energy slave units available.

Such "energy slaves" would represent the amounts of energy conversion disposed of directly by man in the form of personal appliances, heating/lighting energies, autos, telephones, and so forth, as well as those in the industrial network as also available to him, indirectly, in a variety of ways.

We may indicate the gain in such energy-slave availability by noting that, in his Presidential Address to the British Association in 1911, Sir William Ramsay estimated that each British family then had an average of twenty energy "helots" in its service.[38] We may presume that Ramsay's energy "helot" is roughly comparable to the Fuller energy slave as calculated above. From 20 such units per family (of, say, five persons) in 1911, the general European level had risen to approximately 150 by 1940 and over 400 per five-person units by 1960, that is, 81 per capita.

To appreciate the significance of such energy slaves in terms of standard of living advantage, we may show the contrast with Africa as an entire region—whose comparable energy-slave measure remains approximately 10 to 15 up to the present day. See chart below:[39]

[37] *An Introduction to World Resources,* Erich W. Zimmerman, Henry L. Hunker (ed.), Harper & Row, New York, 1964.

[38] "Future Energy Prospects at Home and Abroad," A.R.J.P. Ubbelohde, *Advancement of Science,* September 1965.

[39] Document I, "Inventory of World Resources, Human Trends and Needs," R. B. Fuller and John McHale, Southern Illinois University, 1963.

MAP AREAS	POPULATION 1960	PER CENT OF WORLD POPULATION	ENERGY SLAVES PER CAPITA
Asia	1,679,000,000	56	3
Europe	641,000,000	24.1	81
Africa	254,000,000	8.5	10

A further important characteristic is that such electro-mechanical slave units, though only calculated as doing the work equivalent of humans, are enormously more effective.

> They can work under conditions intolerable to man, for example, 5000° Fahrenheit, with no sleep, to ten thousandths of an inch tolerance, can see at one million magnification of man's vision, have 400,000 pounds per square inch sinuosity, 186,000 miles per second alacrity, and so forth.[40]

All such technological undertakings are now dependent upon vast amounts of inanimate energy supplies to maintain them. Even the extraction, processing, and fabrication of their mineral and metal components would be impossible without such energy inputs.

> The power produced by the Bratask Hydroelectric Power Station alone is greater than the amount of energy that would be obtained by using the muscular efforts of the entire able-bodied population of the U.S.S.R.[41]

We may return, therefore, to closer consideration of such supplies and how we presently use them. Our earlier division of sources is a useful one—into *capital* or stored solar energies, and *income* or renewable daily cyclic sources of naturally occurring energies.

MAJOR ENERGY SOURCES

Capital: the stored, unrenewable energy deposits in the earth.
  1. Fossil Fuels: coal, natural gas, oil (including shale and oil sands).
  2. Nuclear Fuels: those elements which may yield energy through nuclear fission and fusion processes.[42]
The main fossil-fuel deposits have been built up over a 500-million-year geological time period. Their presently prodigal use, with its many deleterious by-product effects, suggests that we review such usages with care in that they do represent a convenient and accessible form of stored

---

[40] Ibid.

[41] *Cybernetics and Problems of Development,* B. V. Akhlibininisky and N. I. Khralenko, Lenizdat Publishing House, U.S.S.R., 1963.

[42] Though earth crust sources of such fuels may be viewed as exhaustible "capital" energy deposits, the extension of the processes to ocean elements such as deuterium might supply an almost unlimited source of energy through nuclear generation.

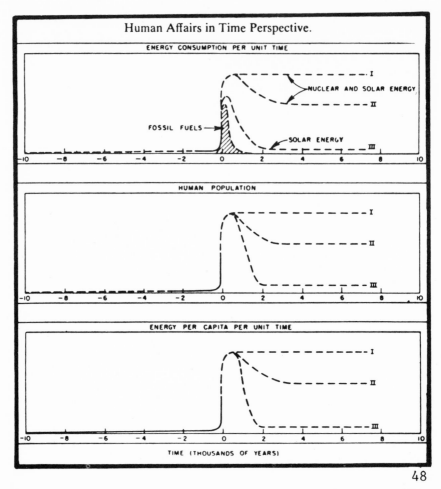

Human Affairs in Time Perspective.

ENERGY CONSUMPTION PER UNIT TIME

NUCLEAR AND SOLAR ENERGY

I

II

FOSSIL FUELS

SOLAR ENERGY

III

HUMAN POPULATION

I

II

III

ENERGY PER CAPITA PER UNIT TIME

I

II

III

TIME (THOUSANDS OF YEARS)

48

energy which could be used now, or in the future, in many different, much more economical and intelligent ways. Nuclear energies, available from the fission of heavy element isotopes and the fusion of lighter elements, though extensible toward an income energy resource through profusion of materials, is presently limited by various factors, for example, including the disposal of its by-product wastes.

Income: the naturally recurring energies available to man by tapping into the regenerative cycles in the ecosystem.

1. Photosynthesis: we have hitherto considered this energy-conversion process only in its food-energy-cycling role. There are many other ways in which energy may be directly extracted from vegetation product cycles, for example, through fuels from tree wood and other sources; by microbial action in "biological fuel cells," and so forth.

2. Other Direct Solar Energy Uses: through concentrating lenses and reflectors into cooling devices; photoelectrical and photochemical fuel cells, and so forth.

3. Hydrological: as derived from the earth gravitational system through rivers, dams, and so forth, and the direct use of tidal and wave power; also, various modes of tapping into the hydrological cycle of evaporation/precipitation.
4. Wind: though this is intermittent and variable, improvements in storage capacities may enable this source to be more widely used.
5. Temperature: temperature differentials between atmospheric and earth/water surfaces yield energy potentials of considerable magnitude.
6. Geothermal: tapping directly into the heat of the earth either through naturally occurring volcanic sources of hot gases and waters or by drilling artificial vents for simpler purposes.
7. Other "Unconventional" Sources: magneto-hydrodynamics, thermionics, and so forth.

The income energies, summarily noted above, have fewer demerits than any of the capital energy sources in terms of pollutant by-products and other noxious side effects to humans, or as yet ascertained effects on the overall function of the ecological system.

Apart from being "cleaner" energy sources, they are also potentially inexhaustible as renewed by the sun, or as occurring in the naturally cyclic ecosystem's operation. In terms of environ redesign, they afford many experimental and innovative directions which are relatively unexplored through our overdependence on the fossil fuels. Aerospace technologies have already given considerable lead here in their utilization of solar-powered communications and other systems dependent on fuel cells of different types.

PRESENT ENERGY USE DISTRIBUTIONS

Our major problem, as stated, is to increase generally the availability of energy so as to aid the development of the more than half of humanity who are presently far below the "industrialized" standard of living. This will mean considerable increases in:
1. the generation of energy
2. its conversion efficiencies
3. the transmission and distribution of energies to where they may be readily available around the earth

It is instructive to compare the location of our present world tension/local war areas and the correlation that exists between these and low energy-conversion availability, population, and food pressures. The key to many of our present world problems lies within the global energy distribution pattern.

Our past and present uses of industrial energies, and the prospects forward from such continued fuel uses, underline the critical nature of

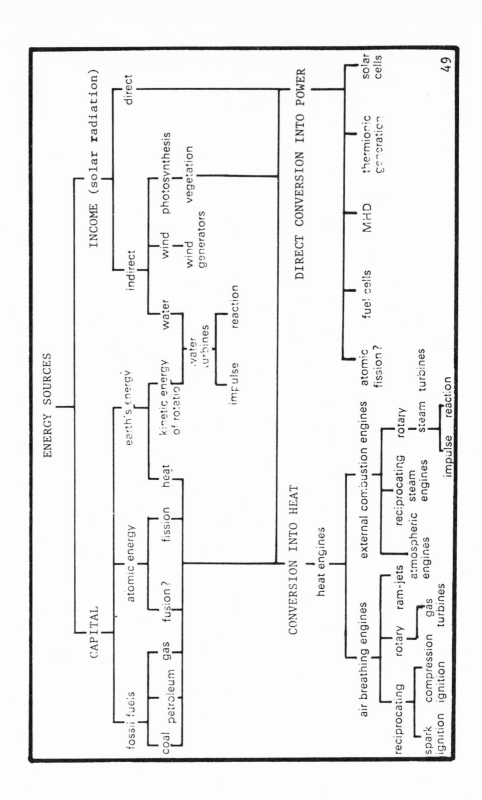

49

[114]

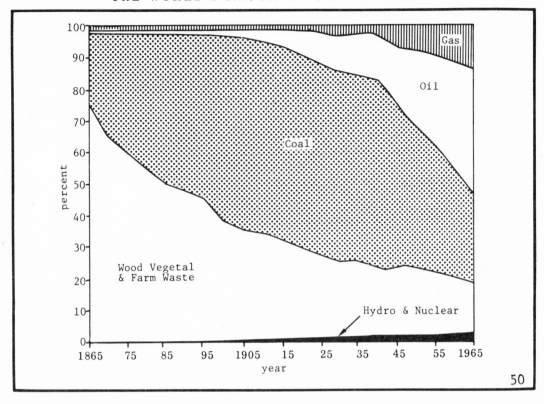

world energy availability both for the developed as well as the underdeveloped regions.

The production of world energy (which parallels, but does not exactly match, consumption figures due to various indirect uses, losses in transmission, and so forth) has increased at the average rate of 3 ¼ per cent annually from 1860 to 1958 with various growth periods when levels rose above five to six per cent. From 1958 to 1961 this annual increase rate has risen considerably. The world's *consumption* of industrial energy from all sources increased by approximately 19 per cent during the period 1961 to 1964.[43] This was an unprecedented rise to a new level which we may expect to be sustained, with higher increase in the present years, due to population rise and the rate of industrialization of underdeveloped regions.

Energy production rose by the same figure during 1961-64, and significant rises were in the area of fossil fuel uses.

Much of the rise in energy consumption was accounted for by increases in the high energy economies, for example, the United States consumed about one third of the world's total industrial energy for less than 7 per

[43] U.N. *World Energy Supplies,* 1961-64.

cent of the world's population; Europe and the U.S.S.R. showed corresponding increases:

> *The industrial regions* dominate the consumption of each of the industrial fuels . . . consumed 77 per cent of the world's most important energy source— coal—in 1963; 81 per cent of world's petroleum; 95 per cent of all natural gas; and 80 per cent of hydroelectricity and nuclear power . . . *the non-industrial world* with 71 per cent of the world's population used 77 per cent of all human energy; 87 per cent of all animal energy and 73 per cent of total fuel wood and waste in 1963.[44]

In round terms, the total energy supply in 1964 was an average of 1.6 short tons (coal equivalent) for each person in the world. The increase in the high-energy economies further dramatizes the gap between these and the low energy-developing regions—in per capita terms, the more fortunate individual in the former consumed *more than fifty times* the industrial energy of his counterpart in the poorer regions.

What this means in other measures may be gauged by the following: As a comparative example, recent figures being more readily available, the United States usage is:

Steel Production   1/3 of the world total
Autos   3/5 of all the world's cars
Trucks   2 out of every 5
Surfaced Roads   1/3 of the world total

Steel Production	1/3 of the world total
Autos	3/5 of all the world's cars
Trucks	2 out of every 5
Surfaced Roads	1/3 of the world total
Electricity	uses 1/3 of all electrical power produced on earth
Railroad Freight	1/4 of world total
Civil Aviation	1/2 the world mileage [45]

When this disparity is compounded with expected population increases in the next few decades, it may be viewed in energy terms as a two-fold dilemma.

Firstly, world population is expected to double by the year 2000, that is, 33 years. No matter what types of controls may be sought or imposed, this figure of approximately 6 billion is unlikely to be much reduced within the time at our disposal. Even given the present distribution of

[44] "The Geography of World Energy Consumption," R. A. Harper, *Journal of Geography,* Vol. LXV, No. 7, October 1966, p. 307.

[45] *U.S. News and World Report,* March 6, 1967.

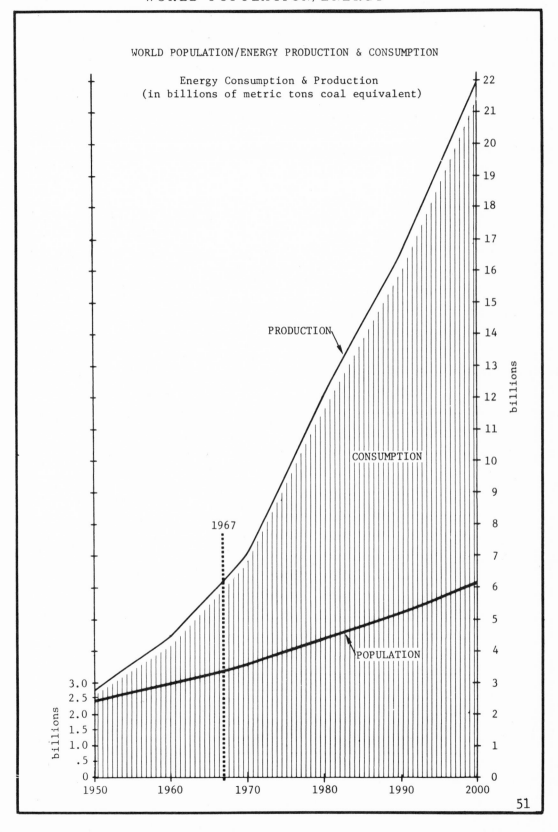

WORLD POPULATION/ENERGY PRODUCTION & CONSUMPTION

Energy Consumption & Production
(in billions of metric tons coal equivalent)

PRODUCTION

CONSUMPTION

1967

POPULATION

billions

billions

51

population and energy resources and the increases in energy conversion efficiencies to be expected from improved technologies, this will still require more than double our present energy production and consumption.

At first glance, this may particularly entail a doubling of present fossil fuel uses—with parallel side effects, unless stringent filtering and more efficient burning is accomplished. The increased use of such fuels raises serious doubts, not only about their reserve capacity but about the wisdom of using up such an accessible, but swiftly exhaustible, store. With a world increasingly dependent on inanimate energies, it seems crass stupidity to clean out the cupboard (or bank balance) before checking on future income or unforeseen emergencies. Given that we maintain our present use level, it may then require more than 10 billion tons of coal equivalent energies annually.

Secondly, however, it is calculated that to maintain double our present world population by the year 2000 will require not double, but about *five times more energy*. Though the rate of industrialization is slow in the developing regions, some already showed a growth rate of electricity consumption of 15 to 22 per cent between 1963 and 1964.

Our present problems, therefore, call for the swiftest increase in the use of other than fossil fuel energies. This may be particularly applicable to the lesser developed regions which are lowest in these resources, but correspondingly high in access to solar, hydro, and tidal power sources. The latter two may be most applicable to systems of large-scale electrical generation with the corresponding increase of industrialization. Augmenting this, we require:

1. the selection and preferred use in such regions of high energy-conversion means;
2. the extension via enlarged transmission networks of electrical power from the presently available, and increasing, concentration of generating plants in the industrial regions;
3. the swift development of locally autonomous power sources, for example, from solar, wind, and hydropower to fuel cell and nuclear power plants for local agri-industrial usage, communications, transport, and other needs;
4. the more efficient and continual redesign of our environ facilities, and their prime mover energy converters, toward extraction of maximum performance per unit of energy invested.

The latter set of requirements may be the more pressing and the most accessible to immediate design solutions:

> ... quite small amounts of power could do a great deal of good. It is interesting to note that the old Dutch wind mills developed only about 2 horsepower apiece, and yet, a relatively small number of these, working steadily, reclaimed large areas of Holland from the sea. An Indian economist has indicated that for a

PROJECTIONS OF ENERGY CONSUMED IN THE YEAR 2000 COMPARED TO 1960 ACTUAL BY WORLD AREAS

10^{12}KwH

Energy consumption in year 2000 **if**

Areas	Actual comsumption	Trend in world consumption from 1950 to 1960 continues	World consumption is at US 1960 per capita level	World consumption is at W. Europe 1960 per capita level	N.America,Europe,Oceania & USSR are at US 1960 per capita level & all other areas are at Europe 1960 level
	1960	(1)	(2)	(3)	(4)
WORLD TOTAL	33.60	179.20	442.40	141.60	200.80
PER CAPITA*	11.12	29.20	72.16	23.04	32.72
North America	12.40	21.44	20.88	6.72	20.88
Latin America	1.12	25.44	41.76	13.36	13.36
Western Europe	6.32	23.84	27.60	8.80	27.60
East Europe,USSR	7.20	36.80	35.92	11.52	35.92
Communist Asia	3.20	40.00	115.20	36.80	36.80
Non-Communist Asia	1.92	23.20	160.00	5.12	51.20
Africa	.64	8.00	42.48	13.60	13.60
Oceania	.40	.80	1.92	6.40	1.92

*values in 10^3 KwH/person. Based on U.N.data,population for the year 2000 is estimated at 6,129,000,000.

52

village of 1000 persons, a power source of slightly more than 100 KW would suffice in the early stages of mechanization, and less than 10 per cent of this would be used for domestic purposes. By contrast, a single American household might require a power supply almost half this size to handle the daily peak loads.[46]

We may also note in relation to the above that such relatively small power sources may supply energies which can play a key "change" role in giving power not only for augmenting food production, and so forth, but

[46] "Power for Remote Areas," H. Z. Tabor, *International Science and Technology,* May 1967, pp. 52-59.

for vital communications—radio, T.V., and small transmitters. In thinking about power for such regions, we often forget the range of power required for various purposes, for example, from a jet airplane at 30,000 horsepower and automobile at 100 horsepower, we go to a household refrigerator at 1/2 horsepower, fluorescent lamp at 1/20 horsepower, and a transistor radio at only 1/1000 horsepower.

The key relation between a high-energy industrial economy and population-growth stability also suggests that we pursue the solution of immediately pressing problems such as population and food supply and distribution on as many levels as possible. This means increasing food production in every possible way with the presently massive logistical support that we already use in war, increasing the rate of local industrialization at both small- and large-scale levels of deployment and concentration, education at all levels and in every type of skill and understanding appropriate to the necessary but abrupt social, cultural, and economic transition.

Power is now the key to expanding food production, as the most immediately pressing problem in the highly populated, less developed, regions. Their need is not merely the stop-gap aid of food surpluses or fertilizer shipments, but energy for transport, communications and distribution facilities, for local fertilizer production, for industrialization and education.

The emergent countries with their dense populations living in small towns and villages need energy badly for light, for village industries, for the irrigation of crops and drainage, and for the local processing of their harvest of sugar, and cotton and jute. Energy for transport is also essential for their development. The solution of their energy problems should, therefore, be one of the first objectives of technical aid, if the gap between the developed and emergent countries is to be reduced.[47]

Simple sharing of existing fuel supplies and industrial machinery would not be enough, however, to alleviate the present imbalance in living standards between such lesser developed regions and the industrial regions. To bring underdeveloped regions up to industrial parity by building up their industries on the same pattern of fuel and major materials consumption which obtains in the developed industrial regions is not possible in present terms. In addition to the required extra energies, it is doubtful if the supply of major metals, for example, would suffice. Progressively lower-grade metal ores are not having to be mined. For example, 100 years ago copper ores used were not less than 10 per cent copper content; today the world average is 1.5 per cent. Even given that metals extracted are progressively recycled, the amount of metals per capita required, at present industrial use levels, would not be available to bring the other 60 per cent of the world's people up to full industrialization.[48]

In terms of the fuel energies necessary, this would entail an approximate 60 per cent rise per year, for example, in our overall use of fossil fuels. Even with our projected reserves as presently known, continued population increase and concomitant energy-use increases would amount to sharing such fuels for about a century or so until presently accessible reserves were exhausted. Though oil and natural gas potential deposits are known to be relatively more enormous than coal, the energies required in processing lower grade mineral ores would be greater, as would the parallel demand for non-fuel uses of oils and gases.

Coal (extrapolating present and projected rates of its use and given that industrialization is not so expanded) may not supply the world energy needs by the year 2000 level for more than 150 to 200 years. Proven oil and natural gas reserves are much greater than the extent of our present knowledge; oil reserve estimates are roughly forty times the world total consumption figures for 1960. Oil, shale, and other sources increase estimates further. The "extent of our knowledge" is the critical factor in projecting such reserves and their utilization. We not only discover more

[47] "World Energy Prospects," Sir Harold Hartley, F.R.S., *World in 1984*, Vol. I, Nigel Calder (ed.), Penguin Books, 1965.

[48] Hence the emphasis, in our present discussion, on increasing performance per unit of invested resources as the only possible way in which this can be done. In terms of industrial energies and materials, the solution may only be sought through prior attention to such technological facts.

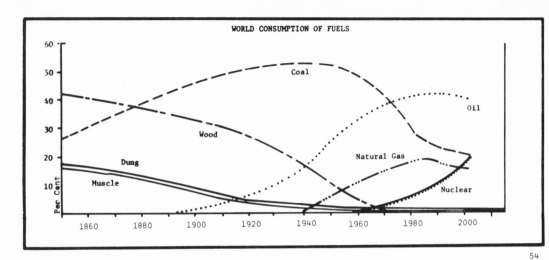

WORLD CONSUMPTION OF FUELS

54

deposits but our knowledge of how to extract more energy from them also increases.

The existence of very large untapped oil fields on the continental shelves and delta lands of Southeast Asia, rivaling those in the Persian Gulf and Caribbean, has been noted in a recent paper:

> Actually it has, by now, become obvious (1) that the world's effective reserves of oil will run into trillions of barrels; (2) that a large part of these reserves exist in the shallow water and delta coastal-plain areas of the Western Pacific and of the Southeastern Asian nations; and that the development of these resources can be of immense benefit to hundreds of millions of people, pending the further "breakthrough" in connection with the harnessing and use of atomic and thermonuclear energies.[49]

One may also speculate as to the relevance of such large-scale oil sources (extending as they do through South Korea, Taiwan, the Philippines, Malaysia, Burma, Cambodia, and the two Vietnams) with

[49] "Major Oil and Gas Deposits of the World's Coastal Lowlands and Continental Shelves—with special reference to those of the Western Pacific," W. Taylor Thom, Jr., F.W.A., President, American Institute of Geonomy and Natural Resource, Supplementary Exhibit, reprinted from the October 1967 *News Letter of the World Academy of Art and Science.*

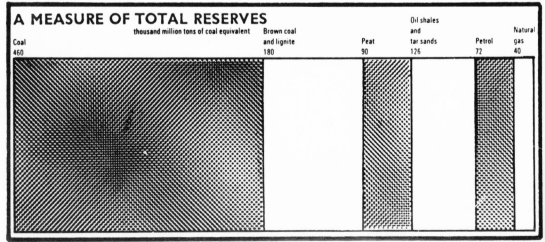

A MEASURE OF TOTAL RESERVES

thousand million tons of coal equivalent

| Coal 460 | Brown coal and lignite 180 | Peat 90 | Oil shales and tar sands 126 | Petrol 72 | Natural gas 40 |

regard to the present power struggle being waged in this area. Unfortunately, there is as yet no world "resource authority" which might decide such conflicting claims in terms of the real needs of the human community.

The point may still be stressed, however, that even with such reserves, both in resources and knowledge, we patently cannot continue our present energy policies with regard to such fuels generally.

Apart from by-product effects and extravagant valuable deposits in "storage," the petro-chemicals and those which may be derived from natural gas are now the basis for innumerable different products, including the swiftly developing range of plastics. Recent advances in microbial research also suggest the bio-synthesis of food materials from such fossil-fuel bases.

Burning up potentially valuable construction materials and an enormous food and medical supply reserve seems even more prodigal than when the oils and gases are considered solely as industrial fuel!

RESOURCE AND USE DIVERSIFICATION

Overshading all other considerations, then, in this regard is that of diversifying our overall world energy economy—of more swiftly developing our "income" energy sources on a massive scale, and of investigating new sources, means of storage, transmission, and more efficient process use.[50]

Hydroelectric power represents less than 10 per cent of the world's energy consumption. Its potential and efficiency of generation are extremely advantageous, particularly as those regions that are poor in other indigenous fuel sources are often well situated to benefit from the use of locally untapped water power. This vast renewable energy resource is obtainable by "tapping in" to the hydro-cycle in combination with the earth gravitational field. Its only demerits for the lesser developed areas are the "energy costs" involved in large-scale harnessing of such power—cost, in terms of trained manpower and material resources allocation, transportation, equipment, and so forth, all of which are in equally short supply in the emergent regions.

Though supplying less than a tenth of the world-energy-consumption total, the regional use of hydro-electrical power as per cent of total contribution, goes as high as 99 per cent in countries such as Norway—down to a low, 5 per cent, in countries such as the United States which are rich in other fuels.

With the level of transnational undertakings increasing, many large joint

[50] We might underline here that the impetus toward this has already been emergency pressured by local ecological malfunction in the advanced regions. The amounts of aerial, water, and soil pollution from current fuel uses now enforce these directions. We might hope that the extension of such ecological regard for human health and survival may be extended to the whole planetary community.

POTENTIAL MARINE ENERGY SOURCES

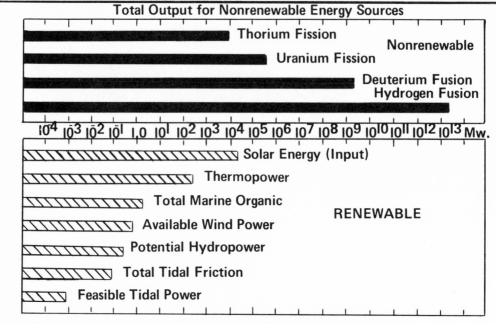

Total Output for Nonrenewable Energy Sources

Thorium Fission

Uranium Fission

Nonrenewable

Deuterium Fusion
Hydrogen Fusion

10^4 10^3 10^2 10^1 1.0 10^1 10^2 10^3 10^4 10^5 10^6 10^7 10^8 10^9 10^{10} 10^{11} 10^{12} 10^{13} Mw.

Solar Energy (Input)

Thermopower

Total Marine Organic

Available Wind Power   **RENEWABLE**

Potential Hydropower

Total Tidal Friction

Feasible Tidal Power

Annual Output for Renewable Energy Sources

"...the sea harbors far more non-renewable energy than the land, in the form of the potential fusion energy of its hydrogen and deuterium.

"The power demand of the world in 2000 has been projected as 14 million megawatts....the ultimate fission and fusion of energy content of the oceans is shown in terms of multiples of that anticipated annual demand.

"Thorium and uranium fission could, in principle, supply this 1.4×10^7 MW for some 700,000 years, whereas deuterium and hydrogen fusion can supply it for times that are greater than the age of the solar system. Although terrestrial sources of fissionable materials are probably greater (and more economical) than the marine, the sea is clearly the predominant source of fusible deuterium and hydrogen.

"Feasible tidal power can supply a tenth of one percent of the total need, but even the entire tidal dissipation in all the oceans of the world represents only ten percent of the total need." --Robert Colbarn, ed.

56

hydro-electrical schemes are planned or already underway. One, for example, due for completion in 1970, as a joint venture between Rumania and Yugoslavia, is expected to meet more than 15 per cent of the energy needs of both countries. A number of such programs are presently underway around the world, for example, the Aswan and Upper Volta dams in Africa. At the largest and most hopeful scale is that of the proposed uses of the Mekong River, "twelfth largest river in the world, 2600 miles in overall length, draining in its lower basin an area larger than France, with a population (in the four countries of Cambodia, Laos, Vietnam, and Thailand) of some 50 million people . . . (presently) less

North America 255,020	U.S.S.R. 140,452	France 97,811	South America 51,500	U.K. 14,700

than 3 per cent of the lower basin is irrigated and almost no hydro-electric power is drawn from the river." [51]

Such world water power harnessed in projects of this scale could provide over ten times more energy than our present coal production. Europe has about 50 per cent of its estimated hydro potential already in use, North America about 45 per cent, though Canada has a considerable unused potential over this figure. Africa, for example, with the largest estimated potential, uses less than 1 per cent.

In terms of overall hydropower use, it has been calculated that about 13 per cent of the estimated potential is presently being developed. If all were developed, however, at present conversion and use rates, it would still not provide more than a part of the world's annual fuel needs.

Tidal power from many of the great river deltas and coastal bays is another powerful hydro source as yet almost untouched. "At present, the only scheme to reach the construction stage is on the Rance estuary near St. Malo, France . . . planned to generate electricity equivalent to annual saving of 400,000 tons of coal." [52] Wave power and the general use of the massive movements of water energy in the oceans we seem to have no direct ways of tapping at this time.

Geothermal power, though used historically in the form of hot springs and other features of recent surface volcanic activity, has been little exploited directly as a large scale energy source. In various areas of the earth the interior heat layers are close enough to the surface for drilled well tapping of steam and hot water fields. The technique is similar to oil and natural gas, but more advantageous in the degree of energy heat more immediately available. Recent pioneer development in the United States [53] has a number of such "wells" operating. An additional important feature of these is their natural occurrence in relation to rich mineral resources, thus providing power for processing, for example, potash fertilizer, one of our currently critical needs.

Wind power has proven itself as an excellent "income" source of energy for centuries—and could be used more widely today, for generator conversion, where small quantities of electricity are required for various

[51] U.N. Office of Information, November 1966. (Note: Present conflict in this area will, no doubt, hold up this scheme considerably.)

[52] *Man and Energy*, A. R. Ubbelohde, Pelican Books, 1963, p. 68.

[53] Magma Power Co., Los Angeles, California, reports vast deposits of steam, chemicals, minerals—and 360,000 parts/million and approximately 700-800 F.—correspondence: B. C. McCabe, President.

local purposes. Rapidly improving storage capacities may make this an excellent autonomous source for more remote areas of emerging regions. Many different "aerogenerators" have been developed experimentally and this is an area particularly suitable for pilot projects in our present program. [54]

Solar energy development has received considerable attention in recent years as the world's total energy-balance sheet has become clarified and general agreement has been reached on the need to find alternative energy sources.

The annual earth receipt from solar radiation is "about 35,000 times the present yearly energy consumption . . . one ten thousandth of this converted directly into power would increase world energy production by about 250 per cent." [55]

One acre of the earth's surface receives energy at the rate of about 6000 horsepower on a clear sunny day. Such conditions vary, of course, around the earth—but, as one writer has observed, if we speak of nuclear reactors, "we should also consider a vast reactor located safely 93 million miles from the earth in space—the sun." [56]

The problems in the use of solar radiation are obvious: intermittency, low density difficulties in storage, conversion, and so forth. But many of these have been overcome technically and various types of radiation-concentration devices have already been proven in direct use of the sun's rays for cooking, cooling, and so forth. Cooling is also an important and obvious factor as areas where the sun is most plentiful and constant are those in need of coolants—a key consideration when the use of solar energy is identified most often with the lesser developed areas, for example, India. Solar water heating has been in use for a long time and a number of "solar" houses utilizing direct and indirectly channelled energies have been built. Many of these intermittent but plentiful income sources of sun and wind power await only more efficient storage for their wide applicability for many of the smaller scale energy tasks.

The most promising overall area of development, and use, has been in aerospace work. The solar cell converting sunlight directly into electrical energy has made possible much of the space exploratory data collected so far. One system of almost 30,000 cells, covering 70 square feet, powered all instruments including cameras and other recorders in a satellite track lasting seven months and covering 325 million miles. Such units in the near future may, therefore, be powering the entire satellite-routed global telecommunications system already partially in operation!

[54] "The Use of Income Energy," R. Buckminster Fuller, *Prague 1967 Newsletter,* World Design Science Decade, November 1966, Southern Illinois University.

[55] "World Patterns of Energy Production," E. W. Miller, *Journal of Geography,* U. S., September 1959, p. 277.

[56] "Power Equals Power," *Xerox Pioneer,* U.S., Fall 1965.

ESTIMATED GROWTH OF
NUCLEAR CAPACITY AND GENERATION

	1960	1970	1975	1980
Total net electricity generation[1] (1,000 million KWh)				
North America	955	1,780	2,380	3,140
Europe	535	1,120	1,570	2,150
Japan	110	300	420	600
Total	1,600	3,200	4,370	5,890
Total output capacity (1,000 million KW)				
North America	192	375	500	650
Europe	131	290	400	540
Japan	23	65	90	130
Total	347	730	990	1,320
Nuclear output capacity (1,000 million KW)				
North America	...	7	30	90
Europe	...	10	40	90
Japan	...	1	5	10
Total	...	18	75	190
Annual nuclear generation[2] (1,000 million KWh)				
North America	...	50	210	630
Europe	...	70	280	630
Japan	...	5	35	70
Total	...	125	525	1,300
Oil equivalent of nuclear heat released (in millions of tons)	...	31	120	305

[1] These figures do not include power stations' own consumption.

[2] Assuming an average annual utilization of 7,000 hours.

58

Note: With all of the above ancillary power sources, we still need energies of sufficient high density of concentration, possible speed of installation, conversion, and of a "continuous" character which might obviate present storage and transmission barriers. Nuclear energy appears to satisfy many of these urgent conditions. The forecasts of the Geneva Conference on the Peaceful Uses of Atomic Energy in 1955 regarding the technical and economic feasibility of its employment have been considerably fulfilled.

Nuclear power has been much emphasized as the fuel source for the future. As we have noted, though, this is presently based mainly on the uranium ores in the earth, so it could be termed a "capital" energy use. But, theoretically, as both fission and fusion processes may be extended to a wide range of elements, nuclear power comes closer to being an "income" source utilizing a wide range of materials. As one pound of fissionable uranium is equivalent in energy to 650 tons of coal, it affords a performance many hundreds of times greater than equivalent fossil-fuel use. Linked also, by its nature, to most advanced technology, ancillary gains via this field may be considerable in the use of radiation energies in medicine, agriculture, and so forth. Part of its present limitation lies in manner of use, that is, to produce steam, and thence to electrical generation, rather than directly producing electricity. Despite these developmental limitations, nuclear reactor installation and successful economic operation have increased considerably.

Its advantages for the underdeveloped regions of the world have been succinctly stated by one distinguished engineer:

> It can function anywhere. It is independent of geography, climate and the general cultural level of the inhabitants. Upkeep is minimal. . . . Needed amounts of nuclear fuel are easily transported, and the consumed weight is negligible. Operation is automatic and can be managed by a limited personnel. And because initial costs are high (and nuclear fuels are and will remain government property), installations will continue to be planned and financed by national or multi-national agencies. They can therefore be placed where they are needed.[57]

This author also draws attention to the facts that the nuclear revolution—of dispersed autonomous power centers as well as those providing large concentrations of power—would be a less difficult transition for developing peoples than the introduction of traditional fossil-fuel-based industries. . . . "Where the airplane is supplanting the bullock cart or dogsled, where radio (and television) directly superseded the village drum for communications, and where manufacturing goes from handicrafts all the way to automation without having to pass through the states symbolized by the steam railway and the assembly line."[58]

As we shall later discuss, the more easeful, swifter, and reasonable pattern of such development may be via nuclear energy, plastics, and electronics—rather than coal, steel and steam! Experience has shown that even if a research reactor initially appears to be a drain on a country's resources, it stimulates overall scientific and technical development in a variety of fields and assists materially in aiding economic and technological takeoff.

The advantages of nuclear power, particularly, lie in its independence of geography; due to the compact and "long-duration" fuel source, plants may be built for use far from the sources of fuels, and located autonomously without need for "continuous" fuel inputs. Portable nuclear reactors have already been constructed for military use. One such type, reported in 1966, weighed less than 15 tons, produced more than 400 kilowatts, and could be transported in an ordinary truck.

Though as compared with present fossil use, it is a "clean" power source, the disposal of radioactive wastes has been and remains a problem—the emergence of nuclear power as a "competitive" source in

[57] "The Impact of the Nuclear Age," Boris Pregel, *America Faces the Nuclear Age*, Sheridan House, New York, 1961, pp. 28-29.

[58] Ibid.

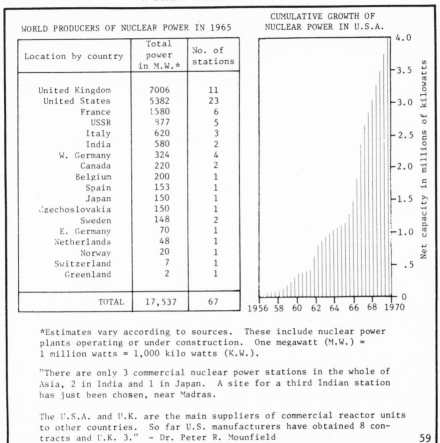

WORLD PRODUCERS OF NUCLEAR POWER IN 1965

CUMULATIVE GROWTH OF NUCLEAR POWER IN U.S.A.

Location by country	Total power in M.W.*	No. of stations
United Kingdom	7006	11
United States	5382	23
France	1580	6
USSR	877	5
Italy	620	3
India	580	2
W. Germany	324	4
Canada	220	2
Belgium	200	1
Spain	153	1
Japan	150	1
Czechoslovakia	150	1
Sweden	148	2
E. Germany	70	1
Netherlands	48	1
Norway	20	1
Switzerland	7	1
Greenland	2	1
TOTAL	17,537	67

*Estimates vary according to sources. These include nuclear power plants operating or under construction. One megawatt (M.W.) = 1 million watts = 1,000 kilo watts (K.W.).

"There are only 3 commercial nuclear power stations in the whole of Asia, 2 in India and 1 in Japan. A site for a third Indian station has just been chosen, near Madras.

The U.S.A. and U.K. are the main suppliers of commercial reactor units to other countries. So far U.S. manufacturers have obtained 8 contracts and U.K. 3." – Dr. Peter R. Mounfield   59

the advanced regions will, however, probably accelerate solutions to this. Recovered wastes from uranium fission have also been used in other types of power plants specifically designed for use in remote areas, for example, in space and for unattended Arctic weather stations. The use of such radio-nuclide fuels leads into other types of more direct energy conversion—thermo-electro and thermionic devices. Fission wastes may then be "viewed as a prime source of such radioisotope fuels ... [and] the anticipated problem of waste storage may be alleviated if this source of useful energy can be exploited and some of these wastes converted into fuels." [59]

ENERGY CONVERSION EFFICIENCY

The efficiency with which energy is converted in various processes is a crucial aspect of the overall energy picture. Present world efficiency is suggested as attaining only about 6 to 8 per cent—at best up to 20 per cent [60]—when we deduct friction, heat, engine wear and malfunction,

[59] "Energy for Remote Areas," J. G. Morse, *Science,* U.S., Vol. 139, No. 3560, March 1963, p. 1175.

[60] "The World Power Conference of 1964," article on main theme of World Power Conference, London 1964, *The Times,* London, September 9, 1964.

poor fuel oxidation, losses in transmission, overweight in loads as presently designed (for example, as in household uses), wastage in nonuse "idling" periods, and so forth.

A great deal may, therefore, be accomplished by increasing our overall energy-conversion efficiency. More rigorous systems design of present uses could more than double the performance per unit of energy invested in many areas.

The automobile is a particularly inefficient example: of the energy in crude oil, 87 per cent remains after refining; 3 per cent is used in transport to the consumer; 25 per cent is converted to work in the engine, but only 30 per cent of this is transmitted to the road (after losses to friction and auto auxiliaries) and further decreases occur through gears and tires. The overall efficiency of the automobile is about 5 per cent—though air drag, braking, and idling reduce this in actual operation.

Other engines represent higher work efficiencies on paper, but closer calculation would probably reveal similar types of loss of energy, even if considerably less than the auto. An interesting example here would be to calculate the duplication and overall loss of energy efficiencies in the average "appliance-equipped" house, as often operating cooling, heating, cooking, lighting, from separately functioning, and different, fuel sources.

A useful case of specific energy-efficiency gains may be elicited from a recent transportation study.

> In 1950, Soviet railroads carried just over 600 billion ton-kilometers of freight traffic and appeared to be straining the upper limit of the possible in doing this. Fifteen years later, they carried more than three times as much traffic with only a modest increase in route mileage, very little rise in the operating labor force, and no increase at all in the number of locomotives.[61]

As the study further indicates, this was accomplished by switching from steam to diesel-electric locomotives, which are more continuously available for work, require less servicing for longer distances, and so forth. The same gains in efficiency might be adduced for diesel electrification of other national railway systems, but the above example shows the swiftest gain over time—which is of critical importance to our central theme.

The division of energies among their various uses—in industrial production, transport, communications, distribution, and so forth—is presently difficult to assess accurately in world terms. In the United States, transportation via trucks, automobiles, and trains has been calculated to require four times the amount of fuel than that required for electrical-power generation. In more recent years, with the rapid expansion of air transport, this may be many times higher, for example, 1966 figures give an estimate of 11,000[62] airplanes in the United States air

---

[61] *Soviet Transport Experience: Its Lessons for Other Countries,* Holland Hunter, The Brookings Institution, Washington, D.C., March 1968.

[62] *Life,* Vol. 60, No. 15, April 15, 1966, p. 40.

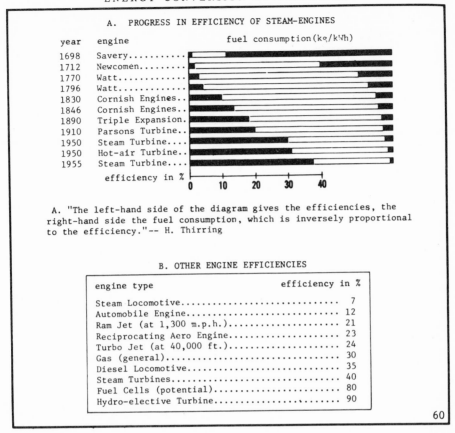

A. PROGRESS IN EFFICIENCY OF STEAM-ENGINES

year	engine	fuel consumption (kg/kWh)
1698	Savery..........	
1712	Newcomen........	
1770	Watt............	
1796	Watt............	
1830	Cornish Engines..	
1846	Cornish Engines..	
1890	Triple Expansion.	
1910	Parsons Turbine..	
1950	Steam Turbine....	
1950	Hot-air Turbine..	
1955	Steam Turbine....	

efficiency in % 0 10 20 30 40

A. "The left-hand side of the diagram gives the efficiencies, the right-hand side the fuel consumption, which is inversely proportional to the efficiency."-- H. Thirring

B. OTHER ENGINE EFFICIENCIES

engine type	efficiency in %
Steam Locomotive.............................	7
Automobile Engine............................	12
Ram Jet (at 1,300 m.p.h.).....................	21
Reciprocating Aero Engine.....................	23
Turbo Jet (at 40,000 ft.)....................	24
Gas (general)................................	30
Diesel Locomotive............................	35
Steam Turbines...............................	40
Fuel Cells (potential).......................	80
Hydro-elective Turbine.......................	90

60

space in any twenty-four-hour period. The general rise of air transport using large quantities of fuel is an obvious factor in our overall energy use increase. This is offset, partially, by the more precise attention to higher fuel-use efficiencies in such advanced technological instruments and their extraction of the highest performance-per-unit-invested, versus weight of equipment, cargo, and so forth.

When we consider only single engine efficiencies, however, the inherent redesigning possibilities are obscured. Such engines only operate within, and as functional components of, larger systems complexes. Possibly, for environ planners, the urban city complex may be a better starting point. We have elsewhere commented that few overall energy budgets are prepared for building, for example, for dismantling as well as construction.

Few detailed energy systems analyses have been applied to urban and other human ecological aggregates, in terms of their overall energy metabolism. Present attention to the malfunction of the auto in cities could be fruitfully extended to lighting, heating, household and public energy uses, including sewage and waste disposal systems, and so forth. Industry, though wasteful of energy in the strict sense, is extremely efficient when compared, even casually, with the average energy-systems management of our urban complexes.

Electrical power generation is probably one of the sectors of industrial energy conversion which has shown most continuous improvement and capacity to switch flexibly from one type of generating fuel conversion to another. Notable in recent years has been the introduction of nuclear-powered generating plants with their highly favorable ratio of fuel input to energy generated—with, however, the earlier caveats about local radiation and thermal pollution.

A recent report from French engineers [63] suggests that we may now design a generator substation at one tenth the size of the present type of unit. This possibility of "miniaturizing" the substations, which are an essential feature of power distribution networks, is accompanied by the additional possibility of extending present transmission radii through ultra-high voltage—carrying power over longer lines with less loss.

Ultra-high voltage transmission with "miniaturized" substations could span enormous areas of the earth and bring electrical power within reach of the energy-poor nations. Many European countries are already running such lines up to 600 miles. The United States and Canada are also concerned with this possibility in transmitting power across sparsely settled plains and mountain areas; "the U.S.S.R. is experimenting with high-voltage D.C. current as part of its plans to transmit power all the way from Siberia to industrial areas in Western Russia." [64] If across Russia, then feasibly from Europe to India or to Africa! The tendency for power networks is to seek the largest interconnectibility for maximal sharing of differential loads at varying peak periods.[65]

In addition to the projection of large-scale technological projects of industrialization for the developing countries, for example, hydro-electric and nuclear power generation, and so forth, it should be borne in mind that:

1. Electrical power "storage" on a large scale is not yet feasible; power must be generated and used within a given transmission grid and large amounts can be efficiently used only if the industrial system is there to use it. Increasing capacities in long-distance transmission of electrical power, mentioned above, offset this economic dependence on locally available industrial use, but the point is an important one.
2. Both ends of the power scale must be kept in proportion. The desired results of eventual large-scale industrial advantage can also be aided considerably by the more immediate and plentiful supply of small- and medium-scale generators and plants. These can supply

[63] "Shrinking the Power Centers," *New Scientist,* U.K., June 16, 1966.

[64] "Cheaper Power Through Higher Voltages," K. Hamill, *Fortune,* June 1959.

[65] "Geosocial Revolution," R. B. Fuller, Document 3 in the present series, 1965, contains specific discussion of this topic.

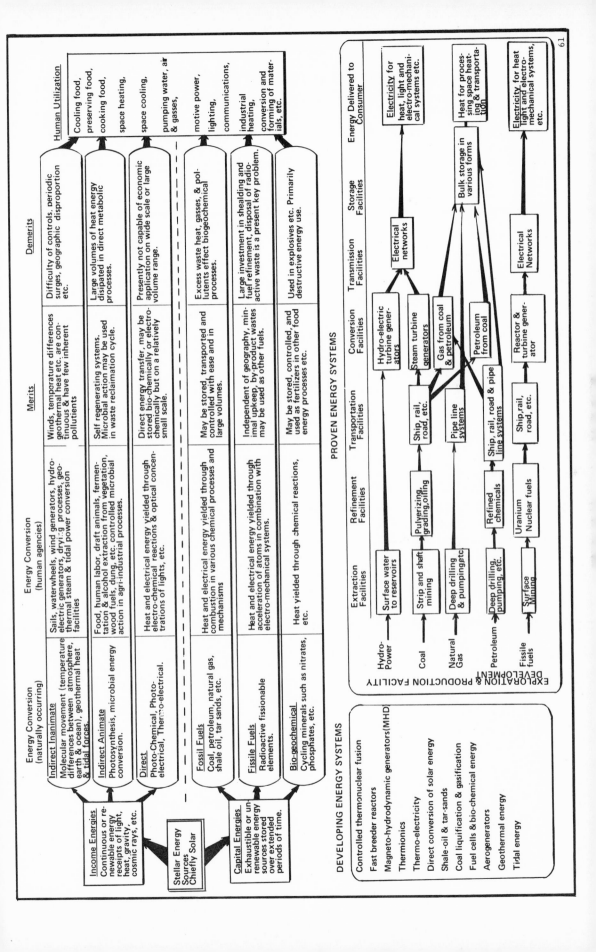

power for increasing food yields through irrigation, and so forth, community utilities, and production facilities of many types. Importantly, also, they can be a key "orientation" agency in speeding the transition from an agriculturally based society to an industrially based one.

An earlier source cited provides a useful typology for the power needs of remote underdeveloped areas as follows:

> **Group 1**—Units delivering a fraction of a watt up to several watts, such as power supplies having roughly the capability of standard flashlight battery and slightly larger, can run radios, transistorized T.V. receivers and small transmitters—providing news, education, entertainment as well as vital communication linkage where telephones and other units are not available.

> **Group 2**—Units from several watts up to one kilowatt, with the capability of an automobile battery, might be used for a microwave relay station, for refrigeration, and for larger communications apparatus.

> **Group 3**—Units comparable to the power of a gasoline lawn-mower engine or larger, providing power for the pumping of water and other agricultural and productive purposes.[66]

This source further stresses the possible uses of income energies of wind and sun used in three classes of devices—wind generators, photo voltaic cells, and thermal engines converting heat (including solar heat) to electrical or mechanical power. The U.N. has also recently issued a 215-page study handbook on this area of autonomous small-scale generation of power for the underdeveloped regions.[67]

In general, we have to avoid the stereotypes of development, for example, that lesser developed regions must necessarily follow the growth patterns of the present high-energy regions. The simple biological parallel of "ontogeny recapitulating phylogeny" may have no real relevance to such development.

Obviously, there are various stages of development, but we may already observe the reality of emerging countries moving into industrial era forms without retracing the earlier stage developments of the advanced regions. Reference is usually made there to cultural barriers, but electric light, cinema, telephone, transistor, and television could not have been more eagerly adopted wherever they have been made available—even in the most traditionally oriented societies. We may note that there appear to be no social cultural barriers in the transfer of advanced military technologies.

---

[66] Power for Remote Areas, H. Z. Tabor, *International Science and Technology*, May 1967. (N.B. see also: *Direct Use of the Sun's Energy*, Daniels (Yale Univ. Press, 1964). *Power from the Wind*, A. Putnam (Van Nostrand Co., 1948), *Solar Energy Quarterly*, Arizona State University, U.S.

[67] *Small Scale Power Generation*, U.N., 1967, 11. B.7.

The most pragmatic attitude toward the redesign of development is a "both/and" one—rather than strict evaluation in either/or terms. The presently advanced countries are characterized by the plurality and variable scale of their energy production and consumption systems. The process of development should also share this plural approach. There are no fixed rules which must be followed—other than those of speed, urgency, and that the most immediate advantage be gauged within a framework of future ecological consequences and contingencies.

There is, for example, the growing trend toward a shared pool of the large-scale world technological instruments, even where this is masked by local "brain drains" and the balance of competitive markets. Advanced global services go increasingly beyond the capacity of even the most powerful countries to wholly sustain and operate—satellites, telecommunicating, world airlines, large-scale energy generation and distribution systems, and so forth. No country has all the necessary resources to develop these entirely alone; few manufacture all the items necessary for their maintenance. They are, by their nature, systems that operate most efficiently in the service of the largest possible numbers of "customers."

We may question, therefore, the often-assumed need in the developing process for the prior build-up and duplication of "heavy industry" in national units. In some, by reason of size, it is obviously impractical; in others, it may be due to "prestige" need rather than actual operative value.

This may also apply to large-scale energy production. Rather than wait for the build-up of specifically national industrial bases, we may need to go further ahead with both variable-scale, locally autonomous, energy generation *and* large-scale regional generation and distribution. Recent developments in ultra-high voltage transmission also suggest that we may increasingly extend our present transmission of energy from concentration in the high-energy areas to those lacking in energy.

Generally, we need to assume that no matter what the artificial constraints may be—those which are customarily put forward such as exchange economics, balance of payments, and so forth—we can no longer afford the disparity between the energy-rich and the energy-poor regions of the world. The present costs in global tensions are already great—the future costs are likely to be ecologically enormous.

Materials

THOUGH OUR main emphasis in this area will be on industrial materials, this is an aspect of the global ecology which has only recently come within more generalized review. The processes of metals and minerals extraction, distribution, use, and circulation in the world industrial networks are now a major subsystem of the biosphere.

As these industrial process cycles begin to approach those naturally occurring in the environ, both in complexity and magnitude of ecological effect, we have been able to identify more clearly the "organic" nature of our physical technologies and their evoluting patterns of growth.

We may, with some conceptual accuracy, refer to the phenomena of industrialization as the externalization of our metabolic systems—as now operable at a global scale in extracting, digesting, and circulating the various major ingredients necessary to the sustenance of our extended human systems operation. We might more fruitfully examine the progressive extractions, flows, and recyclings of such materials in terms of overall "metabolic" or ecological efficiency rather than confine ourselves within the customary economic, fiscal, and trade terms.

The flow of industrial materials and technologies is now as essential to the ecological maintenance of the whole human community as the "natural" flows and cycles of air, water, and light energy. Our present modes of conceptualizing the operation of the industrial eco-networks relate more to a pre-industrial past than to the realities of a critically interdependent global system—whose advanced facilities may only be produced by drawing upon the full array of world resources and only function efficiently when extended to the service of the greatest numbers of men.

Yet—we still operate large sectors of this system in terms of the restrictive barter practices of local agriculturally based societies in marginal survival relations to their environs. Such obsolete modes of accounting and control now clog the efficient operation of the global industrial ecology. They may be as dangerous to its forward and "healthful" maintenance as glandular malfunction in the internal human metabolism or large-scale pollution in the overall ecology.

When we focus upon the historical development of materials, the importance of conceptual orientation becomes clearer. Most of the industrial resources presently in use were not even "conceptually" recognized as such a hundred years ago. Aluminum was a scarce metallic curiosity, radioactivity a laboratory phenomena, and many of our present key metals were regarded as "waste" impurities in other ores. Our material resources and capacities are dependent on the way we view our environment—they are ultimately as we conceive them to be!

We refer to industrial raw materials as those generally found in the earth crust—the ten-mile-thick shell of geologically formed deposits of metallic and nonmetallic ores which we may regard as accessible to extraction and processing within our present technologies. Additional to these crust materials are the elements of the atmosphere and ocean also used in the industrial process. Eight elements make up 98.6 per cent of the earth crust:

Oxygen	46.6 per cent	Cadmium	3.6 per cent
Silicon	27.7 per cent	Sodium	2.8 per cent
Aluminum	8.1 per cent	Potassium	2.6 per cent
Iron	5.0 per cent	Magnesium	2.1 per cent

RELATIVE ABUNDANCE OF METALS

RELATIVE ABUNDANCE OF METALS IN THE EARTH
(present in more than .0009 parts per million)

	P.P.M		P.P.M		P.P.M
SILICON	277,200	COLUMBIUM	24	HOLMIUM	1.2
ALUMINUM	81,300	NEODYMIUM	24	EUROPIUM	1.1
IRON	50,000	COBALT	23	ANTIMONY	1
CALCIUM	36,300	LANTHANIUM	18	TERBIUM	0.9
SODIUM	28,300	LEAD	16	LUTETIUM	0.8
POTASSIUM	25,900	GALLIUM	15	THALLIUM	0.6
MAGNESIUM	20,900	MOLYBDENUM	15	MERCURY	0.5
TITANIUM	4,400	THORIUM	12	BISMUTH	0.2
MANGANESE	1,000	CESIUM	7	THULIUM	0.2
RUBIDIUM	310	GERMANIUM	7	CADMIUM	0.15
STRONTIUM	300	SAMARIUM	6.5	INDIUM	0.1
BARIUM	250	GADOLINIUM	6.4	SILVER	0.1
ZIRCONIUM	220	BERYLLIUM	6	SELENIUM	0.09
CHROMIUM	200	PRAESODYMIUM	5.5	PALLADIUM	0.01
VANADIUM	150	ARSENIC	5	GOLD	0.005
ZINC	132	SCANDIUM	5	PLATINUM	0.005
NICKEL	80	DYSPROSIUM	4.5	TELLURIUM	0.002
COPPER	70	HAFNIUM	4.5	IRIDIUM	0.001
TUNGSTEN	69	URANIUM	4	OSMIUM	0.001
LITHIUM	65	BORON	3	RHENIUM	0.001
CERIUM	46	YTTERBIUM	2.7	RHODIUM	0.001
TIN	40	ERBIUM	2.5	RUTHENIUM	0.001
YTTRIUM	28	TANTALUM	2.1		

RELATIVE ABUNDANCE OF METALS IN THE SEA WATER
(present in more than .0015 parts per million)

	P.P.M		P.P.M		P.P.M
SODIUM	10,561	ALUMINUM	1.9	MANGANESE	0.01
MAGNESIUM	1,272	RUBIDIUM	0.2	LEAD	0.005
CALCIUM	400	LITHIUM	0.1	SELENIUM	0.004
POTASSIUM	380	COPPER	0.09	TIN	0.003
STRONTIUM	13	BARIUM	0.05	CESIUM	0.002
BORON	4.6	ARSENIC	0.024	MOLYBDENUM	0.002
SILICON	4.0	IRON	0.02	URANIUM	0.0016
		ZINC	0.014		62

Other materials of present importance occur in lesser percentages, for example:

Nickel   0.02 per cent

Tungsten   0.005 per cent

Tin   0.0004 per cent.

The major concentrated deposits of these resources are inequably distributed around the earth with little relevance to natural boundaries and "natural" ownerships. This has been an important factor in the location of industries, the growth of the "advanced" nations, and the present disparities in living standards.

Until about two hundred years ago, the numbers of known metals were quite small and the scale of their use comparatively insignificant in our present terms. There were the *noble* metals of gold and silver, and the *base* working metals such as iron, copper, lead and tin; mercury was known but little used. The main alloys were brass and bronze, but their precise combinations of copper, tin, zinc, and antimony were not clearly understood until the eighteenth and nineteenth centuries.

The industrial revolutions of the nineteenth century began the production of metals on an abruptly larger scale than at any other previous period. In the first quarter of the twentieth century more metal of every type was extracted and processed than in the whole of all recorded history; this output was doubled in the second quarter of the century. Ninety per cent of this production was iron-alloyed with a smaller proportion of other metals to form the range of steels which, up till now, have been the fundamental material basis for our present industrial civilization.

From this point on there are three distinct and characteristic phases of industrial growth and materials use which are of signal importance.

The first phase is marked by the localized growth of iron and steel production when large-scale mechanical industry developed in those countries where supplies of iron ore, coal, and limestone were available in close association with developing power and transportation facilities. The swift "takeoff" of the industrially advanced nations owes much to these locally coincident factors of relative self-sufficiency in this brief phase. Even where their own iron ore supplies had to be augmented as production increased, they had the transport facilities, political and trade power to obtain ores from nearby countries. The increased demands for such materials led to a polarity of trade exchange characterized by the flow of manufactured goods from the industrial countries in return for raw materials from the industrially underdeveloped areas. This pattern, with its latent restrictive functions, persists up to our own period.

The second phase occurred in the late nineteenth and early twentieth centuries when new ferrous and non-ferrous alloy production began to require constant access to an array of metallic constituents which were relatively scarce in many of the industrialized countries. Such materials as manganese, tungsten, nickel, cobalt, and so forth, were further, and unevenly, dispersed around the globe—with little relation to previously conceptualized territorial and "power" balances. Within a few decades, the separate national systems of industrialization found themselves acutely dependent for vital alloying and other materials on distant, and often competitively controlled, sources of supply. The whole industrial network, both of manufacturing centers and raw materials areas, became locked in a critically interdependent global relationship—as no one nation could be self-sufficient in the vast range of materials now essential to the maintenance of its industrial system.

> The new century found Great Britain looking to Canada and the Belgian Congo for cobalt, to British Guinea and France for aluminum ore, to Canada for nickel, to India and the Gold Coast for manganese, to China and Burma for tungsten. A new meaning was given to the importance of retaining command, of the seas . . . giving place to command of the air.[68]

All of the other industrial nations were in the same position, even those, such as the U.S., who already possessed a great range of internally available minerals deposits.

Previously neglected, and underdeveloped, regions possessing key materials deposits became the latent focus for a long series of inter-nation power struggles. It is noteworthy that the political slogans accompanying these conflicts rarely referred to their latent content, but were expressed in terms of "living room," "manifest destiny," "self-determination," and the like. We may still locate many of our present or potential tension and conflict areas by direct reference to their production or reserve supplies of key "strategic" materials.

Another marked feature of this second phase of industrial development was that the new key metals and other materials, as such, little changed the prevailing polarity of industrial manufacturing and raw-materials-producing areas. As we have noted, most heavy industry centers had been developed prior to, and independently of, the newer material needs. The heavy industrial base, for example, was steel production and, where iron ore was required in thousands or millions of tons, to sustain this, the vital new alloying metals for successive steel alloy improvements were required in much smaller quantities—less than one tenth of such amounts of iron ore.

The established industrial centers have retained, therefore, their prime position, that is:

1. The general increase in the number of different materials required, as technologies advanced, lessened the relative importance of any one material in determining industry location—particularly as the larger

[68] "Conference on Mineral Resources and the Atlantic Charter," British Association for Advancement of Science, Vol. II, No. 7, 1942.

range of materials needed was more globally dispersed in its various individual supply origins.

2. The relatively smaller quantities of additional alloying materials required less transportation energies—this factor was further reduced by improvement in transportation and intermediate technologies.

3. Further concentration of industrial power in the established metal-working centers was strengthened by the tendency toward the use of scrap, particularly in steel-making.

This polarized pattern—in which the advanced countries continue to develop, at higher standards of living with concomitant reduction in family size and overall population pressure, and the lesser developed countries remain largely restricted to the function of raw materials depositories with much less industrial growth, lower living standards, and rising population pressures—still obtains to a considerable degree.[69] The accompanying tensions and conflicts over control of the strategic material regions is further intensified by the internal imbalance of the overall pattern.

This might be viewed as an ecological malfunction with the overconcentration of highly specialized and developed areas tending toward a latent parasitism on the lesser developed. One key "overconcentration," we may note, has been on steel production as the primary industrial base paired with heavy dependence on coal and oil fuels as the energy resource for such industries.

The third phase, into which we are just entering, is characterized by the possible displacement of steel as *the* prime industrial material (for structural, machine, transport, and other major uses) by other metals, "composite" materials, and plastics. The forward pattern of development may lie in:

1. the pairing of aluminum/magnesium/titanium as prime metals with electrical power from hydro or nuclear sources.

2. in the increased use of metallic and non-metallic composites and plastics in conjunction with similar power sources.

Such trends are already visible, as we shall later discuss. Their future developments could swiftly diversify and alter the present industrial power balance and possibly turn the present prior investment advantage of the older established industrial regions into a restrictive disability.

The speed of technological change no longer favors long-term "stable" amortization in heavy plant equipment as a standing advantage. The rapid recovery of those industrial countries whose capital plant equipment had been largely destroyed in World War II (for example, Germany and Japan) and their subsequent rise to industrial parity and competitiveness with the

[69] For example, regions such as Southeast Asia, Bolivia, Nigeria, and the Congo have long produced together almost 90 per cent of the world's supply of tin, but have had no industrial means for using it internally to their more direct advantage. Advanced countries such as the U.S. consume more than 35 per cent of the world's tin without any major tin mine within their own boundaries.

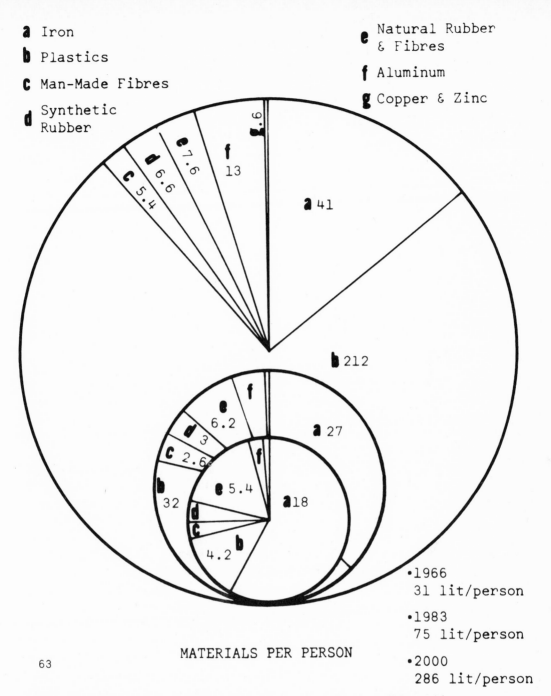

a Iron
b Plastics
c Man-Made Fibres
d Synthetic Rubber

e Natural Rubber & Fibres
f Aluminum
g Copper & Zinc

g .6
e 7.6
d 6.6
c 5.4
f 13
a 41

b 212

f
e 6.2
d 3
c 2.6
b 32
a 27
f
e 5.4
a 18
d
c
b 4.2

•1966
31 lit/person
•1983
75 lit/person
•2000
286 lit/person

63

MATERIALS PER PERSON

other advanced industrial nations, within two decades, is striking evidence of this trending.

In the above synoptic review, we have devoted most attention to metals and metal-working as the prime materials and technologies of industrialization. Many other materials and technologies played major roles in this development, but the main structural and other technical advances have been closely interwoven with, and dependent upon, metallurgical processes. These, in turn, depended upon the general growth of industrial

[141]

chemistry which changed manufacture from being predominantly "mechanical" in nature toward diverse modes of chemical, electro-chemical, and electro-mechanical industrial transformations.

Our present emphasis on metals is based, therefore, on this continuing centrality of their position within the industrial ecology and, even more importantly, on the critical aspects of overall metal resources in our current transitional period. Until other materials are more fully developed and available in the same abundance with the necessary ranges of tensile stress, hardness, durability, energy conductance, forming capacities, and so forth, we are heavily dependent upon the key metals.

The high living standards afforded by advanced technological facilities are predicated largely on the amounts of metals and inanimate energies available. As the amount of metal used in maintaining such living standards increases in overall consumption with the numbers of persons served by an increasing range of industrial facilities, the amount of metals actually available per capita decreases.

Within the immediate range of our present technologies we are dealing with a relatively limited amount of metal resources. Alloying chemistry extends the number of their combinations and provides an increasing range of qualities; the reuse of the metals and their alloys through progressive cycles of scrapping and refabrication in different products means that they are not "lost" or used up.

In the long run, when we consider such factors, metals are inexhaustible. But, if we wish to increase our immediate forward advantage industrially—to serve more men to higher living standards—we can only do this in the shortest possible time by extracting more designed performance from each unit of metal used.

The gain of higher performance per materials-use investment is a "natural" aspect of advanced technological development. Each successive technical improvement is designed to reduce materials and energy "costs" per function. This is dramatically evident in the progressive miniaturization of many devices; in the reduction of materials weight, prime mover and maintenance energies in advanced technologies of transportation, communication, information handling (see chart on computer performance gains).

Extending advanced living standards to more peoples despite decreasing amounts of available metals and other materials per capita is only feasible, therefore, through redesign toward more efficient performance in the use cycle of our major materials. Though inherent within technological development, the swift increase in the overall amounts of materials used, in the range of industrial facilities, and the greater number of users, require that we more consciously redirect and hasten this process—or we may be overtaken by the inevitable conflicts which our present "have/have not" disparities engender.

KEY METALS

Some brief comment on selected key metals may be pertinent here. Notes above, on the interdependence of manufacturing and raw materials areas, and the increasing world consumption of these metals may be related to the tables on reserves, production, and consumption in this section.

Iron/Steel Though now constituting our main metal usage, it is interesting to reflect that this enormous dependence on iron is relatively recent. Iron came into tool and weapon use only after copper and bronze. Too soft to use in the pure state, it took many centuries for man to control the amount of carbon in iron mixtures to produce a sufficiently hard steel. Our present range of steel alloys mostly originated in the past hundred years. The development of their precise alloying techniques may be accounted one of the most important in our period—when man was able to predict, consistently control, and flexibly manipulate the structural qualities of his major materials on a large scale for the first time.

With iron as the major component in combination with varying amounts of other metals, steels may be produced with a vast range of required properties: of great tensile strength, degrees of hardness, wear, rust and acid resistance, and so forth. They may be non-magnetic, of high electrical resistance, low coefficient of expansion—or possess these and other characteristics in various combinations.

The main alloying metals used are manganese, chromium, nickel, molybdenum, tungsten, cobalt, and vanadium. Chromium and nickel are used to produce rust-, acid-, or heat-resisting steels; manganese gives particular wear-resisting properties. High speed tool and cutting steels are generally formed with tungsten and/or molybdenum with lesser quantities of chromium, vanadium, and cobalt.

No material presently used, and required, in such large quantities wholly rivals the range of qualities available in steels for general purposes. But this is now changing quite rapidly as aluminum, magnesium, composites, and plastics have entered the field in bulk production. A further factor influencing this shift is the limitation of steel in loss of strength. At very high temperatures, in aerospace and supersonic aircraft work, where atmospheric re-entry heats and "lead-edge"-materials conditions go beyond the melting point of most steels, it has been superseded by ceramic refractory coatings and refractory alloys of other metals.

The growing usages of aluminum, other metals, and plastics in areas previously served by steel have, however, forced its development toward higher yield strengths and other properties. Current high tensile strength steels of 18 to 22 tons per square inch are likely to be doubled in strength yield in the next period, and the possibility of high-strength steels of up to 200 tons per square inch also seems feasible within the next few decades.

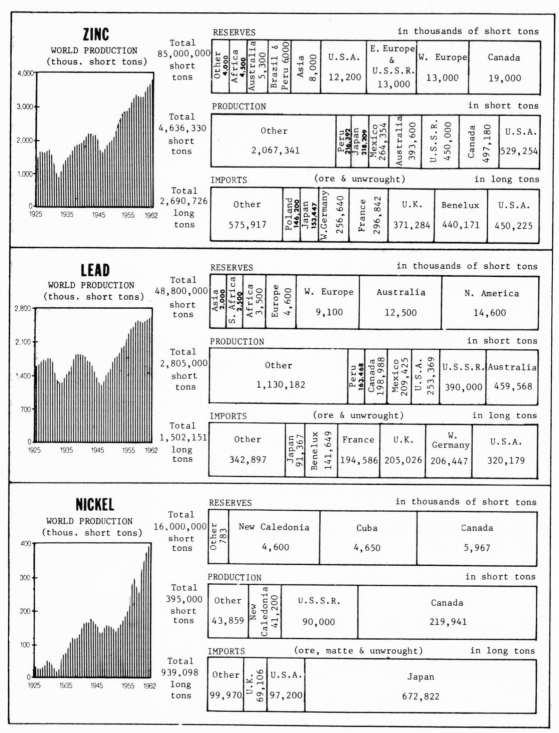

Recent changes in its production technologies have kept steel in a favored position by increasing production, though more direct and "continuous" processes have also contributed.

The enormous investment in steel industries and their central position in the various national economies sustain constant emphasis on steel as the

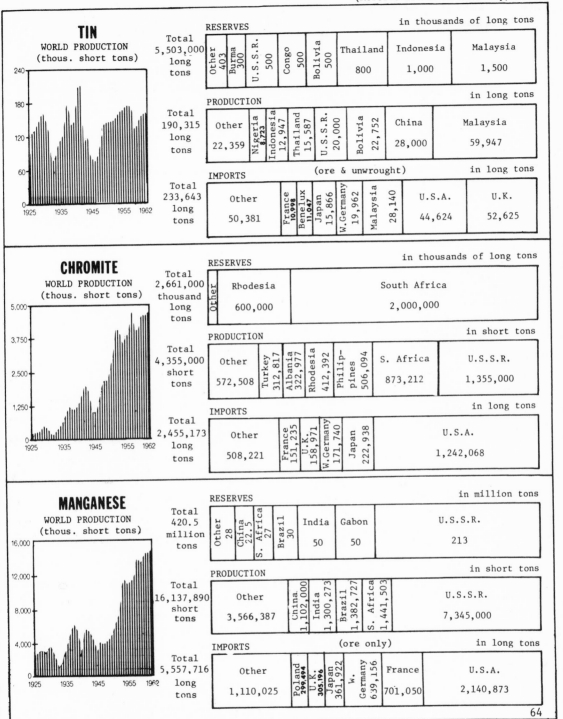

key industrial base and index of economic development. As we shall later discuss, however, this might no longer obtain for newly developing countries whose major developmental direction may lie with the "light metals" or structural plastics as the preferred developmental base.

As we have noted, the location of iron ore deposits was a prime factor

[145]

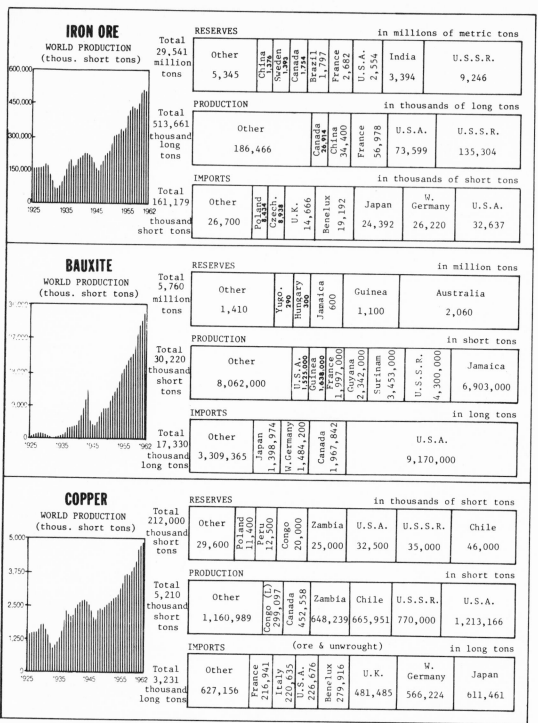

IRON ORE

WORLD PRODUCTION (thous. short tons)

RESERVES — in millions of metric tons — Total 29,541 million tons

Other	China	Sweden	Canada	Brazil	France	U.S.A.	India	U.S.S.R.
5,345	1,376	1,393	1,754	1,797	2,682	2,554	3,394	9,246

PRODUCTION — in thousands of long tons — Total 513,661 thousand long tons

Other	Canada	China	France	U.S.A.	U.S.S.R.
186,466	26,914	34,400	56,978	73,599	135,304

IMPORTS — in thousands of short tons — Total 161,179 thousand short tons

Other	Poland	Czech.	U.K.	Benelux	Japan	W. Germany	U.S.A.
26,700	8,434	8,938	14,666	19,192	24,392	26,220	32,637

BAUXITE

WORLD PRODUCTION (thous. short tons)

RESERVES — in million tons — Total 5,760 million tons

Other	Yugo.	Hungary	Jamaica	Guinea	Australia
1,410	290	300	600	1,100	2,060

PRODUCTION — in short tons — Total 30,220 thousand short tons

Other	U.S.A.	Guinea	France	Guyana	Surinam	U.S.S.R.	Jamaica
8,062,000	1,525,000	1,638,000	1,997,000	2,342,000	3,453,000	4,300,000	6,903,000

IMPORTS — in long tons — Total 17,330 thousand long tons

Other	Japan	W.Germany	Canada	U.S.A.
3,309,365	1,398,974	1,484,200	1,967,842	9,170,000

COPPER

WORLD PRODUCTION (thous. short tons)

RESERVES — in thousands of short tons — Total 212,000 thousand short tons

Other	Poland	Peru	Congo	Zambia	U.S.A.	U.S.S.R.	Chile
29,600	11,400	12,500	20,000	25,000	32,500	35,000	46,000

PRODUCTION — in short tons — Total 5,210 thousand short tons

Other	Congo (L)	Canada	Zambia	Chile	U.S.S.R.	U.S.A.
1,160,989	299,097	452,558	648,239	665,951	770,000	1,213,166

IMPORTS (ore & unwrought) — in long tons — Total 3,231 thousand long tons

Other	France	Italy	U.S.A.	Benelux	U.K.	W. Germany	Japan
627,156	216,941	220,635	226,676	279,916	481,485	566,224	611,461

in the development of our major industrial centers in the West. That the availability of local ores is now of lesser importance is evidenced by the growth of the steel industry in, for example, Italy and Japan—as more dependent on the importation and re-use of scrap than primary ore. The scrap cycle has also steadily gained in importance in the long established

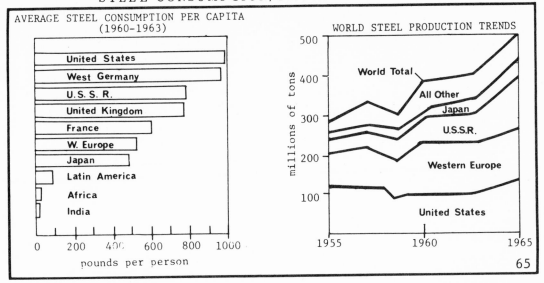

AVERAGE STEEL CONSUMPTION PER CAPITA (1960-1963)

WORLD STEEL PRODUCTION TRENDS

65

centers where local high-grade ores have been exhausted or are no longer sufficient to meet demand.

Copper Though probably the first metal used by man, copper has retained a central position relative to steel, even though it is used in far lesser quantities for high ductility, alloying qualities, and electrical conductivity.

CONSTRUCTION MATERIALS

PROPERTIES OF CONSTRUCTION MATERIALS
(Ranked by Tensile Strength)

Material	Tensile Strength 1,000 psi	Tensile Modulus mil. psi	Fabricability into Complex Shapes	Corrosion Resistance
EPOXY, Unidirectionally (glass-reinforced prepreg)	100	3	poor	excellent
STRUCTURAL STEEL	60	27	poor	poor
DIE-CAST ALUMINUM	40	9	good	good
POLYESTER, (glass-fiber-reinforced)	20	0.2	good	excellent
EPOXY, Cast unfilled	10	0.5	good	excellent
RIGID VINYL	8	0.4	excellent	excellent
PHENOLIC (general-purpose)	7	0.1	excellent	excellent
POLYSTYRENE (general-purpose)	6.5	0.5	excellent	excellent
POLYETHYLENE (high-density)	5	0.2	excellent	excellent
GLASS	5	10	good	excellent
WHITE PINE (with grain)	5	1.1	poor	good

66

Variations in volume copper use in industrial sectors and its use movement from sector to sector in power generation/transmission, communications, and transportation reveal successive gains in performance per unit in various technologies. For example, where a technical advance enables more messages to be conveyed per wire transmission, or "wire" use is superseded by wireless, and so forth, this is reflected in the decrease in volume copper use in that sector or by acceleration in the scrapping pattern. Other indications, such as the electrification of transportation and other systems, increase in armaments production, and so forth, are reflected in the shift of copper from one sector to another, and so forth.[70]

> About a quarter of the world's production is used in generators, motors, switchboards and other electrical apparatus; over 8 per cent for transmission lines for power and lighting; and 5 per cent for telephones and telegraphs. Other rod and wire uses consume 12 per cent; bearings, bushes, and fittings 4 per cent; radio sets over 3 per cent; and the remaining 43 per cent or so serves for the various copper alloys and other uses.[71]

The main alloys of copper are the brasses of the copper-zinc group, the duralumins where copper is a minor but key constituent, the copper-nickel and copper-beryllium alloys. The use of copper and its alloys is a critical area in industrialization, as underlined above, and the concentration of ore production in various world regions has led to those nations with limited access to such ores emphasizing the search for substitute conducting materials. The concomitant growth in other conducting metals has also moved copper away from various prime use sectors, for example, its partial replacement by aluminum for long-distance electrical transmissions due to the lesser weight and loss of the latter metals.

Copper has a high recovery rate in its scrapping and re-use cycles; for example, in the U.S. about 40 per cent of the copper used in manufacture is derived from scrap. In 1963, scrap recovery equaled 80 per cent of domestic U.S. mines production. More is recycled in the form of brass and other alloys.

Aluminum More abundantly present in the earth's crust than iron, aluminum's volume use was relatively much less until recent years for two main reasons. First, earlier bulk production required much more energy input than iron and was a more complex technical process, for example, one ton of aluminum required approximately twenty times more coal equivalent in extraction and processing energies than a ton of iron; second, development in aluminum alloys did not progress as swiftly as in steel.

Today the light, strong alloys of aluminum (and magnesium, a somewhat similar case) now provide many of the physical qualities of steel

[70] See copper chartings in Document 2 of this series, "The Design Initiative," R. B. Fuller.

[71] *Minerals in Industry,* W. R. Jones, Pelican Books, 1963, p. 88.

at less than one third of its weight, and with relatively high electrical conductivity.

From half a million tons of annual production twenty years ago, aluminum world production is now almost 6 million tons. Its chief uses are in construction and transportation; in the latter area, its availability in high-strength alloy forms has paced the development of aircraft and aerospace technologies. More and more uses are developing constantly for aluminum as its increasing volume and improvements in alloys reduce overall costs against gains in weight/performance ratios.

The consumption of aluminum in the various countries gives a useful picture of their degree of material development, for example, for 1961, per capita aluminum use was as follows: [72]

U.S.   23 lbs.   Australia   8 lbs.
U.K.   15 lbs.   Japan   4 lbs.
Other European countries, less than 10 lbs. per person.

The extraction of aluminum from its basic ore, bauxite, requires large amounts of electrical power and, therefore, favors local primary processing close to ore sources—where such power is, or can be made, available. The coincidence of large bauxite deposits and potential hydropower in many of the lesser advanced areas has already led to their combined development, for example, in Jamaica, Ghana, and to projected large developments in Surinam, Guinea, and Indonesia. Apart from Canada and the U.S.S.R., most of the other major users of aluminum are more or less dependant on imported bauxite for their needs. Scrap recovery and re-use in production is high, approximately 25 per cent in developed industrial countries.

Tin   Important deposits of tin ores occur in few parts of the world and these are, significantly, in the lesser developed regions—Southeast Asia (Malaya, Thailand, Indonesia), Bolivia, Nigeria, the Congo—and China. The main industrial powers possess little or no domestic tin ore, but consume the world's major production of tin annually. The relative importance of tin as a "strategic" metal lies in alloying—phosphor bronzes, so-called gun metals, and importantly for bearings, valves, and bushings, accounting for approximately 40 per cent of consumption.

About 20 per cent is used in the form of solders. With such key uses, the conflicts around the control of tin-ore-producing areas have furnished the latent background for considerable political and economic maneuvering, for example, the countries initially occupied by Japan in W.W.II were those producing over 60 per cent of the world's tin, and we may note that these areas still furnish a central focus for intensified international conflict.

[72] Note: In terms of such indexing of development, more refined indices could be prepared relating per capita key metals use; performance per unit of invested capability—as shown by access to advanced transport/communication services; information processing equipment, and so forth. Such indices would go beyond the ordinary economic indicators of gross national products and so forth, to measure more accurately the degree of environmental advantage indicated by access to and use of not only material resources but advanced technological services.

Various tin compounds, mainly tin oxides and chlorides, constitute a further essential and important use for this metal in industrial undertakings. Both these uses, and others above, including the extensive one of tin-plating, give a scrap recovery rate of approximately 30 per cent from all form of tin used with the least recovery from various chemical uses.

Nickel   As with tin, the occurrence of nickel ores of workable use constitute another anomaly in metals distribution around the world. More than 80 per cent of the world nickel supply is obtained from one area in Canada. The other producing areas are again of some strategic significance: the U.S.S.R. (from the Finnish mines acquired during W.W.II), Cuba, and New Caledonia.

Most of the nickel is used in steel-alloying. Either alone or in combination with other alloying elements, it is used to produce steels requiring great strength and durability—for aero-engines, turbines. In specific combination with chromium for nickel-chrome steels, it provides a range of indispensable heat-resisting metal alloys. Nickel-iron and nickel-copper alloys give particular magnetic properties and electrical resistance required in telecommunications, electrical engineering, and instrumentation.

OTHER KEY METALS

We could continue the above review through the extensive range of metals now essential to the maintenance of the world industrial network. Our intention here, however, is not to survey these metals in detail—such information may be found in the many excellent and comprehensive metals handbooks—but rather to sketch certain global relations of patterns of production and use, and to indicate approaches toward such metal usage which may be fitted within our ecological viewpoint. This will become more apparent when we consider in more detail the circulation and recycling patterns of materials in a further section.

Some other critical metals should be mentioned, however, in passing:

The Ferrous Alloying Elements   *Manganese* is not, strictly speaking, an alloying material, but functions much more basically in the steel-making process as a "cleansing" agent that removes various impurities in the steel melt which might otherwise impair the finished steel's properties. Some of the main deposits and main production of manganese are again in regions which have least domestic use for the ore. The main flow is, therefore, from these areas to the industrial center regions. Apart from the U.S.S.R., which has by far the largest mine production of manganese, others are India, Brazil, China, Ghana, the Congo—stressing again a dependence polarity of certain ore-producing and industrial-use centers.

Cobalt is another such alloying element, whose main source is the Congo Republic, producing approximately eight times (60 per cent of the world total production) more than the next bulk areas, Rhodesia, Finland, and Canada. Major uses of cobalt are in high-speed cutting tool steels and for high-temperature engines such as jets; a second important use, accounting for over a quarter of the world production, is in permanent magnetic alloys.

Tungsten afforded the first improvement on carbon steels for high-speed cutting tools, armorplate, and projectiles, and came early in the steel alloy development before W.W.I. Its main uses are still in this area, with tungsten carbide steel as one of the hardest known cutting metals. With the highest melting point of any metal, another important use is in electric bulb filaments. Though using less than 2 per cent of the world's production in this form,[73] it is an interesting example of high performance per unit of material. Tungsten filament is considered to be 4½ times as efficient as carbon filament for such purposes and its use has resulted in tremendous savings in electrical energies, bulbs, and other materials.

The major ore producer is China, about three-fold that of the next producers in order—United States, South and North Korea, Bolivia and Portugal.

Chromium has been referred to earlier in relation to nickel-chrome alloys. Its chief use is in such corrosion-resistant chromium steels, accounting for about 45 per cent of production with the remainder in the form of chromite ore used for refractory furnace linings and about 15 per cent for other chemical processes, for example, the range of chromates in tanning, dyeing, photography, and so forth. Major ore producers are the U.S.S.R., South Africa, the Philippines, Southern Rhodesia, and Turkey.

Vanadium, though used in fractional quantities for forging, spring, and high-speed cutting steels, has become of key interest in recent years from its role in special alloys of machine parts requiring high reliability such as transmissions, gears, springs, and so forth.

Rare metals deserving mention here are a group of metals usually referred to as the "rare earths." Though including tungsten and vanadium from above, these were originally referred to as "rare" because of their difficulty of isolation in the pure state. The most familiar to emerge in recent years are molybdenum (long used in steel alloys), titanium, beryllium, columbium, zirconium, and tantalum. To these we could add a long list of others that are of growing importance in a wide range of new alloys developed mainly for, and in, aerospace and military research. Titanium has now reached volume production as a major structural metal in its own right with very high strength-to-weight ratios outperforming columbium and magnesium alloys for many purposes. For example, in 1965 the latest Mach 3 aircraft was one of the first all-titanium aircraft

[73] "Less than 2 tons of tungsten metal supply filaments for 100 million electric bulbs . . . in 1960 the total annual world consumption for light filaments was little more than 200 tons." *Minerals in Industry,* W. R. Jones, Pelican Books, 1963, p. 269.

and the new supersonic transports are expected to use large quantities of this metal.[74]

In this area of "rare-metals" use, we should also note the direction of development in the use of, for example, germanium and other elements in transistors, solid-state circuits, semi-conductors, and so forth, now the basis of our massive developing communications and computer technologies. First, these are made ultra pure, then design modified by minutely controlled impurities for specific functions of the crystal lattice at the molecular level. We shall comment later upon a similar direction in the use of pure "whisker" reinforcement in a swiftly developing range of filament-reinforced composite materials.

Uranium—the successive developments of atomic weapons and other nuclear energy uses have made uranium, radium, thorium, and plutonium the most sought-after metals in the past few decades. As the result of intensive worldwide search, many such radioactive ore sources of different types have been located. Because of the critical nature of these, in relation to nuclear strategies, information on their distribution, production, and so forth, tends to be somewhat uneven and, where given, may be misleading. The major sources for the West are those in Canada, the United States, and the Congo, but new discoveries of uranium deposits have occurred in Australia, New Zealand, and Japan in recent years.

The importance of these metals for future energy production may be underlined here as the potential reserve of such material will be a key factor in future years. Estimates of the uranium and thorium reserves in the United States alone are of the order of "hundreds of thousands of times greater than the world's initial supply of fossil fuels [indicating] ... almost unlimited supplies of energy from the fissionable and fertile isotopes of uranium and thorium."[75]

Silicon is an interesting example here of the most plentiful element in the earth's crust now "at the heart of many of the most explosive areas of modern growth; computers, home entertainment, military electronics, and the control of power—not only at signal power levels but also at bulk power levels."[76]

Note: The introduction of these new element uses, and of the "nuclear" elements below, presages a new phase in our resource thinking that we shall discuss later. In this forward development, which we may call the fourth phase, the level of organized knowledge, that is, research, and its capacity to "restructure" materials to almost any desired range of physical properties, will further erode all the previous notions of the need

---

[74] One of the most productive titanium ore deposits is in India, producing the third-highest amounts, after the U. S. and Canada, in the past two decades.

[75] *Energy Resources*, Pub. 1000-D, National Academy of Sciences, National Research Council, U.S., 1962.

[76] Statement of Dr. G. Guy Suits, Director of Research, General Electric Co., Panel on Science and Technology, 7th meeting, 89th U.S. Congress, 1966.

for the separate national and other groupings to compete for the inequably distributed, naturally occurring, material resources.

METAL RESERVES AND FUTURE USES

Most analyses of world resource materials deal in "years of supply in exploitable reserves." For example:

Aluminum	570 years	Copper	29 years
Iron	250 years	Lead	19 years
Zinc	23 years	Tin	35 years

The use of such estimates, while useful for general economic criteria, is limited by lack of appreciation of the limited degree to which such metals are actually "used up."

As we have noted, most of them are highly recoverable through their scrapping cycles and are, therefore, used over and over again. Our "reserves," therefore, include all metals in present use and those recoverable from the lowest-grade ore deposits in the earth crust, which are not usually accounted for in terms of "exploitability"—as not being economically exploitable in present terms.

Of course, present availability is important, as we have stressed, in the next critical transition in access to industrial parity for the poorer nations. In dealing with energy resource reserves, the key question is how we may bring the underdeveloped nations up to better standards of living, that is, as measured by present materially advanced regions. It has been noted, for example, "that the U.S. with only 6 per cent of the world's population, consumes approximately 30 per cent of the world's total current production of minerals."

We might then ask how much more would be required to bring the total world population up to the same level of material consumption? This comes out to about five times the present world production of minerals—far more than we can presently attain to with present levels of materials and energy performance efficiencies.

Using an ordinary example, suppose we tried to extend the 1960 level of U.S. automobile use (at roughly 1 auto per 3 persons) to the entire world population. This would require approximately 2300 million tons of steel—as against total world steel production (1963) of only 425 million tons.

In the same way, when we consider extending full-scale electrification to the underdeveloped nations, the average use of copper per capita in fully industrialized nations is approximately 120 pounds per capita. The increase of even one pound per-capita consumption in present world-population terms would require about a 36 per cent increase in world copper production. Even the slightest rise in living standards can require vastly increased amounts of metals use in our present terms.

Again this underlines that the only way to advance the living standards of the underadvantaged countries, by bringing them up to industrial

	YEAR	1966	1970	1980	1985	1990	2000
	POPULATION						
	(billions)	3.4	3.7	4.6	5.0	5.6	7.0
Metals	IRON						
	Mil. tons	469.0	560.0	900.0	1130.0	1400.0	2250.0
	Lbs./person	304.0	332.0	431.0	497.0	550.0	706.0
	ALUMINUM						
	Mil. tons	7.7	11.3	32.0	55.0	90.0	250.0
	Lbs./person	5.0	7.0	15.0	24.0	35.0	79.0
	COPPER						
	Mil. tons	5.4	6.2	9.2	10.0	13.5	20.0
	Lbs./person	4.0	4.0	4.0	4.0	5.0	6.0
	ZINC						
	Mil. tons	4.3	5.0	7.2	8.7	10.4	15.0
	Lbs./person	3.0	3.0	4.0	4.0	4.0	4.0
	TOTAL METALS						
	Mil. tons	486.0	582.0	948.0	1204.0	1514.0	2535.0
	Lbs./person	315.0	345.0	453.0	503.0	594.0	795.0
	Mil. cu. m.	64.0	78.0	129.0	167.0	215.0	384.0
	Liters/person	19.0	21.0	28.0	33.0	38.0	55.0
Synthetics	PLASTICS						
	Mil. tons	16.0	27.0	105.0	240.0	420.0	1700.0
	Lbs./person	10.0	16.0	50.0	116.0	165.0	535.0
	SYNTHETIC RUBBERS						
	Mil. tons	3.9	5.5	11.5	16.0	23.0	44.0
	Lbs./person	2.0	3.0	6.0	7.0	9.0	14.0
	MAN-MADE FIBERS						
	Mil. tons	5.6	7.2	13.0	17.0	24.5	46.0
	Lbs./person	4.0	4.0	6.0	7.0	10.0	15.0
	TOTAL SYNTHETICS						
	Mil. tons	25.5	40.0	130.0	273.0	467.0	1790.0
	Lbs./person	17.0	24.0	62.0	121.0	183.0	563.0
	Mil. cu. m.	23.0	35.0	114.0	236.0	409.0	1564.0
	Liters/person	6.8	9.5	25.0	47.0	73.0	224.0
Natural Products	NATURAL RUBBER						
	Mil. tons	2.2	2.5	2.6	2.7	2.8	3.0
	Lbs./person	1.0	2.0	1.0	1.0	1.0	1.0
	NATURAL FIBERS						
	Mil. tons	19.0	21.5	30.2	35.0	41.5	60.0
	Lbs./person	12.0	13.0	15.0	15.0	16.0	19.0
	TOTAL NATURAL PROD.						
	Mil. tons	21.2	24.0	32.8	37.7	44.3	63.0
	Lbs./person	14.0	14.0	16.0	17.0	17.0	20.0
	Mil. cu. m.	18.4	20.7	27.7	31.9	37.5	53.2
	Liters/person	5.4	5.6	6.0	6.4	6.7	7.6
Totals	Million tons	533.0	646.0	1111.0	1515.0	2025.0	4388.0
	Lbs./person	345.0	385.0	530.0	667.0	794.0	1379.0
	Mil. cu. m.	105.0	134.0	271.0	435.0	662.0	2001.0
	Liters/person	31.0	36.0	59.0	87.0	118.0	286.0

The paper from which the preceeding table has been adapted suggests that we use _volume_ as against _weight_ measures, particularly in relation to the comparative use of plastics -- whose weight consumption does not reflect their increasing use volume. This is an important point. With the density differential involved, one pound of plastic may replace up to eight pounds of metal. As strength to weight ratio increases in the synthetics, weight alone may be less important than space volume per performance.

parity, is through increase in the overall performance of all of our resources, and through a radical reorganization and ecological redesign of our major socio-economic activities. This is, as we have noted, inherent in the advanced technological development processes. It requires, however, to be more immediately realized and used as a conscious design principle in the less technologically advanced areas of our environment facilities.

The "reserves" table in this section may then be viewed as a useful guide for long-range future planning, as indicating where it may be more practical to concentrate on the highest extraction of performance from present above-grade already mined and processed metals—so as to keep an amount of "exploitable" reserves in storage against future, unforeseeable emergencies.

In thinking about such "reserves" of metals, it is important to keep in mind: 1. their recycling nature in actual use, that is, that they are not exhausted by use; 2. that exploitable refers only to present limits of economic return, in processing metal ores, against energy cost inputs.

Given abundant supplies of energy, that is, through more efficient use of *capital* energies and more access to *income* energies, we may secure almost inexhaustible supplies of further minerals from the earth's crust and oceans plus the developing capacity to increasingly "construct" or synthesize materials from many different element sources. The critical period lies in our present transition from one "kind of world" to another—of more equable distribution of life advantages.

Oceans   So far, we have hardly touched upon the potential of ocean exploration for metals and other materials. Sodium and chlorine, via common salt and bromine, have long been extracted from sea water; magnesium is already being produced on a large scale where it occurs as one part to 800 parts of water. Various bodies of sea water, for example, the Red Sea, may be considered as fluid ocean mines. Further extraction of other materials is now projected with the development of large-scale desalination plants.

The more immediate bulk production source for ocean ores may be that of the nodule deposits recently discovered on the ocean floor. In many areas, thick concentrations of high-grade ore nodules have been located with a manganese content up to 50 per cent; cobalt, nickel, and copper to 3 per cent respectively; and other metals in varying amounts. One specifically interesting quality of these nodules is their continuing growth formation. Referring to the speed with which such nodule deposits grow, one authority has suggested that ". . . as these nodules are being mined, the minerals industry would be faced with the interesting situation of working a deposit that grows faster than it could be mined or consumed." [77]

In terms of "ecological design" of using the naturally occurring growth

[77] *The Mineral Resources of the Sea*, J. L. Mero, Elsevier Publishing Co., 1965.

cycles, the above has interesting connotations! Further examples may be adduced which are of relevance to oceans' use. A number of plants and animals have been found to have the power of concentrating elements found in sea water, as land plants and animals selectively accumulate soil elements. Seaweeds concentrate iodine from its normal dispersion of 0.001 per cent in sea water to up to 0.5 per cent; certain coral species take up iodine to 8 per cent levels. Oysters concentrate copper from sea water, and a particular sea slug has the capacity to concentrate vanadium in its body though the quantity in its environ is quite minute.

When we consider that, apart from the minerals already present in the ocean waters and floor, it has been estimated that in the United States some 200 tons of copper, in various forms, are lost to the oceans in sewage per year for each million persons, together with 50 tons of each of such metals as manganese, lead, aluminum, and titanium. Such naturally occurring agents could possibly be designed into processing systems for minerals concentration and recovery. Our use of domesticated land food, plants, and animals is precisely such an ongoing system for intermediate processing of food energies and materials.

A further balancing aspect relative to metals use and the general pattern of reserves and recycling of materials is the third phase shift to composites, to non-metallic and plastic substitutes for many of the previous functions of metals.

THE SYNTHESIS OF MATERIALS

Reference to "synthetic" and "man-made" materials is, in some senses, misleading. We do not make new materials but, rather, discover new ways to "rearrange" the elements in various configurations and combinations that give us similar desired properties to some naturally occurring configuration, for example, synthetic wood or stone. Or, we may rearrange the molecular configuration to give a range of material properties that are not available in nature, for example, as in the plastics.

Strictly speaking, man has always been "synthesizing" his environ constituents in re-forming and re-structuring them to his specific needs—from the earliest use of fire, foods, fibers, metals, and so forth, up to the latest alloys and plastics.

There is no "intrinsic" difference, therefore, between natural and synthetic materials; the one is not "truer to nature" than the other. Our division here on the synthesis of materials merely established the degree of balance of man's restructuring and redesigning materials over that of using those naturally occurring forms.

The first commercial plastics, that is, the cellulose nitrates or celluloids, were made in the late 1860s, though one of the synthetic resins, polystyrene, was isolated in 1831. The Bakelites, phenol-formaldehyde resins, were introduced in 1909, and, for the next 20 years, celluloids and Bakelites were the major plastic materials in use. The next large-volume

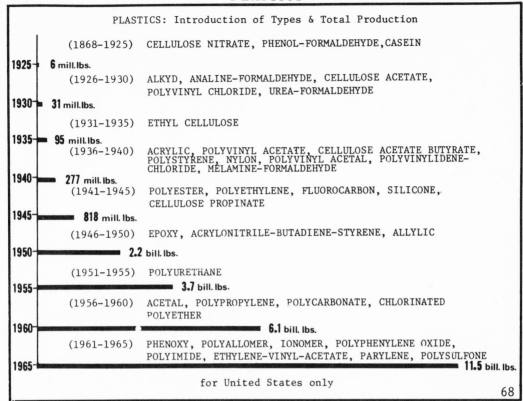

PLASTICS: Introduction of Types & Total Production

(1868-1925) CELLULOSE NITRATE, PHENOL-FORMALDEHYDE, CASEIN

1925→ **6** mill. lbs.

(1926-1930) ALKYD, ANALINE-FORMALDEHYDE, CELLULOSE ACETATE, POLYVINYL CHLORIDE, UREA-FORMALDEHYDE

1930→ **31** mill. lbs.

(1931-1935) ETHYL CELLULOSE

1935→ **95** mill. lbs.
(1936-1940) ACRYLIC, POLYVINYL ACETATE, CELLULOSE ACETATE BUTYRATE, POLYSTYRENE, NYLON, POLYVINYL ACETAL, POLYVINYLIDENE-CHLORIDE, MELAMINE-FORMALDEHYDE

1940→ **277** mill. lbs.
(1941-1945) POLYESTER, POLYETHYLENE, FLUOROCARBON, SILICONE, CELLULOSE PROPINATE

1945→ **818** mill. lbs.

(1946-1950) EPOXY, ACRYLONITRILE-BUTADIENE-STYRENE, ALLYLIC

1950→ **2.2** bill. lbs.

(1951-1955) POLYURETHANE

1955→ **3.7** bill. lbs.

(1956-1960) ACETAL, POLYPROPYLENE, POLYCARBONATE, CHLORINATED POLYETHER

1960→ **6.1** bill. lbs.

(1961-1965) PHENOXY, POLYALLOMER, IONOMER, POLYPHENYLENE OXIDE, POLYIMIDE, ETHYLENE-VINYL-ACETATE, PARYLENE, POLYSULFONE

1965→ **11.5** bill. lbs.

for United States only

68

COMPOSITE MATERIALS

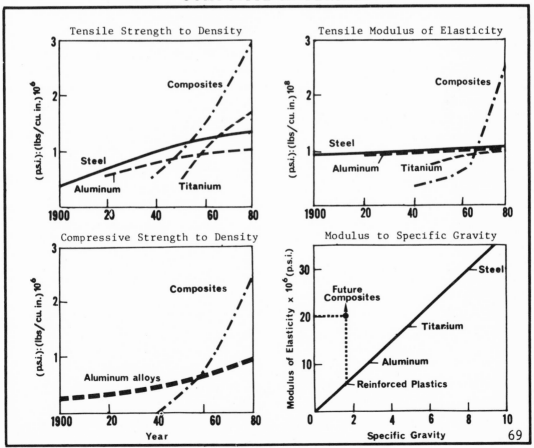

Tensile Strength to Density

Tensile Modulus of Elasticity

Compressive Strength to Density

Modulus to Specific Gravity

69

introduction of two of our present key plastics groups, the cellulose acetates and vinyl resins, occurred significantly [78] in 1927. Polystyrene became available in bulk in 1938 and the polyethylenes in 1942. Since then, a major new group of plastics with unique properties has been introduced approximately every year. Today the volume and diversity of these groups defies any summary listing. The world total volume consumption of all such "synthetics" in 1966 was about one third of the volume consumption of all metals, and by the 1980s it is calculated that the volume use of plastics will surpass that of all iron products.

Composites This most recent class of designed materials, developed particularly in the past few decades, affords a bridge between the metal alloys and the non-metallics in the ceramics and plastics range. One group of composites may be regarded as a "subform" of alloy, consisting of minute amounts of lower-melting-point metals embedded in a refractory metal to give better forming ductility to the latter without impairing its other properties. Another consists of the range of metallic and non-metallic composites reinforced with high modulus fibers, or filaments, of boron, graphite, beryllium, glass, and so forth. This class also uses pure "whisker" reinforcements of various metals which give extremely high strength in their whisker state. Solid forms of various types, made from high-melting-point oxides, are in development which may be glazed with refractory ceramics for superior performance to metals at very high temperatures.

In general, the promise of very high tensile strength structural materials through the use of these composite techniques, in particular those of the filament-reinforcement type, has already been borne out in aerospace work. Metallic composites are already in such use, or in advanced development, and have the inherent possibility of achieving unprecedented strengths most nearly approaching, and surpassing, the highest theoretical yield limits of their separate constituent materials. The accompanying curve charts show the predicted gain in performance over the next period based on test results of composites reinforced with high modulus filaments of boron, graphite, glass, and beryllium.

Structural Plastics of glass-fiber-reinforced epoxy resin, and other bases, are similar to the above group of filament composites and have become one of the most important ranges of plastic materials. The impact resistance of such fiber-reinforced plastics having a given strength-to-weight-ratio has already risen 1000 per cent in the past ten years compared to aluminum and plywood.

[78] Significance here refers to 1927 as the beginning of a period of grave economic and political crises which continue up through the depression years of the 1930s. The "lack of fit" between such events and underlying "real" developments is striking when we consider that 1932 also marked the year of completion of the elements table, the initiation and a swiftly ensuing number of scientific and technical developments, many of whose full impacts are only now emerging into economic and political "reality." (For more detailed discussion of this point, see Document 2, "The Design Initiative," 1964, R. B. Fuller, in the present series.)

ESTIMATED REPLACEMENT OF SELECTED MATERIALS BY PLASTICS IN 1970

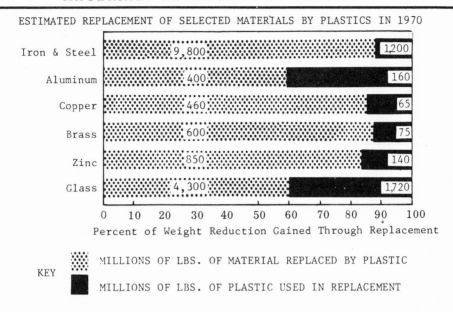

Iron & Steel	9,800 / 1,200
Aluminum	400 / 160
Copper	460 / 65
Brass	600 / 75
Zinc	850 / 140
Glass	4,300 / 1,720

0 10 20 30 40 50 60 70 80 90 100

Percent of Weight Reduction Gained Through Replacement

KEY

MILLIONS OF LBS. OF MATERIAL REPLACED BY PLASTIC

MILLIONS OF LBS. OF PLASTIC USED IN REPLACEMENT

ESTIMATED USE OF PLASTICS IN APPLIANCES & AUTOMOBILES

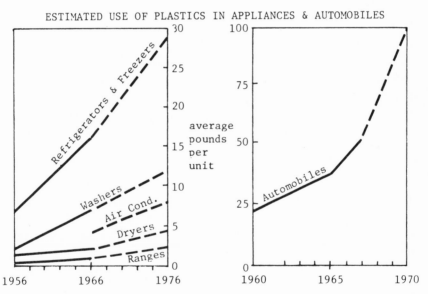

"Since 1955 the average plastic has dropped in price by about 35%, whereas steel has increased in price by more than 20%....On a weight basis, plastics probably never will be as cheap as steel; but on a volume basis the price difference could all but disappear.

"....Tooling costs are lower for plastics than for metals. Also, complex shapes can be molded in a single operation, and finishing of parts is virtually eliminated. A metal part often involves the assembly of several components -- this means additional labor cost and a higher price for the finished part." --"Chemicals and the Auto Industry," Special Report, Chemical and Engineering News, October 22, 1962, p. 117.

70

MINERALS	WORLD PRODUCTION	LEADING COUNTRY	PRODUCTION
Natural Gas	28,384,031 MIL. CU.FT.	U.S.A.	18,171,325
Nickel	481,269 S.T.	Canada	246,954
Nitrogen	23,784,000 S.T.	U.S.A.	6,048,000
Petroleum	12,889,705,000 B.B.L.	U.S.A.	3,215,742,000
Phosphate Rock	86,969,000 S.T.	U.S.A.	39,770,000
Platinum Group	3,154,434 T.O.	U.S.S.R.	1,900,000
Potash	16,861,197 S.T.	U.S.A.	3,299,000
Salt	111,304,000 S.T.	U.S.A.	38,958,000
Silver	260,820,000 T.O.	Mexico	37,939,498
Steel	543,080,000 S.T.	U.S.A.	127,213,000
Sulfur	17,247,167 L.T.	Canada	2,073,413
Tin (mined)	211,664 L.T.	Malaysia	72,121
Titanium (imenite)	2,959,965 S.T.	U.S.A.	935,091
Tungsten	38,690,000 LBS.	U.S.A.	13,860,000
Uranium	17,058 S.T. (Non-Comm. World)	U.S.A.	9,125
Vanadium	10,595 S.T.	U.S.A.	4,963
Zinc (mined)	5,175,463 S.T.	Canada	1,248,977

S. T.	Short Ton	C.	Carat
L. T.	Long Ton	T. O.	Troy Ounce
B. B. L.	Barrel	F.	Flask

72

WORLD PRODUCTION OF MAJOR MINERALS AND METALS BY COUNTRY

(Revised to 1968)

MINERALS	WORLD PRODUCTION	LEADING COUNTRY PRODUCTION	
Aluminum	8,285,415 S.T.	U.S.A.	3,269,259
Antimony	64,402 S.T.	S. Africa	14,216
Asbestos	3,359,006 S.T. (1966)	Canada	1,479,281
Bauxite	43,612,000 L.T.	Jamaica	9,121,000
Cement (all hydraulic)	2,813,855,000 B.B.L.	U.S.S.R.	497,208,000
Chromium	5,110,833 S.T.	U.S.S.R.	1,731,000
Coal (all grades)	3,002,581,000 S.T.	U.S.S.R.	656,000,000
Cobalt	20,045 S.T.	Congo (Kinshasa)	10,709
Copper (mined)	5,435,787 S.T.	U.S.A.	954,064
Fluorspar	3,150,488 S.T.	Mexico	785,114
Gold	45,610,000 T.O.	S. Africa	30,532,880
Gypsum	49,629,000 S.T. (1966)	U.S.A.	9,647,000
Iron Ore	618,308,000 L.T.	U.S.S.R.	165,347
Lead (mined)	3,132,887 S.T.	U.S.S.R.	440,000
Magnesium	202,608 S.T.	U.S.A.	97,406
Manganese	18,650,000 S.T.	U.S.S.R.	7,940,000
Mercury	242,042 F.	Spain	50,000
Mica	319,943,000 LBS. (1966)	U.S.A.	226,267,000
Molybdenum	125,363,000 LBS.	U.S.A.	88,930,000

[polymers] ... are becoming bona fide structural materials of real consequence. They are already replacing many metals in consumer products to such a degree that in United States' industry as a whole the volume of polymers used already exceeds the volume of steel ... [due to] the density difference averaging about seven times in favor of polymers. But relative growth rate of usage is such that polymers will soon overtake steel, even on a weight basis, and they may have already done so ... polymers will indeed become the basic materials of the future. We will be manufacturing the bulk of our products, and even the machines that make them from new, man-made, synthetic polymers. And, inevitably, the elements from which we will fashion these new polymers are common inexpensive ones.[82]

When we extend discussion of plastics into the non-structural area, including synthetic rubbers, man-made fibers, and so forth, we may see the increased range of human activity in which these are now employed. Through packaging, clothes, all types of tools and appliances, to large-scale agricultural and other uses, we engage not only with polymers but with the entire range of the electro-chemical industries, now extending into the scale incorporation of bio-electro-chemical techniques. These industries are now the forward core base of industrialization rather than the steel-producing complex—with which, of course, they are closely associated.

This brings many other issues into fresh perspective, particularly that of the use of fossil fuels. The chemicals derived from these fuels are the basic materials for most of the synthetic resins and elastomer plastics, and, importantly, for the synthetic rubbers—a further important reason to reconsider our presently prodigal energy extraction from these fuel deposits.

We have earlier referred to this third phase of industrialization with its shift from earlier dependence on steels and associated direct use of fossil fuels. By moving out of this dependence, we shift also from the *capital* depletion bias of our resources use till now—to that of a more ecologically oriented "tapping in" to the basic *income* sources of energies and materials.

When we begin to use the most commonly available and abundant elements in the earth crust, atmosphere, and oceans in "designed" combinations with the rarer elements within a pattern of comprehensive recycling and re-use, we come to an almost entirely different picture of our material resources.

Questions of resource balances, reserves, the dependence of industries and whole economies on access to this or that resource will change radically. This is demonstrated by the above examples of the newer alloys, the "electronic" and "nuclear" elements, and even more in the plastics and other designed and man-made materials.

[82] Statement by Dr. G. Guy Suits, Vice President and Director of Research, General Electric Co., 7th Panel on Science and Technology, 89th U.S. Congress, January 1966.

We will be less and less dependent on the given configurations and properties of naturally occurring "rare" deposits, on the ownership and control of strategic minerals, but rather more on the possession of organized knowledge, that is, trained human beings, their requisite standards for full creative living, and the material facilities for their continued pursuit of further knowledge. Unfortunately, the earlier polarity established between advanced and less advanced world regions is only further intensified in this dimension during our present transition period. The accumulated industrial wealth, associated higher living and educational standards, and research facilities of the former still maintain their earlier advantage.

The actual trends in materials research and development suggest that if we are able to assist the advance of the lesser developed peoples more swiftly, and survive this period of laggard disparities, then many of the older bases for conflict over "scarce" and inequably distributed resources will disappear. Conflict and competition will be reoriented toward other areas of human activity. Notions of territoriality, strategic rights, and control of material resource deposits will shift to the "brain mines" of the world—and these are, perhaps, not so amenable to the older forms of political and economic control.

Returning briefly to our central topic of the development of the world's less advantaged regions, we may note, again, that the emerging patterns of new material types and uses discussed above restress new directions for such development. The old patterns of steel, heavy industry, massive centralization, and so forth, are no longer viable.

The developing nations would be better encouraged by, and for, the world community of nations to move directly into the forward phases of industrialization, into the age of polymers, light metals, nuclear power generation, and the full range of automated production, transportation, and communication facilities.

Questions as to how, at what monetary cost, and by whom supported, are increasingly irrelevant as we begin to spend more materials, energies, and human lives in our present global conflicts than have been even fractionally used on behalf of human advancement.

Ecological Redesign

THOUGH CONCENTRATING on the more immediate and positive advantage which may be sought through increasing the efficiency of energy and materials usage in our technological systems, we have also underlined the necessary long-range redesign of these so that they may be more compatible with the overall ecological system.

Until recently our technological systems were hardly considered as an "organic" part of the ecology; hence little attention was given to this aspect of their function. Now when they have begun to degrade environ usage and soil various preferred sectors of the air, earth, and waters with their discarded materials and energy use by-products, we are beginning to examine their "pathology"—without, in a sense, having engaged first in some overall assessment of their physiology.

Generally, when the problem is stated simply in terms of "technological hazards," this tends to produce various piecemeal programs of filtering industrial smoke or car exhausts, or checking the level of effluents into rivers and streams, or legislating natural conservation and "beautification" projects. Laudable as these may be, they do not pose the problem in large-enough terms.

Fortunately, the various scientific bodies in different countries which have been called upon to consult on the "pollution problem" have already reframed this within the larger context of some overall "management" of air, water, and other physical resource utilization at the various regional and national levels.

They have addressed themselves not only to the quantitative aspects of such resource management but also to the quality of the environment.

We have referred to technology as an extension of the human metabolism—one which processes millions of tons of materials each day; yet we have no very clear picture of its operation even to the extent that we have such knowledge of our own internal workings.

We need to reconceptualize our global, man-made environ facilities within more comprehensive and coherent schemes. For example, even where refined and advanced econometric models of whole regional and national economics are presently used, they concern themselves largely with the inputs and outputs of the industrial system almost solely from the viewpoint of its economic operation, in terms of fiscal and material balances. There is little sense of the complex ecological relationships

CLOSED ECOLOGICAL SYSTEM

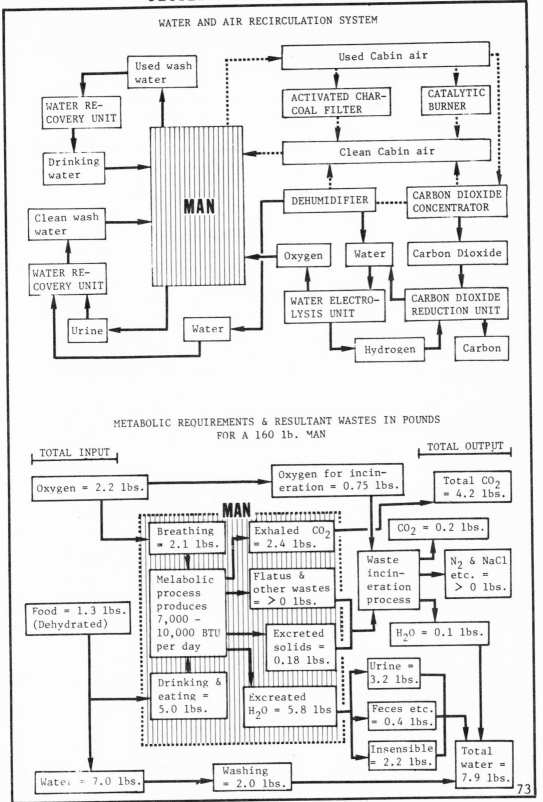

WATER AND AIR RECIRCULATION SYSTEM

METABOLIC REQUIREMENTS & RESULTANT WASTES IN POUNDS
FOR A 160 lb. MAN

73

which obtain even when we consider the industrial-economic system in isolation.

A great deal is known about the overall operation and linkages of the different components of the industrial complex, so patently many of the inefficiencies, wastages, and breakdowns occur—not through lack of such operational knowledge—but through lack of adequate conceptuality of the whole system's operation. We need to reanalyze our industrial systems in terms of models that are not based on simplistic notions of production/consumption.

We do not "produce" things in the sense of manufacturing them out of new raw materials only—then "consume" them so that they and their constituent materials no longer exist.

We extract materials out of the earth in one part of the globe, transport them to another area halfway around the world, process them with other locally available materials, elsewhere in the system, or go directly into human use.

We do not, then, "consume" products in any kind of *end* sense. They are used in a well-defined life cycle, then broken down in such use and are repaired, or discarded and replaced. Some of their material constituents are returned to the process and fabrication cycle directly or indirectly in various time lags of secondary uses; others are further decomposed, returned in part to the earth or atmosphere, or "flushed" into the oceans.

Though the above schema seems repetitive and simplistically drawn, we generally design and use our environment as if we had no knowledge of its existence! As has been repeatedly underlined, most of our currently prodigal modes of using the earth and biosphere systems are potentially dangerous. We dissipate vast quantities of capital energies which may be needed in future emergencies, and we disperse valuable concentrations of materials that we have no present means of reconstituting. Referring earlier to the concept of "spaceship earth," we may quote another version of this:

> The closed economy of the future might similarly be called the "spaceman" economy, in which the earth has become a single spaceship, without unlimited reservoirs of anything, either for extraction or for pollution, and in which, therefore, man must find his place in a cyclical ecological system which is capable of continuous reproduction of material form even though it cannot escape having inputs of energy....[83]

This extends to our use of "income" resources, to the use of soils, of air, water, and to our understanding of our complex interdependence on other organic life forms. We have already used up and destroyed a great many other living species with little inquiry as to their possible functional relation to our own survival.

In redesigning our environmental, and particularly our industrial, facilities as ecological subsystems, we need to determine the gainful and

[83] "The Economics of the Coming Space-ship Earth," K. E. Boulding, *Environmental Quality in a Growing Economy, Essays from the Sixth RFF Forum*, Henry Jarrett (ed.), Baltimore, Maryland: Johns Hopkins Press, for Resources for the Future, Inc., 1966, pp. 3-14.

75

GROWTH IN ONE-WAY BOTTLE USE

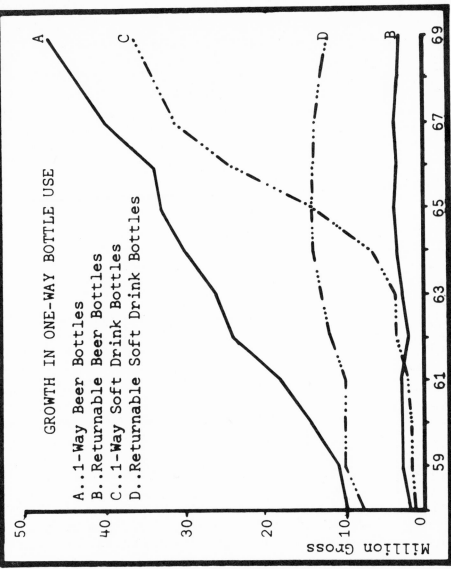

A..1-Way Beer Bottles
B..Returnable Beer Bottles
C..1-Way Soft Drink Bottles
D..Returnable Soft Drink Bottles

Million Gross

N.B. It has been estimated that each non-returnable bottle costs 30¢ to collect and dispose of in New York State. (Industrial Research, November, 1969.)

PACKAGING COSTS OF SELECTED PRODUCTS   74

As a percentage of product sales price, f.o.b. factory

Product and packages	Percent [a]
Paint in an aerosol can	16
Paint in a conventional metal can	5
Toy in a film-overwrapped carton	14
Toy in a blister pack	8
Motor oil in a metal can	26
Motor oil in a fiber can	10
Small appliance in a corrugated carton	6
T.V. set in a corrugated carton	1
Beer in a tinplate can	43
Beer in a one-way glass bottle	36
Frozen food in a boil-in-bag and carton	10
Frozen fish in a carton	5
Moist pet food in a metal can	17
Dry pet food in a carton	9
Cereal in a folding carton	15
Cornmeal in a paper bag	5
Analgesic in a plastic bottle	10
Antibiotic in a plastic bottle	1
Baby food in a glass jar	36
Baby juice in a metal can	33

[a] The figures above are not presented as averages. In any given product field, the cost ratio may vary widely even among the same size packages made of the same materials.

more efficient linkages which may be established between separately functioning processes. To this end, the various major cycle charts, and those of the closed aerospace ecologies, may be usefully related and compared with industrial networks or with the systems function of a community, or with a large-scale building complex.

We may ask how the overall energy flows are disposed relative to each use and function in the latter systems, and how more performance may be gained through different relations. In such extended reviews we might redesign materials throughout so that the wastes and by-products, the discards and residues of one sector of the network may become the raw materials (or energy source) of another. In general, this direction has already been broached in some areas, but requires much larger-scale investigation and application.

One convenient focus of attention lies, specifically, in the scrapping and re-use cycles of materials. We customarily design our structures and other facilities and artifacts only in terms of one cycle use—with design calculation given to the eventual disassembly of components and their direct re-use, or their scrapping and re-entry into the processing cycle.

This is not only confined to buildings and autos, though these are particularly obvious cases, but may be extended, for example, to the myriad artifacts of metal, glass, plastics, and other materials that are used daily.

Unless we begin to account for each phase in this cycle, we cannot, in any real sense, design "ecologically" or in terms of overall efficiency of performance.

The metals and metallic alloys are an example here where very little has been known about their actual re-use and discard cycles. For each billion tons of main metal ores mined, about two thirds is "waste" rock or mine tailings discarded at the mine site. From this point on through foundry processing and fabrication there is some control of "process" scrap, but as the finished products go into use, such control is lost and the scrap-return cycle has been left to the haphazard operations of the "salvage" market. The obscurity of this pattern leads many authorities to talk about metals being "used up" through manufacture when, in effect, most metals are almost wholly recoverable—or could be with adequate "cycling" design. We may ask then:

> To what extent are they lost in use? To what extent do they follow man-made cycles like the well-known carbon cycle in nature, so that the world stock is not depleted? [84]

The only cycle here that has been delineated approximately is that of the ferrous metals, as large amounts of scrap have long been re-used in steel making. The detailed scrap and re-use cycles of copper, lead,

[84] "The Recovery of Metals from Scrap," Sir Harold Hartley, *Advancement of Science*, Vol. II, No. 7, 1942. (Note: Despite the date, this remains one of the classical and most informative papers in this area.)

IRON & STEEL SCRAP INDUSTRY

IRON & STEEL
million of net tons (U.S.)

1885 — 1895 — 1905 — 1915 — 1925 — 1935 — 1945 — 1955 — 1965

0   500   1000   1500   2000

Estimated total inventory of potentially recoverable iron and steel that will become obsolete from marketed products as measured by the LIFE CYCLE OF PRODUCTS

in primary use during 1955-1965

materials too costly to recover

materials in secondary use, i.e., held in standby or for parts

materials not being used and not yet sold as scrap

scrap sold to dealers and which is held or sold depending upon the market price fluctuation.

MINED ORE → BLAST FURNACES → PIG IRON

iron and steel foundry castings

process scrap

steel mill products

machine shop fabrication and production

prompt industrial scrap

obsolete scrap

MARKET CLASSIFICATION	%	AVERAGE LIFE CYCLE OF PRODUCTS (years)
Shipbuilding & Marine equipment	100	
Rail Transportation equipment	86	
Contractors' products	87	
Foundry	100	
Ordnance & other Military equipment	36	
Electrical machinery & equipment	75	
Mining, Quarrying, & Lumbering	91	
Machinery & Industrial tools	94	
Agricultural equipment	99	
Containers	13	
Automotive	100	
Other domestic & commercial equipment	57	
Oil & Gas drilling equipment	100	
Appliances, Utensils, & Cutlery	76	
Aircraft	100	

0   5   10   15   20   25   30   years

RECOVERABLE SCRAP PERCENT

aluminum, and so forth, are less clear, though figures of scrap generated and collected in various sectors of industry give some knowledge of the recycling of such metals. Through these we may ascertain the cycle of a given material in its "use-life" in various products—but we have no clear picture, for example, of the changing pattern of "new" metal vs. scrap use in specific industries, or of the various inputs of energy required at different parts of the scrap/re-use cycle, and so forth, and how these relate to the overall "energy costs" of various use performances in different product cycles.

As we have earlier emphasized, were it not for such "regenerative" cycling of industrial materials, we would not have enough metals, and so forth, to take care of expanding technological requirements.

Some indication of the importance of the scrap cycle may be gauged from the following figures, as well as those introduced earlier in our materials discussion:

> About 957,000 tons of copper were recovered from scrap in 1963. This represented about 40 per cent of the total supply of copper in the U.S. for that year and 80 per cent of the total copper produced by domestic mines. The lead recovered from scrap amounted to about 494,000 tons—almost double the 253,000 tons of lead produced in the U.S. during 1963. The annual volume of aluminum scrap is about 25 per cent of the total aluminum supply.[85]

The increasing number of exotic alloys now used in advanced technologies, their high energy cost in manufacture and strategic importance in missiles and aerospace, for example, have led the military to examine the possibility of clearly identifying metal alloys in use so that they may be more easily recovered.

> In the future, any one of the jet blades, or any component part of a jet aircraft engine, will have the type of metal stamped on it . . . so that regardless of use or wear the type of metal will be known and identifiable. [86]

This example of the scrapping and re-use pattern of metals may seem a narrowly specific one, at some distance from our overall ecological viewpoint. In actuality it is, however, a useful "systems model" aspect of the entire industrial pattern and its ecological function. This scrap re-use cycle is a parallel of the larger, naturally occurring cycles in the ecosystem, and will furnish the "systems model" for the solution of many other problems in the redesign of our major environment facilities.

The human systems that we have evolved are now global in their

[85] "Restoring the Quality of the Environment," *Report of the Environmental Pollution Panel,* President's Science Advisory Committee, The White House, November 1965.

[86] Proceedings: 37th Annual Convention, U.S. Institute of Scrap Iron and Steel, Jan. 1965; comments by B. J. Outman relating to a report entitled, "Marking of Aircraft and Missile System Parts Fabricated From Critical High Temperature Alloys," Air Force and Navy Defense Procurement Department, June 29, 1964.

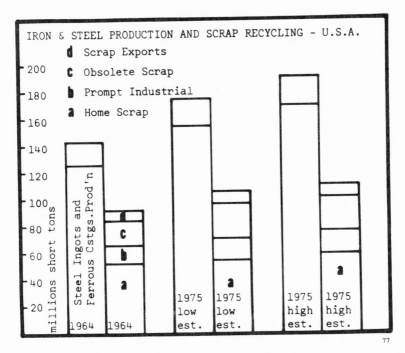

IRON & STEEL PRODUCTION AND SCRAP RECYCLING - U.S.A.

operation and their efficient ecological operation is now interlocked with the maintenance of the entire human family on the planet.

The present level of these extended human activities already interferes substantially with the natural cycles of energy and materials in the biosphere within which all of our major life processes are sustained:

> Is it too soon to inquire if these factors, plus others, may be contributing to an upset of nature's delicate balance? Are we slowly overturning the oxygen-carbon dioxide system upon which all life is dependent? Is that cycle being disturbed by high oxygen consumption and low oxygen yield? Are we thus shifting certain basic weather patterns upon which our various civilizations have come to depend? [87]

The minimal set of basic questions we need to ask ranges far beyond those required for local solutions to our various problems. Many of the problems are only problems because of a parochial concern with this or that economically or politically "convenient" set of solutions. There are no wholly local solutions any more—as there are no major human problems that are not also global. The basic questions revolve around the overall ecological maintenance of the entire human community.

What are the optimal conditions for human society on earth? There is obviously no fixed answer to such a question. But there are the various physical factors of adequacy in food, shelter, health, general welfare, and the concomitant access to the individually preferred physical and social facilities that make life meaningful and enjoyable. We have gradually arrived at sets of such conditions, as in the various bills of human rights—like that of the United Nations.

[87] "Second Progress Report of the Subcommittee on Science Research and Development," Committee on Science and Astronautics, 89th U.S. Congress, 1966.

[173]

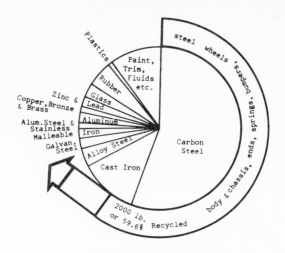

WEIGHT DISTRIBUTION AND SCRAP RECYCLING
1966 Plymouth (3355 lb.)

Whether such "ground rules" may be practical or not, we do in effect approach them, however tentatively, when we try to legislate for some human-welfare or environmental-control measure. The time is overdue for much more than tentative or local measures. To design our way forward through our present critical transitions, we need to adopt some more positive and operational indicators of the optimal conditions for the fulfillment of human life. By this, we do not mean optimal determinants that may be valid for all time and all people, that is, some set of absolutes. The variable and changing nature of human values makes this not only undesirable but unrealistic, in that one set of values in development may considerably modify others. But such considerations may still be flexibly accommodated and yet allow adequate definition.

We may tackle this in other ways by asking various fundamental questions about our planetary society. Which activities are most inimical to this; which more positively sustain, and forward, the human enterprise?

What are *the physical limits and constraints in the overall ecosystem,* with regard to our growing technological systems?

What are *the relevant human limits,* for example, the biological limits; air, food, water; temperature, space, speed, and noise tolerances?

What are *the irreplaceable resource limits,* for example, both the physical energy and material resources, and the human individual, social, and genetic resources?

In many ways, the core of our discussion has revolved around the same inquiry, repeated in different ways:

What are the physical operational parameters for the planet—the ecological or housekeeping rules that govern human occupancy?

These are very large questions, but they are those to which we must now apply ourselves—in many different ways and over a very long period. Some of the answers we already know, in part. Others are, in some senses, ultimately unanswerable. That they may be so is the more reason to ask them—if only to probe the limits of our knowledge.

Selected Reading Lists[*]
The Ecological Context

Achievements of Western Civilization, Joan Thompson. Harper & Row, 1965.

The Art of Conjecture, B. De Jouvenel. Basic Books, Inc., New York, 1966.

Change and Habit, Arnold J. Toynbee. Oxford University Press, New York, 1966.

Chronology of the Modern World, Neville Williams. Barrie and Rockliff, 1966.

Computers and Thought, E. Feigenbaum and J. Feldman (eds.). McGraw-Hill Book Co. 1963.

The Human Condition, Hannah Arendt. Doubleday-Anchor Books, 1959.

Ideas and Integrities, R. Buckminster Fuller. Prentice-Hall, Inc., New Jersey, 1963.

Impacts of Western Man, William Woodruff. St. Martin's Press, New York, 1966.

Information, Scientific American (ed.). W. H. Freeman and Co., London, 1966.

Man and His Future, G. Wolstenholme (ed.). Little, Brown and Co. Ltd. (Canada), 1963.

Man on Earth, S. P. R. Charter. Angel Island Publications, Inc., 1962.

Man's Role in Changing the Face of the Earth, William L. Thomas, Jr. (ed.). The University of Chicago Press, 1956.

The Meaning of the Twentieth Century, Kenneth Boulding. Harper & Row, New York, 1964.

Men, Machines and History, S. Lilley. Lawrence and Wishart, London, 1965.

Modern Science and Technology, R. Colborn. Van Nostrand Co., New Jersey, 1965.

The Next Hundred Years, Harrison Brown, James Bonner, and John Weir. Viking Press, 1957.

Nine Chains to the Moon, R. Buckminster Fuller. Southern Illinois University Press, 1963.

Our Polluted World, John Perry. Franklin Watts, Inc., New York, 1967.

"Prospects for Humanity," *Saturday Review,* August, September, October, 1964.

Resources and Man. Committee on Resources and Man, National Academy of Sciences—National Research Council. W. H. Freeman and Company, San Francisco, 1969.

Science and the Future of Mankind, Hugo Boyko (ed.). University of Indiana Press, 1964.

Science in our Lives, Ritchie Calder. New American Library, New York, 1962.

The Science of Man in the World Crisis, R. Linton (ed.). Columbia University Press, 1945.

Scientific Basis for World Civilization, L. J. Baranski, Ph.D. Christopher Publication, 1960.

Scientific Change, A. C. Crombie. Basic Books, Inc., New York, 1963.

Statistical Yearbook 1965, United Nations. New York, 1966.

Three Worlds of Development, I. L. Horowitz. Oxford University Press, 1966.

2000+, John McHale. "Architectural Design," London, 1967.

MAN IN THE BIOSPHERE

Advances in the Astronautical Sciences, American Astronautical Society. Plenum Press, 1961.

[*] *Note:* Though grouped for convenience, under the various chapter headings, many of these books deal broadly with the entire range of topics under discussion.

Animal Ecology, S. Charles Kendeigh. Prentice-Hall, Inc., 1961.

Bioastronautics Data Book, National Aeronautics and Space Administration. U.S. Government Printing Office, 1962.

"Biology and Human Environment," *Ekistics,* Vol. 21, No. 123, February 1966.

Biotechnology: Concepts and Applications, Lawrence J. Fogel. Prentice-Hall, Inc., 1963.

Cybernetics and Management, Stafford Beer. English University Press, Ltd., London, 1959.

Ecology, Eugene P. Odum. Modern Biology Series, Holt, Rinehart & Winston, Inc., 1963.

Energy Exchange in the Biosphere, David M. Gates. Harper & Row, New York, 1962.

Fundamentals of Ecology, E. P. Odum. W. B. Saunders Co., London, 1959.

Geography of World Affairs, J. P. Cole. Pelican Books, 1963.

Global Geography, G. T. Renner and Associates. Thomas Y. Crowell Company, 1944.

Human Ecology, A. H. Hawley. Ronald Press Co., New York, 1950.

Human Species, Anthony Barnett. Pelican Books, Ltd., 1957.

The Human Species, Frederick S. Hurse. Random House, New York, 1965.

Human Use of the Earth, Philip L. Wagner. The Free Press, New York, 1960.

Life Support System for a Near Earth or Circumlunar Space Vehicle, Garland B. Vhisenhunt, Jr. Plenum Press, 1961.

Mankind Evolving, Th. Dobzhansky. Yale University Press, New Haven, 1962.

Manned Space Cabin Systems, Eugene B. Konecci. Advances in Space Science, Academic Press, 1959.

The Meaning of the Twentieth Century, K. Boulding. Harper & Row, 1964.

New Views of the Nature of Man, J. R. Platt (ed.). University of Chicago Press, 1965.

A Regenerative Life-Support System for Long-Term Space Flight, J. J. Konikoff. *Advances in the Astronautical Sciences,* Vol. VIII, Plenum Press, 1963.

Science and Survival, B. Commoner. The Viking Press, 1966.

Space Biology, James S. Hanrahan and David Bushnell. Basic Books, Inc., 1960.

Spacecraft Life Support Systems, Dan C. Popma. National Aeronautics and Space Administration, Langley Research Center, Paper No. CP 63-693, April 1963.

Waste-Recovery Processes for a Closed Ecological System, Wesley O. Pipes. National Academy of Sciences-National Research Council Publication 898, 1961.

Weather and Climate Modification, Problems and Prospects. Vol. I and II. National Academy of Sciences, Washington, D.C., 1966.

THE PHYSICAL ENVIRONMENT

Abundance of Chemical Elements, V. V. Cherdyntsev. University of Chicago Press, 1961.

After the Seventh Day, Ritchie Calder. New American Library, New York, 1961.

Bioastronautics—Fundamentals & Practical Problems. Vol. 17, W. C. Kaufman (ed.). AAS/ AAAS Symposium, Cleveland, Ohio, 1963.

Biochemical Evolution, E. Florkin and S. Morgulis. Academic Press, New York, 1949.

"Carbon Dioxide and Climate," Gilbert N. Plass. *Scientific American,* July 1959.

The Chemical Elements, Helen Miles Davis. Ballantine Books, 1959.

Climatic Change, Harlow Shapley (ed.). Harvard University Press, 1953.

"Climatic Changes of the Past and Present," *American Scientist.* 48, pp. 341-64, 1960.

Conquest of the Sea, Cord-Christian Troebst. Harper & Row, New York, 1962.

Down to Earth, C. Croneis and W. C. Krumbein. Harper & Row, New York, 1951.

Draft of a General Scientific Framework for World Ocean Study. Intergovernmental Oceanographic Commission, UNESCO, Paris.

The Earth and Its Atmosphere, D. R. Bates (ed.). Basic Books, 1957.

Earth and Space Science, C. W. Wolfe (ed.). Heath and Co., Boston, 1956.

Environmental Hazards Coordination, (Pesticides) Committee on Government Operations, U.S. 89th Congress. U.S. Government Printing Office, 1966.

Environmental Pollution: A Challenge to Science and Technology, Committee on Science and Astronautics, U.S. 89th Congress. U.S. Government Printing Office, 1966.

The Fitness of the Environment, L. J. Henderson. Macmillan, New York, 1913.

The Forest and the Sea, Marston Bates. Random House, 1960.

Geography of Economic Activity, Richard S. Thoman. McGraw-Hill, Inc., 1962.

Global Impacts of Applied Microbiology, M. P. Starr. John Wiley and Sons, Inc., New York, 1964.

Impact of Space Exploration on Society, W. E. Frye (ed.). Symposium, San Francisco, 1965.

Man's Physical World, J. E. VanRiper. McGraw-Hill, Inc., New York, 1962.

Migration and Environment, H. L. Shapiro. Oxford University Press, New York, 1939.

The Mineral Resources of the Sea, John L. Mero. Elsevier Publishing Co., New York, 1965.

The Nature of Natural History, M. Bates. Scribner's, New York, 1950.

The Ocean of the Air, D. J. Blumenstoek. Rutgers University Press, New Jersey, 1959.

Physical Geography, R. K. Gresswell. Hulton Educational Publishers Ltd., London, 1958.

Physiological and Performance Determinants in Manned Space Systems, P. Horowitz (ed.). Symposium, Northridge, California, 1965.

The Planet Earth, Scientific American (ed.). Simon and Schuster, Inc., New York, 1957.

The Processes of Ongoing Human Evolution, Baker. Wayne State University Press, 1960.

Science and Economic Development: (New Patterns of Living), (second edition), R. L. Meier. M.I.T. Press, 1965.

A Special Report on Water Power. June 1966.

The World of Life, W. F. Pauli. Houghton Mifflin, Boston, 1949.

THE HUMAN SYSTEMS

Anthropology Today, A. L. Kroeber (ed.). University of Chicago Press, 1953.

Bibliography of International Relations and World Affairs, E. H. Boehm. Clio Press, Santa Barbara, Calif., 1965.

Changing Human Behavior, John Mann. Scribner's, New York, 1965.

The Chemical Revolution, a Contribution to Social Technology, A. Clow and N, Clow. London, 1952.

The City of Man, W. Warren Wagar. Houghton Mifflin Co., Boston, 1963.

Communication and Social Order, Hugh Dalziel Duncan. The Bedminster Press, 1962.

Conflict Resolution and World Education, Stuart Mudd (ed.). Published by Dr. W. Junk, The Hague and Indiana University Press, 1966.

Continuities in Cultural Evolution, Margaret Mead. Yale University Press, 1964.

The Control of Human Heredity and Evolution, T. M. Sonneborn (ed.). Macmillan, 1965.

The Crisis of Cultural Change, Myron Bloy. Seabury, 1965.

Cultural Foundations of Industrial Civilization, J. U. Nef. Cambridge University Press, 1958.

Cultural Patterns and Technical Change, M. Mead (ed.). Mentor Books (UNESCO), 1955.

The Culture Consumers, Alvin Toffler. The Macmillan Company, Ltd., 1964.

Economic Man, Vols. I and II, C. Reinhold Noyes. Columbia University Press, 1948.

Education Automation, R. Buckminster Fuller. Southern Illinois University Press, 1963.

Education, Manpower & Economic Growth: Strategies of Human Resource Development, Frederick Harbison and Charles A. Myers. McGraw-Hill Book Company, 1964.

Empire and Communications, H. A. Innes. Oxford University Press, 1953.

Essays in Sociological Theory, Talcott Parsons. Free Press, New York, 1964.

The Evolution of Culture, L. A. White. McGraw-Hill Book Company, New York, 1959.

Free Men and Free Markets, R. Theobald. Doubleday and Co., Inc., New York, 1963.

The Future as History, R. L. Heilbroner. Grove Press, Inc., New York, 1961.

Handbook of Modern Sociology, R. L. Faris (ed.). Rand McNally and Co., 1964.

The Human Dialogue, F. W. Matson and Ashley Montagu (ed.). The Free Press, New York, 1967.

Human Ecology, J. W. Bewr. Milford, London, 1935.

The Human Meaning of the Social Sciences, D. Lerner (ed.). World Publishing Co., New York, 1959.

Human Values on the Spaceship Earth, K. E. Boulding and Henry Clark. National Council of the Churches of Christ in the U.S.A., 1966.

The Influence of Culture on Visual Perception, M. H. Segall, Donald T. Campbell and Melville J. Herskovits. Bobbs-Merrill Co., Inc., New York, 1966.

International Cooperation and You, Louis Verniers. Union of International Assoc. Document No. 12., U.I.A. Publication No. 177, 1962.

International Institutions, Paul Reuter. Rinehart and Co., New York, 1958.

In the Human Grain, W. J. Ong. Collier, Macmillan Ltd., London, 1967.

Language, Thought and Reality, Benjamin Lee Whorf. John Wiley and Sons, 1956.

Manpower Report of the President, U.S. Government Printing Office, 1964.

Mirror for Man, C. Kluckhohn. Fawcett Publications, Inc., 1963.

The New Sociology, I. L. Horowitz (ed.). Oxford University Press, Galaxy Books, 1965.

The Next Generation, Donald Michael. Vintage Books, New York, 1965.

On Human Communications, Colin Cherry. Chapman Hall, 1957.

Of Time, Work & Leisure, Sebastian de Grazia. The Twentieth Century Fund, 1962.

People or Personnel, Paul Goodman. Random House, 1963.

Physiology of Man in Space, J.H.U. Brown (ed.). Academic Press., 1963.

The Scientific Estate, D. K. Price. Harvard University Press, 1965.

Social Indicators, Raymond A. Bauer (ed.). M. I. T. Press, 1966.

Sociology, T. B. Bottomore. Allen and Unwin Ltd., London, 1962.

The Silent Language, E. T. Hall. University of Illinois, 1960.

The State of the Nation (Social Systems Accounting), Bertram M. Gross. Travistock Publications, London, 1966.

The Study of Culture at a Distance, Margaret Mead and Rhoda Metraux (ed.). University of Chicago Press, 1953.

Study of Thinking, J. S. Bruner, J. J. Goodnow and G. A. Austin. Chapman & Hall, Ltd., 1956.

The Technological Order, C. F. Stover (ed.). Wayne State University Press, 1963.

Technology and Social Change, Eli Ginzberg (ed.). Columbia University Press, 1964.

Theories of Society, Vol. I and II, T. Parsons, E. Shils, K. Naegele, J. R. Pitts (eds.). The Free Press, New York, 1961.

Understanding Media, Marshall McLuhan. McGraw-Hill Book Company, 1964.

World Communications. UNESCO Publications Center, 1964.

World Handbook of Political and Social Indicators, Russett, Lasswell and Deutsch. Yale University Press, 1964.

World Technology and Human Destiny, R. Aron (ed.). University of Michigan Press, 1963.

POPULATION AND FOOD

Asia's Population Problems, S. Chandrasekhar (ed.). With a discussion of population and immigration in Australia. George Allen and Unwin Ltd., London, 1967.

Born to Hunger, A. Hopcraft. Houghton Mifflin Company, Boston, 1968.

The Challenge of Man's Future, H. Brown. Martin Secker & Warburg, Ltd., London, 1967.

Economic History of World Population, Carlo Cipolla. Pelican Books, 1964.

Family Planning and Population Programs: A Review of World Developments. B. Berelson et al (eds.). University of Chicago Press, 1966.

The Geography of Hunger, Josue de Castro. Little, Brown & Company, Boston, 1952.

Global Impacts of Applied Microbiology, Mortimer P. Starr. John Wiley and Sons, Inc., New York, 1964.

Hungry Nations, W. and P. Paddock. Little, Brown & Company, Boston, 1964.

The Hungry Planet: The Modern World at the Edge of Famine, G. Borgstrom. The Macmillan Company, New York, 1965. Paperback edition, Collier Books.

India's Food Resources and Population, P. C. Bansil. Vora, Bombay, 1958.

Land Requirements for the Production of Human Food, J. Wyllie. University of London Press, 1954.

Lands for Tomorrow, L. Dudley Stamp. Indiana University Press, 1952.

The Limits of Man: An Enquiry into the Scientific Bases of Human Population, H. Nicol. Constable & Company, Ltd., London, 1967.

Man Must Eat, Sir William Slater. Chicago University Press, 1964.

Our Crowded Planet: Essays on the Pressures of Population, F. Osborn (ed.). Doubleday & Company, Inc., Garden City, 1962.

The Population Bomb: Population Control or Race to Oblivion?, P. R. Ehrlich. Ballantine Books, Inc., New York, 1968.

The Population Crisis: Implications and Peace for Action. L. Ng (ed.), Stuart Mudd, co-editor. Indiana University Press, 1965.

Population Dynamics; Causes and Consequences of World Demographic Change, R. Thomlinson. Random House, Inc., New York, 1965.

The Population Explosion and World Hunger, A. McCormack. Burns, Oates & Washbourne, Ltd., London, 1963.

Population and Food, M. Cepede, F. Houtart and L. Grond. Sheed & Ward, Inc., New York, 1964. (Translated from the French.)

Population: The Vital Revolution, F. Freedman. Doubleday & Company, Inc., New York, 1964.

Population and World Politics, P. M. Hauser. The Free Press, Glencoe, Ill., 1959.

Proceedings of the High Lysine Corn Conference, June 21-22, 1966, E. T. Mertz and O. E. Nelson (eds.). (Purdue University, Lafayette, Indiana.) Washington, D.C., Corn Industries Research Foundation, a division of Corn Refiners Association, Inc., 1966.

The Rich Nations and the Poor Nations, Barbara Ward. W. W. Norton and Co., Inc., 1962.

The Soil That Supports Us, C. E. Kellog. Macmillan Co., New York, 1941.

The Third World, P. Worsley. University of Chicago Press, 1964.

World Without Want, Paul G. Hoffman. Harper and Row, New York, 1962.

ENERGY

America Faces the Nuclear Age, J. E. Fairchild and D. Landman (eds.). Sheridan House, New York, 1961.

Applied Solar Energy Research (a directory of World Activities and Bibliography of Significant Literature), J. S. Jensen (ed.). University of Arizona, 1959.

A Chronological History of Electrical Development, E. S. Lincoln (ed.). New York, 1946.

Direct Energy Conversion, Sutton. McGraw-Hill, 1966.

The Economics of Atomic Power, Sam H. Schurr. *Bulletin of the Atomic Scientist*, January 1965.

Economic Aspects of Atomic Power, Schurr and Marschak. Cowles Commission for Research in Economics by Princeton University, 1950.

Electricity Without Dynamos, J. W. Gardner. Pelican Books, Inc., 1964.

Energy for Man, Hans Thirring. Indiana University Press, 1958.

Energy: Its Production, Conversion and Use on the Service of Man, Philip Sporn. Pergamon Press, New York, 1963.

Energy in the Future, P. C. Putman. D. Van Nostrand Co., New York, 1953.

Energy Research and Development and National Progress. Superintendent of Documents, U.S. Government Printing Office, Washington, D.C.

Energy Resources of the World. U.S. Government Printing Office, Washington, D.C., 1949.

Energy Resources (a report to the Committee on Natural Resources of the National Academy of Sciences), M. Hubbert. National Academy of Sciences, Washington, D. C., 1962.

Energy Life and Animal Organization, J. A. Riegel. English University Press, London.

Energy Policy (problems and objectives). Organization for Economic Co-operation and Development, Paris, 1966.

Energy Research and Resources of the World, N. B. Guyol. Department of State Publication 3428, U.S. Government Printing Office, Washington, D. C., 1949.

"Energy," Sam H. Schurr. *Scientific American*, September 1963.

Energy and Society, Fred Cottrell. McGraw-Hill Book Company, Inc., 1955.

Energy Sources-The Wealth of the World, E. Ayers and C. Scarlott. McGraw-Hill Book Company, Inc., 1952.

A History of Civil Engineering, Hans Straub. M.I.T. Press, Cambridge, Mass., 1964.

"Home Generation of Power by Photovoltaic Conversion of Solar Energy," J. F. Elliott. *Electrical Engineering*, Vol. IXXC, No. 9, September 1960.

"How Many Energy Slaves Can a Nation Maintain?," Professor A. R. Ubbelohde. *New Scientist*, September 9, 1965.

"Longer Range View of Nuclear Energy," Weinberg and Wigner. *Atomic Science*, Vol. XVI, No. 10 (Bulletin).

Maximum Plausible Energy Contributions from Wind Power, Palmer C. Putnam. Solar Energy Research, University of Wisconsin Press, 1955.

New Frontiers for Energy. Power, July 1966.

Panel Heating in Polar Buildings, J. M. Stephenson. *Air Conditioning, Heating and Ventilation*, Vol. LIX, No. 6., June 1962.

Peaceful Uses of Atomic Energy, Vol. 1. United Nations, New York, 1956.

Power from the Wind, P. C. Putnam. Van Nostrand, New York, 1948.

"Power—Today and Tomorrow," F. Sherwood Taylor. *Sources of Energy*, Chapter 1. Frederick Muller Ltd., London, 1954.

Proceedings of the International Conference on the Peaceful Uses of Atomic Energy, Vol. 1. United Nations, New York, 1965 (Geneva, 1955).

Proceedings of the 3rd International Conference on the Peaceful Uses of Atomic Energy, Vol. 1. United Nations, New York, 1965.

Social Implications of the Peaceful Uses of Nuclear Energy, O. Klineberg (ed.).

Solar Energy Research, Daniels, Farrington and John A. Duffie (eds.). University of Wisconsin Press, 1955.

Solar Power Plants, M. L. Ghai. Solar Energy Research, University of Wisconsin Press, 1955.

Statistical Yearbook of the World Power Conference, No. 9, Frederick Brown (ed.). Lund, Humphries and Con, Ltd., London, 1960.

Technology and Social Change, Eli Ginsburg (ed.). Columbia University Press, 1964.

Tidal Power and the Severn Barrage, H. Headland. Proceedings of the Institution of Electrical Engineers, Vol. 96, Part 2, June 1959.

"Towards Power Generation by MHD," *New Scientist*. No. 365, Nov. 14, 1963.

"World Fuel Picture for 1980," *New Scientist*, August 4, 1966.

World Energy Supplies. 1957-1960. United Nations, Ser. J. No. 5. New York, 1962.

World Energy Supplies. Statistical Papers Series J. No. 9 1961-1964. United Nations, 1966.

MATERIALS

Agricultural Mechanization, United Nations, New York, 1963.

Computers and the World of the Future, Martin Greenberger. M.I.T. Press, 1964.

European Steel Trends, United Nations, New York, 1949.

The Geography of Economic Activity, R. S. Thomas. McGraw-Hill Book Co., 1962.

A History of Industrial Chemistry, F. Sherwood Taylor. Abelard-Schuman, New York, 1957.

History of Metals, L. Aitchson. MacDonald and Evans, 1960.

History of the Strength of Materials, S. P. Timoschenko. London, 1953.

History of Technology (5 volumes), C. Singer, E. J. Holmyard and A. R. Hall (eds.). Oxford University Press, 1954.

History of Western Technology, Friedrich Klemm. M.I.T. Press, 1964.

A History of Science and Technology—18th and 19th Century, R. J. Forbes and E. J. Dijksterhuis. Pelican Books, 1963.

Industrialism and Industrial Man, Clark Kerr, John T. Dunlop, Frederick Harbison and Charles A. Myers. Harvard University Press, 1960.

Industrial Standardization in Developing Countries. United Nations, New York, 1964.

Industrial Scrap Generation. U. S. Department of Commerce Business and Defense Services, 1957.

Industrial Wastes. Lipsett. C. H. Atlas, 1951.

Iron and Steel Scrap, Survey and Analysis of Availability. U. S. Department of Commerce, 1957.

International and Metric Units of Measurement. Marvin Green Chemical Publishing Co., New York.

Landmarks of Tomorrow, P. F. Drucker. Harper and Row, 1959.

Long Term Economic Growth 1860–1865. Bureau of the Census, Washington, D. C., 1966.

Machines and the Man, R. P. Weeks (ed.). Appleton-Century-Crofts, Inc., New York, 1961.

Man-Computer Symbiosis, J. C. R. Licklider. Institute of Radio Engineers Transactions on Human Factors in Electronics. Vol. HFE-1, No. 1, March 1960.

Man's Place in the Dybosphere, R. R. Larrderr. Prentice-Hall, Inc., 1966.

Medieval Technology and Social Change, Lynn White, Jr. Oxford University Press, 1962.

A Methodology for Systems Engineering, Arthur D. Hall. Van Nostrand, 1962.

Mineral Facts and Problems, 1965 ed. Bureau of Mines, U. S. Department of the Interior, Washington, D. C., 1965.

Mineral Resources, Dean F. Frasche. National Academy of Sciences, 1962.

Modern Technology and Civilization, C. R. Walker. McGraw-Hill Books, 1962.

Natural Resources and International Development, Marion Clawson (ed.). Johns Hopkins Press for Resources for the Future, Inc., 1964.

Origin of Invention, Otis T. Mason. M.I.T. Press, 1966.

Planning for Balanced Social and Economic Development. United Nations, New York, 1964.

Plastics in the Service of Man, E. G. Couzens and V. E. Yarsley. Penguin Books, Ltd., 1956.

Prospective Changes in Society by 1980. Denver, Colorado , 1966.

Psychological Principles of System Development, Gagne (ed.). Holt, Rinehart & Winston, 1962.

Resources in America's Future, Landsberg, Fischman and Fisher. Johns Hopkins Press.

The Rise of Chemical Industry in the Nineteenth Century, F. L. Haber. Oxford University Press, 1958.

Science and Resources, Henry Jarrett (ed.). Johns Hopkins Press, 1959.

Stages of Economic Growth, W. W. Rostow. Cambridge University Press, 1960.

Statistical Summary of the Mineral Industry, 1959-64. Mineral Resources Division, Overseas Geological Survey, London, 1966.

Statistical Yearbook, 1965. Statistical Office of the United Nations Department of Economic and Social Affairs, New York, 1966.

The Story of the Plastics Industry. The Society of the Plastics Industry, Inc. John B. Watkins, 1966.

Studies in Long-Term Economic Projections for the World Economy. United Nations, New York, 1964.

Survey and Analysis of the Supply and Availability of Obsolete Iron and Steel Scrap. Business and Defense Services Administration, U. S. Department of Commerce, January 1957.

System Engineering. Goode and Machol. McGraw-Hill, 1960.

Systems: Research & Design (Proceedings of the First Systems Symposium at Case Institute of Technology), Donald P. Eckman (ed.). John Wiley & Sons, Inc., 1961.

Technology & Social Change, John F. Cuber. Appleton-Century-Crofts, Inc., 1957.

Technological Trends in Major American Industry. Bulletin No. 1474. U. S. Dept. of Labor, Washington, D. C., 1966.

The Unfinished Epic of Industrialization, R. Buckminster Fuller. Jargon Press of Jonathan William's Nantahala Foundation. Heritage Press, 1963.

World Economic Development, D. W. Fryer. McGraw-Hill Book Co., Inc., New York, 1965.

World Economic Survey, 1964. United Nations, New York, 1965.

World Resource Statistics (2nd ed.), John C. Weaver and Fred Lukerman. Burgess Publishing Co., Minneapolis, Minnesota, 1953.

World Trade and Investment, The Economics of Interdependence, Donald Bailey Marsh. Harcourt, Brace and Company, 1951.

The World in 1984, Vol. 1/2, Nigel Calder (ed.). Penguin Books, Baltimore, Maryland.

World Prospects for Natural Resources, Fisher and Potter. Johns Hopkins Press, Maryland.

ECOLOGICAL REDESIGN

The Chasm Ahead, Aurelio Peccei. The Macmillan Company, 1969.

Closing the Cycle From Use to Reuse. The Fusion Torch. Bernard J. Eastlund and William C. Gough. U. S. Atomic Energy Commission, 1969.

Communitas: Means of Livelihood & Ways of Life, P. and P. Goodman. Vintage Press, New York.

Conversion of Organic Solid Wastes Into Yeast, Floyd Meller. Bureau of Solid Waste Management. U. S. Department of Health, Education, and Welfare, 1969.

Design With Nature, Ian McHarg. Natural History Press, Garden City, New York, 1969.

Ecology and Resource Management, Kenneth Watt. McGraw-Hill Co., New York, 1968.

The Environmental Handbook, Garrett De Bell (ed.). Ballantine Books, New York, 1970.

Fertility From Town Wastes, J. C. Wylie. Faber and Faber, Ltd., London, 1955.

Industrial Wastes and Salvage, Charles Lipsett. Atlas Publishing Co., 1963.

The Role of Packaging in Solid Waste Management 1966 to 1976. U. S. Department of Health, Education, and Welfare Bureau of Solid Waste Management, Rockville, Maryland, 1969.

The Social Costs of Private Enterprise, K. William Kapp. Harvard University Press, 1950.

Solid Waste Management/Composting; European activity and American potential. U. S. Dept. of Health, Education, and Welfare Public Health Service. Environmental Control Administration, Cincinnati, 1968.

Towards a Liberatory Technology, Lewis Herber. *Anarchos,* No. 3, Spring 1969.

World Resources Inventory Series (Southern Illinois University):

Document One [1963]	*Inventory of World Resources, Human Trends and Needs*	R. B. Fuller and John McHale
Document Two [1964]	*The Design Initiative*	R. B. Fuller
Document Three [1965]	*Comprehensive Thinking*	R. B. Fuller
Document Four [1965]	*The Ten Year Program*	John McHale
Document Five [1967]	*Comprehensive Design Strategy*	R. B. Fuller
Document Six [1967]	*The Ecological Context: Energy and Materials*	John McHale

The Subversive Science, Paul Shepard and Daniel McKinley (eds.). Houghton Mifflin Company, 1969.

The Challenge of Abundance, R. Theobald. New American Library of World Literature, Inc., New York, 1962.

The Environment Game, N. Calder. Martin Secker & Warburg, Ltd., London, 1967.

Future Environments of North America, F. F. Darling and J. P. Milton (eds.). The Natural History Press, Garden City, N. Y., 1966.

The Peace Race, S. Melman. Ballantine Books, Inc., New York, 1961.

Rich Lands and Poor, G. Myrdal. Yale University Press, New Haven, Conn., 1964.

Science and Survival, B. Commoner. The Viking Press, Inc., New York, 1966.

Transforming Traditional Agriculture, T. W. Schultz. Yale University Press, New Haven, Conn., 1964.

Will the Human Race Survive?, H. Still. Hawthorn Books, Inc., New York, 1966.

Chart Reference List

1. *Steam Power Plant Site Selection.* Energy Policy Staff, Office of Science and Technology, U.S. Government Printing Office, 1968.

2. "Restoring the Quality of our Environment." U.S. Department of Health, Education, and Welfare, U.S. Government Printing Office, 1966.

3. *Statistical Abstracts of the U.S.* (86th edition). U.S. Department of Commerce, Bureau of Census, 1965, p. 173.

4. *The Fusion Torch: Closing the Cycle from Use to Re-use,* Bernard J. Eastlund and William C. Gough. U.S. Atomic Energy Commission, May, 1969.

5. *Time* magazine, July 11, 1969, p. 56.

6. *The Population Crisis and the Use of World Resources, Vol. II* (Chapter—"Housing and Population Growth," Robert Cook and Kaval Gulhati). Published by Dr. W. Junk, The Hague, 1964.

7. (1) *Population and Food Supplies: The Edge of the Knife,* Roger Revelle. National Academy of Sciences, Washington, D.C., 1966, pp. 24-47.

(2) *International Reference Day Book: 1970.* Professional & Technical Programs, Inc., New York, 1969.

8. Ibid.

9. National Security Seminar, 1966, p. 163.

10. Compiled from various sources.

11. Compiled from various sources.

12. (1) *Fundamentals of Ecology,* E. P. Odum. Holt, Rinehart & Winston, New York, 1959, p. 18

(2) "Photosynthesis," E. I. Rabinowitch, *Scientific American,* 1948, pp. 30-31.

13. (1) "Food for the World," Howard W. Mattson. *International Science and Technology,* December 1965, p. 34.

(2) "Photosynthesis," H. A. Spoehr, Chemical Catalog Com. Inc., 1926, pp. 31-40.

(3) "Direct Use of the Sun's Energy," Farrington Daniels. *American Scientist,* Vol. 55, January, 1967, p. 16.

14. (1) "Solar Radiation Power," POWER, September 1957, p. 24.

(2) *Fundamentals of Ecology* (Second Edition), Eugene P. Odum. W. B. Saunders Company, Pennsylvania, 1959, pp. 46-47.

(3) "Energy Resources," M. K. Hubbert, National Academy of Sciences.

15. Compiled from various sources.

16. "World of Opportunity," *Science and Technology for Development,* Vol. 1, United Nations, 1963.

17. Compiled from various sources.

18. *The Ecological Context,* John McHale. Carbondale, Illinois, 1967, p. 25.

19. (1) "Biology and Human Environment," C. H. Waddington. *Ekistics,* Vol. 21, No. 123, February 1966.

(2) "World Fishing," *Barclays Bank Review.* Barclays Bank, February 1967.

(3) "Food and the World Fisheries," Anthony D. Scott. *Natural Resources and International Development,* Marion Clawson (ed.). Johns Hopkins Press, Washington, D.C., 1963, pp. 134-37.

20. (1) "World Water Cycle," *Time* magazine, October 1, 1965.

(2) "Water," *Life Science Library, Life* magazine, p. 38.

(3) "Water—A Special Report," POWER, June 1966, pp. S8, S10.

21. (1) "Carbon Dioxide and Climate," *Scientific American,* Vol. 201, 1959, pp. 41-47.

(2) "Photosynthesis," *Scientific American,* Vol. 79, August 1948, p. 25

(3) *The Realm of Carbon,* Horace G. Deming. John Wiley & Sons, New York, 1930, pp. 259-261.

22. "Carbon Dioxide and Climate," Gilbert N. Plass. *Scientific American,* Vol. 201, July 1959.

23. (1) *Minerals in Industry,* W. R. Jones. Penguin Books, New York, 1963.

(2) *Phosphate in Agriculture,* Vincent Sanchelli. Rinehart Publication Corp., New York, 1965.

(3) *Fundamentals of Ecology,* E. P. Odum. Holt, Reinhart and Winston, Inc., New York, 1959.

24. Compiled from various sources.

25. Compiled from various sources.

26. "The Biological Trace Elements," Henry A. Schroeder. *Journal of Chronic Disease,* Vol. 18, 1965, pp. 226-227.

27. *The Future of the Future,* John McHale. George Braziller, Inc., New York, 1969, p. 165.

28. *Health & Disease,* René Dubos, Maya Pines & editors of *Life.* Time Inc., New York, 1965, pp. 193-195.

29. *Time: Its Breadth and Depth in Biological Rhythms,* John J. Grebe. Annals of the New York Academy of Sciences, Vol. 98, Article 4, October 30, 1962.

30. (1) International Industrial Development Center Study, Stanford Research Institute.

(2) *Science and the Future of Mankind,* Hugo Boyko (ed.). World Academy of Art and Science, published by Dr. W. Junk, The Hague, 1961.

(3) *Change/Challenge/Response.* Office of Regional Development, Albany, New York, 1964.

31. *Deadline for Survival,* Peter Golmark. Transactions of the New York Academy of Sciences, Vol. 31, 1969, p. 589.

32. (1) "Frequency Spectra Chart," Douglas Aircraft Company, California, 1962.

(2) "New Techniques of Communication," F. J. D. Taylor. *Discovery Magazine,* Vol. XXV, No. 10, October 1964.

33. (1) *1965 World Almanac,* Hansen Editor. New York *World-Telegram and Sun,* New York, 1965.

(2) *World Geo-Graphic Atlas,* Bayer. Container Corporation of America, Chicago, Illinois, 1953.

34. (1) *Music of the Spheres,* G. Murchie. Houghton Mifflin Company, Boston, 1961.

(2) Lecture Series: Harlow Shapley, Southern Illinois University, 1964.

35. (1) *Science and Engineering and the Future of Man,* W. Taylor Thom, Jr. Science and the Future of Mankind, W.A.A.S., 1963.

(2) *The Process of Man's Occupancy of the Earth,* Hans Carol. Department of Geography, York University, Ontario, 1964.

(3) *Technology and Social Change,* Allen and others. Appleton-Century-Crofts, Inc., 1957.

36. "Science, Technology, and Change," John McHale. *The Annals of the American Academy of Political and Social Science,* Vol. 373, September 1967, pp. 120-140.

37. *Civilization at the Crossroads,* Radovan Richta. International Arts and Sciences Press, Prague, 1969.

38. Ibid.

39. "World Population Projections 1965-2000," *Population Bulletin,* Population Reference Bureau, Inc., October 1965, pp. 94-95.

40. *The Ten Year Program,* John McHale. Carbondale, Illinois, 1965, p. 8.

41. *Human Trends and Needs,* B. Fuller and J. McHale. World Resources Inventory, Southern Illinois University, Carbondale, Illinois, 1963, p. 40.

42. "Food Resources of the Ocean," J. Holt. *Scientific American,* September 1969, p. 188.

43. "The Role of Goals and Planning," H. Ozbekan. *Mankind 2000,* R. Jungk, J. Galtung, Allen and Unwin, United Kingdom, 1969.

44. (1) "Food and the World Fisheries," Anthony D. Scott. *Natural Resources and International Development,* Marion Clawson (ed.). Johns Hopkins Press, Washington, D.C., 1963, pp. 134-37.

(2) "The World Food Crisis," G. Borgstrom. *Futures,* June 1969.

(3) *OECD at Work.* OECD, Paris, 1969.

(4) *Our Nation and the Sea.* U.S. Government Printing Office, 1969.

45. "The World Food Crisis," G. Borgstrom. *Futures,* June 1969, p. 344.

46. *Energy Resources,* Publication 1000 D, Committee on Natural Resources, National Academy of Sciences—National Research Council, Washington, D.C., 1962.

47. *The Ecological Context,* John McHale. Carbondale, Illinois, 1967, p. 66.

48. *Energy Resources,* M. King Hubert. U.S. National Academy of Sciences, 1962.

49. *Energy into Power,* E. G. Sterland. National History Press, Garden City, 1967, pp. 120-121.

50. *Energy for Man,* Hans Thirring. Harper & Row, New York, 1962, p. 218.

51. Data compiled from U.N. and other sources.

52. *World Prospects for Natural Resources,* J. Fisher and N. Potter. Baltimore, Maryland.

53. *World Energy Supplies 1961-1964.* Department of Economic & Social Affairs, Statistical Office of the U.N., United Nations, New York, 1966, Series I, No. 9.

54. *Barclays Bank Review,* May 1969.

55. Ibid.

56. "Earth Science and Oceanography," Robert Colbarn (ed.). *Modern Science & Technology,* 1965, p. 622.

57. *Resources and Man.* National Academy of Sciences, W. H. Freeman Company, San Francisco, 1969, pp. 212-213.

58. *Energy Policy: Problems & Objective.* Organization for Economic Cooperation & Development, 1966, p. 61.

59. (1) "Nuclear Power in the World Today," Peter R. Mounfield (notes from lecture given at S.I.U., May 9, 1967, pp. 4 and 5).

(2) "Environment Contamination from Nuclear Reactors," Malcolm L. Peterson. *Science & Citizen,* November 1965, p. 1.

60. (1) *Energy for Man,* Hans Thirring. Harper & Row, New York, 1962, p. 54

(2) Document 4, *The Ten Year Program,* John McHale. World Resources Inventory, Carbondale, Illinois, 1965, p. 53.

61. (1) "The Nature and Sources of Energy," Zimmerman, *Introduction to World Resources,* p. 68.

(2) Energy R. & D. and National Progress, Inter Department Energy Study, Washington, D.C., 1964, p. 40.

62. "Metals and Mineral Processing—How Metals Are Recovered," Marshall F. Sittig. *Engineering & Mineral Journal,* June 1958.

63. "Materials, Polymers," W. F. Watson. *Technological Forecasting and Corporate Strategy,* G. Wills, D. Ashton, B. Taylor (eds.). American Elsevier Company, New York, 1969.

64. (1) "Minerals," Julian W. Feiss. *Scientific American,* September 1963, p. 131.

(2) *1964 Minerals Yearbook, Vol. I.* U.S. Department of Interior, Bureau of Mines, Washington, D.C., 1965.

(3) *Mineral Facts and Problems, 1965 ed., Bulletin 630.* U.S. Department of Interior, Bureau of Mines, Washington, D.C., 1966.

(4) *Statistical Summary of the Mineral Industry 1959-1964.* Overseas Geological Survey, Mineral Resources Division, London, 1966.

65. "Transition," Vol. 8, No. 2. Nystrom & Company.

66. "Plastics Primer," *1962 Western Plastics Directory,* p. 5.

67. "The Synthetics Age," R. Houwink, *Modern Plastics,* McGraw-Hill, Inc., August 1966, Table 1, p. 99

68. (1) *The Epic of Steel,* Douglas A. Fischer. Harper & Row, New York, 1963, p. 304.

(2) *Impact of Western Man,* William Woodruff. Macmillan Company, New·York, 1966, pp. 210-13.

69. David L. Grimes, Vice President, Wittaker Corporation, San Diego, California.

70. (1) *Technology Behind Investment.* A. D. Little, Inc., New York, 1965.

(2) "Cost-Price Squeeze Tightens Materials Battle in Major Appliances," *Steel,* July 1966.

71. (1) *Trends in Application of Structural Composite Materials,* David L. Grimes. Advisory Group for Aerospace Research & Development, Washington, D. C., November, 1965, p. 11.

(2) *Metals Handbook,* Vol. 1 (Eighth edition), American Society for Metals, Ohio, 1961.

72. *Minerals Yearbook, 1967, Vols. I and II.* Bureau of Mines, U.S. Department of Interior, 1968.

73. (1) *Douglas Missile & Space Systems Development Interplanetary Mission Life Support System,* E. S. Mills, R. L. Butterton, 1965.

(2) ASD Report TR 61-363, NASA.

74. *Modern Packaging,* 40(9): 93, May 1967.

75. Bureau of the Census, Department of Commerce, BDSA, U.S. Government Printing Office, Washington, D.C.

76. (1) *Survey & Analysis of the Supply and Availability of Obsolete Iron & Steel Scrap* (Revised edition). Batelle Memorial Institute, Ohio, 1957.

(2) *Iron & Steel Scrap: Consumption Problems.* U.S. Department of Commerce, U.S. Government Printing Office, Washington, D.C., 1966, p. 4.

77. *Iron & Steel Consumption Problems,* U.S. Department of Commerce, Washington, D.C., 1966.

78. Institute of Scrap Iron & Steel and Chrysler Corporation, Washington, D.C., June 1967.